Germany's Past and Europe's Future

TITLES OF RELATED INTEREST

Coker *Drifting Apart?*

Deibel & Gaddis *Containing the Soviet Union: A Critique of U.S. Policy*

Dougherty & Pfaltzgraff *Shattering Europe's Defense Consensus: The Antinuclear Protest Movement & the Future of NATO*

Drown et al. *Western European Arms Cooperation*

Goldstein *Fighting Allies: Tensions within the Atlantic Alliance*

Griffith et al. *Security Perspectives of the German Left: The SPD & the Greens in Opposition*

Grove & Windass *The Crucible of Peace: Common Security in Europe*

Langer *Transatlantic Discord & NATO's Crisis of Cohesion*

Rothschild *Peace for Our Time*

Sloan *NATO in the 1990s*

Stahlberg *A Question of Allegiance*

Wettig *High Road, Low Road: Diplomacy & Public Action in Soviet Foreign Policy*

RELATED PERIODICALS (sample copies available upon request)

Armed Forces Journal International

Defense Analysis

Middle East Strategic Studies Quarterly

Survival

Germany's Past and Europe's Future

THE CHALLENGES OF WEST GERMAN FOREIGN POLICY

Edwina S. Campbell

PERGAMON-BRASSEY's
International Defense Publishers, Inc.

Washington • New York • London • Oxford
Beijing • Frankfurt • São Paulo • Sydney • Tokyo • Toronto

U.S.A. (Editorial)	Pergamon-Brassey's International Defense Publishers, Inc. 8000 Westpark Drive, Fourth Floor, McLean, Virginia 22102, U.S.A.
(Orders)	Pergamon Press Inc., Maxwell House, Fairview Park, Elmsford, New York 10523, U.S.A.
U.K. (Editorial)	Brassey's Defence Publishers Ltd., 24 Gray's Inn Road, London WC1X 8HR, England
(Orders)	Brassey's Defence Publishers, Headington Hill Hall, Oxford OX3 0BW, England
PEOPLE'S REPUBLIC OF CHINA	Pergamon Press, Room 4037, Qianmen Hotel, Beijing, People's Republic of China
FEDERAL REPUBLIC OF GERMANY	Pergamon Press GmbH, Hammerweg 6, D-6242 Kronberg, Federal Republic of Germany
BRAZIL	Pergamon Editora Ltda, Rua Eça de Queiros, 346, CEP 04011, Paraiso, São Paulo, Brazil
AUSTRALIA	Pergamon-Brassey's Defence Publishers Ltd., P.O. Box 544, Potts Point, N.S.W. 2011, Australia
JAPAN	Pergamon Press, 5th Floor, Matsuoka Central Building, 1-7-1 Nishishinjuku, Shinjuku-ku, Tokyo 160, Japan
CANADA	Pergamon Press Canada, Suite No. 271, 253 College Street, Toronto, Ontario, Canada M5T 1R5

Copyright © 1989 Pergamon-Brassey's International Defense Publishers, Inc.

Pergamon-Brassey's books are available at special discounts for bulk purchases for sales promotions, premiums, fund-raising, or education use through the

Special Sales Director
Macmillan Publishing Company
866 Third Avenue, New York, NY 10022.

Excerpts from *Begegnungen un Einsichten* by Willy Brandt. Copyright © 1976 Willy Brandt. Reprinted by permission of the publisher.
Excerpts from *Memoirs* by Jean Monnet. Copyright © 1978 by Doubleday, a division of Bantam, Doubleday, Dell Publishing Group, Inc. Reprinted by permission of the publisher.
Scattered quotes from Jon Jacobson, *Locarno Diplomacy: Germany & the West, 1925–1929.* Copyright © 1972 by Princeton University Press.

Library of Congress Cataloging-in-Publication Data

Campbell, Edwina S., 1950—
 Germany's past and Europe's future : the challenges of West German foreign policy/Edwina Campbell.—1st ed.
  p. cm.
 Bibliography: p.
 Includes index.
 ISBN 0-08-036737-2
  1. Europe—Foreign relations—Germany (West) 2. Germany (West)—Foreign relations—Europe. 3. Germany (West)—Politics and government—1982– I. Title.
 D1065.G3C36 1989
 327.4304—dc19   89-30654   CIP

PRINTED IN THE UNITED STATES OF AMERICA
10 9 8 7 6 5 4 3 2 1

To Charlotte
Zwanzig Jahre Freundschaft und Zusammenarbeit

contents

foreword

For the United States and Western Europe, the founding of the Federal Republic of Germany (FRG) in 1949 represented in itself an event of historic importance. Born in the bitter legacy of World War II, the West German state arose not as a result of any consciously contrived postwar plan foreseen in the closing days of World War II, but instead as a direct consequence of the inability of the four occupying powers to reach agreement on the future of Europe. Because of its geographic location in the middle of a divided Europe, the Federal Republic of Germany was destined to become the linchpin of the Western deterrence framework embodied in the Atlantic Alliance. Just as there could be no forward defense of NATO without the participation of the FRG, so was West German Alliance membership the essential precondition for forward defense itself. The FRG became not only an indispensable member of the Atlantic Alliance but also a crucially important part of the European Community. Politically, the FRG has achieved a degree of democratic stability and internal cohesiveness that, for reasons amply discussed by Dr. Edwina Campbell, eluded the ill-fated Weimar Republic as the successor state to the Wilhelmine Germany defeated in World War I. Founded as a provisional state, pending eventual German reunification, the FRG has enjoyed, both at home and abroad, a degree of acceptance and respectability—of political consensus—denied to the Weimar Republic, which was widely described as a "republic without republicans."

Historians will long debate the precise circumstances and causal factors that have contributed to the evolution of the FRG as a West German state in the European setting of the late twentieth century. Since its founding in 1949, the FRG has been host to an understandable discussion of the impact of modern German history on the present and future role of Germany in the international arena. Although the present generation is not directly accountable for the actions of its predecessors, nevertheless, the lessons of the past must always inform the words and deeds of this and future generations. Thus the FRG exists amid the unprecedented abundance of material goods and political stability with the searing memory of an episode that nearly extinguished Western civilization. Hence, to view the world and in particular Europe and the transatlantic relationship, as well as more proximate interests on both sides of the inner German border, through German eyes is to behold the same panorama but with a different lens from that of the outsider. To cast oneself in the position of the beholder with respect to a state's foreign policy is in itself vitally important, whether for the student or practitioner. In light of the German experience of the twentieth century, such an exercise is a crucial component of the study or practice of statecraft for all who would address the issues directly associated with the role of the FRG in late twentieth-century Europe. The present volume furnishes, in this respect, a basis for understanding the forces that have shaped the FRG in the years that have passed since its founding, as well as those elements that are likely to play an indispensable role in determining the FRG's place in the European setting of the 1990s and beyond.

Among the many factors differentiating the FRG from the German states before it, as Edwina Campbell suggests, are the number and quality of transnational relationships that emerged both to buttress and to sustain the intergovernmental links that were forged by the political leadership of Western Europe in the years after World War II. The mobility of persons, together with the proliferation of contacts of various kinds across once forbidding frontiers, shaped the evolution of the European integration movement and helped to strengthen identification with the Western roots of European civilization as an alternative to the destructive German nationalism then so recently vanquished. It was deemed essential for the FRG to establish a transformed relationship in which the enmity that had existed with France was replaced by a partnership whose longevity will soon equal the length of time of that dark period in their relationship between the end of the Franco-Prussian War (1871) and the outbreak of World War I (1914). As Dr. Campbell clearly demonstrates, the Franco-German relationship formed the bedrock of the FRG's *Westpolitik*. Yet, if Germans were to move beyond the irrevocable legacy of the years before 1945, they had to establish peaceful relations with states to the east and west along and beyond the frontiers of the FRG and, more broadly, the German nation. The value of Dr. Campbell's work lies in the extent to which she has set forth in vivid fashion the forces that decisively shape the contemporary German perspective within the emerging Europe of the 1990s.

For the FRG a principal question remains the extent to which the circumstances giving rise to the remarkable success of *Westpolitik* can continue to be fulfilled on a broader scale. The author indicates the sharp differences and discontinuities from conditions operative in the West to those that have faced Bonn in pursuit of its *Ostpolitik* and with respect to relations with the German Democratic Republic in the *Deutschlandpolitik*. West German membership in NATO and in the European Community framework formed a counterweight to the East as well as an association of pluralistic societies based on representative government and private sector economies united by a commonly perceived threat. Nevertheless, the *Ostpolitik* of the FRG, which Dr. Campbell describes in measured yet interpretative fashion, flowed as a logical necessity in the German mind from the tragic history of the first half of the twentieth century. Its achievements were designed to put to rest issues that, so long as they existed, served to deepen the harsh wound inflicted by the Third Reich upon the German psyche. What remains, of course, is the question of the extent to which the FRG, within the context of its historic dilemma, will be able to achieve an appropriate reconciliation between its inner needs and geostrategic circumstances. The present work is instructive in offering to the outside observer of the evolving German scene vitally important insights into those forces likely to shape the foreign policy of the FRG in the years leading toward the end of this century and into the third millennium.

Robert L. Pfaltzgraff, Jr.
President
Institute for Foreign Policy Analysis
and
Shelby Cullom Davis Professor of
International Security Studies
The Fletcher School of Law and Diplomacy
Tufts University

preface

This book would not have been possible without the assistance and friendship of individuals and organizations on both sides of the Atlantic. In the United States, Donald Abenheim and David Gress of the Hoover Institution provided the critical comments and personal encouragement necessary to its completion. During the period in which the final revisions took shape, the entire staff of Eagle Research Group (ERG), with great good humor and patience, put up with the author's tribulations; only because space does not permit, thanks to Marlene Korenstein, Robert Popolow, Laura Rounds, Robert Squire, and Jeanette Wimberly are meant for all of my colleagues at ERG.

The Robert Bosch Foundation, the Institute for Foreign Policy Analysis, the German Marshall Fund, and the Stiftung für die Deutsche Wissenschaft all provided financial support for the residence and travel in Europe that made this book possible.

At the same time, friends and professional colleagues from many nations made those two years in Europe both productive and pleasant. Chief among them were Christine and David Simmons, Günther and Beate Schulz, Reinhold and Hildegard Geimer, Monika and Karen Feldhof, and Peter Hertel. In addition, thanks are owed to all those who made possible my work as a Robert Bosch fellow at the Bundestag and the Auswärtiges Amt, notably Eugen Selbmann, Horst Ehmke, Dietrich Stobbe, Karsten Voigt, Michael Bock, Klaus Holderbaum, Horst Holdhoff, Klaus Hildebrand, and Herbert and Corinna Quelle. The staff of the Robert Bosch Foundation, notably Rüdiger Stefan and Uta Ehle, were welcome friends in Stuttgart, as well as financial benefactors.

The U.S. Embassy in Bonn made possible my participation in more than two dozen seminars throughout West Germany in 1986 and 1987, an invaluable opportunity provided by Prof. William Griffith to discuss the country's foreign policy with Germans from all walks of life and political convictions. My thanks to all who welcomed my participation in their discussions, including the Bundeswehr Zentrum für Innere Führung (Koblenz), the Friedrich Ebert Stiftung (Bergneustadt), the Friedrich Naumann Stiftung (Gummersbach), and the Ostkolleg (Cologne). Special thanks to Manfred Stinnes, Manfred Strack, Trudel Scheiger, Jörg Ludwig, Bernd Herbert, Hartmut Gimmler, and all the USIS program officers who became friends in the course of our work together.

After my year as a Robert Bosch fellow, Adela Jabine at the German Marshall Fund, Robert Pfaltzgraff, Jr., at the Institute for Foreign Policy Analysis, and the Stiftung für die Deutsche Wissenschaft made possible my prolonged stay in Bonn and my travel to Stockholm, Paris, and Vienna to discuss Franco–West German relations and the work of the Conference on Security and Cooperation in Europe. Those who gave their valuable time for interviews are listed in the bibliography, but their welcome is also gratefully acknowledged here. A special thanks to Michael, Kyllikki, Oliver, Anton, and Anna Pitts, who made me a part of their family in Stockholm.

Finally, all the friends who made of Bonn a place to come home to are too numerous to mention, but they will, I hope, know that they are all warmly remembered with my thanks to Susan Higman, Janice Carter, Alan Cole, Geoff and Jenny Ediss, John Kohan, John Newsome, and Tony and Evi Taylor. To Matthew's parents, David and Christine Simmons, who literally put a pillow under my head and a cup of tea in my hand when I returned to Bonn from my wanderings: I couldn't have done it without you.

Those whose support and encouragement I have acknowledged enabled me to expand on work begun nearly two decades ago, when I first had the pleasure of studying German history with Carl Anthon at the American University. His enthusiasm led me to a Fulbright fellowship in West Germany and to an M.A.L.D. thesis on the postwar Franco–West German "Locarno from below" for Robert Pfaltzgraff, Jr., at the Fletcher School.

My initial work on the Federal Republic owed much to both of those professors, and to the excellent seminar on the Locarno treaties given by Professor Mieletz at the University of Freiburg in 1972. That work would not have been possible without the support of Ulrich Littmann at the Fulbright Commission, David Klein at the American Council on Germany, Heinz Engelhardt at the International Mayors Union, and all those practitioners of the Frankreichpolitik who spent many hours with a young American full of questions. They included too many French and German mayors, civil servants, and private individuals to mention, but in Freiburg, Besançon, Bordeaux, Stuttgart, Niedersachsen, and the Seine-

Maritime, I hope they know who they are. Anita Gratet in Freiburg was typical of them all.

Finally, affectionate thanks to my first and enduring German family, that of Gunther and Dorothee Hartmann, who gave me and many other Americans a home near the "most beautiful tower in Christendom."

Special thanks to Michael D'Ambrosio, and to Vicki Chamlee, Don McKeon, and Franklin Margiotta at Pergamon-Brassey's, thanks for the professional advice and good humor that made this book a reality.

introduction

"AS LONG AS THE BRANDENBURG GATE IS CLOSED"

In May 1989, the Federal Republic of Germany celebrated its fortieth anniversary. As is usual with significant dates in modern German history, the occasion was an ambiguous one. A product of the east-west Cold War that settled over Europe from 1947 to 1949, the Federal Republic was ultimately the result of German policies of conquest and extermination, of Nazi Germany's war and defeat in 1945. Many of its founders, at home and abroad, had worked for the defeat of their own country in its National Socialist years. They knew that the future of Europe, and of Germany itself, had depended on the destruction of the Third Reich and the reestablishment of a German democracy.

Many more Germans had done all they could for German victory. Millions of them had lost everything with the defeat: family, friends, homes they would never see again. As the extent of the Third Reich's crimes became clear in 1945, they found that knowing in one's head that Germany's defeat was for its own good in the long run was one thing, but feeling it in the heart was quite another. The founding of the Federal Republic on May 9, 1949, almost four years to the day from Germany's capitulation, could not be as unambiguous as July 4, 1776, is for Bonn's American ally. Whether the fortieth anniversary of the West German state was a cause for celebration, mourning, or simply commemoration still divided Germans in 1989.

As a result, the West German government has always had trouble identifying and reflecting the public patriotism that comes easily to other countries. The division of Germany is not primarily physical. One German historian wrote, "No discussion can take place anymore, given this horrible division that has so split us apart that one can hardly speak of being one nation any longer."[1] Theodor E. Mommsen was not describing the postwar division of his country, but the effect on Germany of its fatal attraction to Nazism. The deepest cleavages in West German public opinion still relate to the nature of German guilt and of West German responsibility. For those who claimed that they could not see what was happening to their country until it was too late: Mommsen reached the above conclusion in a letter written to a friend in Rome, Felix Gilbert, on February 18, 1933.

Gilbert's correspondents in those crucial months saw all too clearly what was happening to Germany. His aunt, Edith Mendelssohn Bartholdy, wrote from Leipzig on March 12, 1933, "We can only hope that this bitter cup too will pass from our poor country. But by the time it does, mightn't culture and even civilization be completely lost?"[2] A German colleague in Italy wrote with great prescience, "The nerve, the self-confidence, the optimism that [the political upheaval] has cost us—we will probably be able to assess . . . only at some later date. And only now can we begin to assess slowly how deep Germany's fall is not only in political but also in cultural respects."[3] The date was May 30, 1933, four months to the day from Hitler's appointment as the last chancellor of the Weimar Republic, and the fall had just begun.

Over fifty years later, setting a self-confident and optimistic tone for the citizens of their country was still difficult for the political leaders of the Federal Republic. In attempting to define a public mood appropriate to the fortieth anniversary of the end of World War II in Europe, Bonn stumbled badly. As its failed attempt at a ceremony of reconcilation with the United States at Bitburg showed, May 8, 1945—for its allies so unambiguously Victory in Europe Day—could not be that for the Federal Republic.[4] Three years later, the fiftieth anniversary of the organized mob violence of Kristallnacht, November 9, 1938, again found the political leadership and people of the Federal Republic involved in an angry debate over the German past and its meaning for West Germany's and Europe's future.

Unlike Bitburg, which had directly involved an American president, the controversy over Philip Jenninger's Kristallnacht speech, resulting in his resignation as president of the West German parliament (on, of all days, November 11, 1988, the seventieth anniversary of the German defeat in World War I),[5] passed rather quickly from the television screens and thoughts of most Americans. However, the underlying problem in both cases was the same: the ambiguous historical legacy of the Federal Republic. Felix Gilbert's correspondents identified the problem correctly when the Third Reich was still in its infancy. The Federal Republic is condemned to the search for the culture, civilization, nerve, self-confidence, and optimism that Germany lost from 1933 to 1945. This book is about one aspect of that quest, as defined by West German foreign policy.

In the 1990s and probably beyond, the Federal Republic will still be working out the implications of policies pursued by Nazi leaders long since dead. The war and the holocaust, remembered personally by only a handful of aging individuals, will remain primary determinants of West German domestic and foreign policies. Exhortations, whether from West German politicians or Bonn's allies, to be proud of the accomplishments of the Federal Republic, to assume a greater political and military role globally, and to abandon seemingly endless soul-searching and self-criticism are unlikely to have much effect on a country whose lack of soul-searching and self-criticism once inflicted such misery on the world. The Federal Republic can work out its historical inheritance only over time.

As it does so, American foreign policy will have to deal with an ally responding to the problems of the 1990s, to a far greater extent than any of the other western countries, against the backdrop of the 1930s and 1940s. This is not necessarily a cause for concern, provided that Bonn's allies do not lose sight of its unique problems. Since 1949, West Germany's politicians, diplomats, and soldiers have been remarkably imaginative and pragmatic, in the best sense of both words, in defining a foreign policy role for the Federal Republic. As West Germany begins its fifth decade, the United States has no reason to doubt the vitality of that pragmatic imagination, but the goals it serves may be misunderstood abroad.

Certainly, if the foreign policy of the Federal Republic is discussed only in terms of West German economic interests and security concerns, the pursuit of its goals *will* be misunderstood abroad. The discord and disarray within the western alliance in the early 1980s reflected the failure of Bonn's allies to understand the historical component of its foreign policy. As they scrambled to cope with West Germany's activist east-west diplomacy and increasingly militant peace movement, Washington, Paris, and London generally failed to see that neither West German jobs nor the range of Soviet missiles was the primary issue: German history was.

For the Federal Republic, it always has been. From the very beginning, in 1949, Bonn's foreign policy has dealt fundamentally with only one question: definition of an acceptable role for Germans—initially in Europe and, since the early 1970s, globally—in the shadow of the Third Reich. The role of the Federal Republic was, of course, also defined with regard to the changing political, economic, and security interests of West Germans and their allies over the past four decades. Unlike its allies, however, Bonn was never free to define those interests in a way relatively independent from its historical burden: the fears of its neighbors and the self-doubt of Germans themselves were too great. The imperialism of the Wilhelmine Empire, the suicide of the Weimar Republic, and the murderous racism of Nazi Germany have always been major factors in West Germany's view of the world and of its own role in world politics.

One of the earliest manifestations of this worldview was Bonn's *Frankreichpolitik*, the policy toward France articulated by the first government of the Federal Republic and its Christian Democratic chancellor, Konrad Adenauer. This book uses the German word, as it uses the words *Westpolitik*, *Ostpolitik*, and *Deutschlandpolitik*, to discuss West German foreign policies toward, respectively, France, the countries of western Europe and the Atlantic Alliance, the members of the Warsaw Pact, and the German Democratic Republic. In each case, Bonn's policy was one of detente, and the use of the German word seeks to convey this parallel. I have also chosen not to capitalize "east" and "west" when referring to the European countries and their respective alliances, since turning "east" and "west" (and their variations) into proper nouns to me seems to indicate a permanent ideological and political division contrary to the historical reality of Europe.

East-west detente began officially for the Federal Republic and its western allies in 1967, with NATO's Harmel Report on the Future Tasks of the Alliance; *west*-west detente had begun for Bonn in 1949. The Frankreichpolitik was a conscious process of detente, leading, Bonn hoped, to entente and cooperation with France. Simultaneously, Bonn's Westpolitik initiated the same process with the United States, Canada, and the Federal Republic's neighbors in western Europe; and twenty years later, the Ost- and Deutschlandpolitik of Willy Brandt and Walter Scheel applied the lessons of the Frankreichpolitik to West Germany's relations with the countries of eastern Europe.

In the months when the Brandt-Scheel Ostpolitik was taking shape, my mind was on Konrad Adenauer and the "hereditary enmity" between France and Germany that had been a political constant of pre-1945 Europe. I wrote, in 1970 and 1971, an undergraduate paper on the significance of the 1963 Franco-German (Elysée) Treaty of Friendship and Cooperation. In the fall of 1972, I spent a semester at the University of Freiburg studying the 1925 Locarno treaties among France, Germany, Britain, Belgium, and Italy and the nature of the relationships among the three principal Locarno powers from 1925 to 1929. In 1974, I completed a master's thesis on the grassroots basis of rapprochement between the Federal Republic and France in the 1950s and 1960s: the role of sister cities and the concept of a "Locarno from below," in which rapprochement between the two countries was not left to their professional diplomats and politicians, as it had been in the 1920s.[6] While the world watched Willy Brandt, I listened to private citizens on both sides of the

Rhine talk about the relationship between France and Germany in their lifetimes.

What they described was nothing short of a revolutionary change in the nature of the "hereditary enmity." The catalyst for that change was a revulsion at the susceptibility—of Germans in particular, but also of other Europeans—to the "totalitarian temptation"[7] that had brought western civilization to the abyss in 1945. That revulsion led western Europe, especially the Federal Republic and France, to a fundamental rethinking of what Ernest May first called *axiomatic* foreign policies more than a quarter century ago: the reinterpretation of past events in ways that result in new or changed *calculated* policies.[8] Specific calculated policy decisions made by Bonn and Paris—their support for the European Coal and Steel Community (ECSC), the integration of the Saarland into the Federal Republic, West German membership in NATO, and the establishment of the European Community (EC)—reflected these new axiomatic policies. So did Washington's role in western Europe after 1947. The abandonment of its initial occupation policy in Germany (decartelization, denazification, demilitarization) in 1947, the 1948 Marshall Plan for European Recovery, and the North Atlantic Treaty signed in 1949 were all calculated policies resulting from the United States's new axiomatic policy: no appeasement of totalitarian dictators.[9]

The origins of the new axiomatic policies in Bonn and Paris were somewhat different. Although the nature of Hitler's and Stalin's foreign policies was of prime importance to Washington in its move from one axiomatic policy (no entangling alliances) to another (no appeasement), the relationship between France and Germany prior to 1945, before as well as during the Third Reich, was the chief concern of policymakers in Bonn and Paris and at the local level in both countries. The threat posed by the Soviet Union was *relatively* of secondary importance. Startling though this seems to Americans, whose view of and role in the world were irrevocably changed by the east-west Cold War, it was not the principal factor impelling France and West Germany to pursue detente with each other in the 1950s. The Cold War determined some of the forms that detente took, notably West German membership in the North Atlantic Treaty Organization, but the prime impetus to Franco–West German rapprochement was the history to which Germany had subjected itself and the rest of Europe in the twentieth century.

One of the changed axiomatic policies that shaped Bonn's and Paris's calculated policies was a new interpretation of both world wars as a second Thirty Years' (civil) War, into which Europe had plunged itself in the three decades after 1914 and for which no nation—not even National Socialist Germany—bore sole responsibility. This interpretation contrasted sharply with the "war guilt" clause of the 1919 Versailles Treaty and the vitriol poured on practitioners and advocates of Franco-German rapprochement in both countries in the 1920s. The true miracle of the 1950s was not West German economic recovery but the articulation of a successful process of detente with France. This success led to the institutionalization of the Frankreichpolitik as a model for the Ost- and Deutschlandpolitik of the 1970s.

To someone as imbued with the detente process between France and the Federal Republic as I was, the Brandt-Scheel coalition's policies toward eastern Europe obviously reflected the same change in axiomatic policies that had heralded a new Frankreichpolitik twenty years before. This change included Bonn's acceptance of a political and military status quo in which West Germany's military options were nonexistent and its diplomatic options limited, together with the conviction that the use of force was no longer an acceptable or productive means to alter that status quo. One principal difference between the policies of west-west detente in the 1950s and of east-west detente in the 1970s was the lack of certainty that Moscow, Warsaw, Prague, and East Berlin shared with Bonn a long-term—and not merely a tactical—commitment to the establishment of a cooperative relationship among their governments and nations.

Still, initiation of *both* the Frankreichpolitik and the Ost- and Deutschlandpolitik was a gamble for Bonn. West German statesmen in both the 1950s and the 1970s wagered that each policy would, in the long term, produce positive results for their country. They gambled that Bonn's initially limited influence and room to maneuver could be expanded and applied more effectively through the pursuit of west-west detente after 1949 and east-west detente after 1969. One of the critical components of both policies, given Bonn's overriding interest in coming to terms with the catastrophic results of German foreign policy before 1945, was the articulation of a concept of "capillarizing" detente, that is, establishing it firmly among ordinary citizens rather than only at the level of interstate cooperation.[10]

This concept, increasingly evident in West German relations with eastern Europe only in the late 1980s, was at the heart of the Frankreichpolitik from the beginning. It was the Locarno from below that French and German mayors had begun to practice even before the Federal Republic of Germany was created as their reaction to the failure of the two countries to achieve a lasting rapprochement in the 1920s. When the foreign ministers of France, Germany, and Britain met for the first time at Locarno, Switzerland, in October 1925, their meeting ushered in four years of dialogue and consultation on the foreign policy issues facing their countries. Germany joined the World War I victors as a member of the League of Nations, with a permanent seat on the

League Council. British troops withdrew from the Rhineland. France welcomed Germany as a signatory to the 1928 (Kellogg-Briand) Pact of Paris, renouncing war as an instrument of national policy. However, the personal and political rapprochement of Aristide Briand, Gustav Stresemann, and Austen Chamberlain, the "spirit of Locarno," never spread outward and downward through the political leadership and citizens of France and Germany.

After World War II, local and national leaders sought to rectify their catastrophic failure to support Stresemann's and Briand's foreign policies by instituting a Locarno from below through cultural, educational, and sister cities programs. West Germans, reeling from Germany's experience with a government that had conceived of public opinion as an object of state manipulation, embarked on a foreign policy designed to make such manipulation unlikely, if not impossible, in the future. Active and widespread involvement of the citizenry in the rapprochement process was to be the key. Transnational ties between private individuals and organizations served a twofold purpose: (1) to create domestic constituencies in both France and the Federal Republic for foreign policies of cooperation and competition (but not confrontation) and (2) to break the characteristic and counterproductive quid pro quo cycle of historical Franco-German relations, in which each country had seen itself as a player in a zero-sum game of advantages and concessions.

Bonn's Frankreichpolitik was a policy of asymmetrical linkage. Both France and West Germany were able to link the resolution of their priority issues in ways that shattered the zero-sum perceptions that Stresemann and Briand had failed to overcome in the 1920s. The Federal Republic's achievement of equality at the Schuman Plan negotiating table in 1950 and France's achievement, de facto, of oversight of West German coal and steel production in the 1951 ECSC treaty were the first of Bonn's and Paris's goals to be met by this pattern of asymmetrical linkage. The development of the Franco–West German Locarno from below made possible the abandonment of the old public demands for an immediate quid pro quo. The constituency that saw the mutual interest of the two countries in long-term cooperation was both creating and created by the specific cultural, educational, and economic programs of the 1950s and 1960s. This constituency enabled asymmetrical linkage to become such an ingrained part of French and West German foreign policies that the alternative, asymmetrical quid pro quo policy, seemed completely anachronistic to both countries by the 1970s.

The same, however, did not hold true when Bonn looked eastward at the beginning of that decade. When Willy Brandt's political adviser, Egon Bahr, enunciated his concept of *Wandel durch Annäherung* (change through communication) in 1963, its prospects for success were regarded as virtually nonexistent.[11] The totalitarian governments of the Warsaw Pact, Bahr's critics charged, were little interested in change or communication. Neither the Kiesinger-Brandt Grand Coalition government of 1966 nor the Brandt-Scheel government of 1969 found a Jean Monnet or a Robert Schuman on the Spree or the Vistula. What did exist, as it had along the Seine in 1950, was the Warsaw Pact countries' interest in simultaneously containing the military potential of West German industrial strength while profiting from its contribution to trade and economic growth.

What also existed, as it had in the late 1940s and early 1950s, was pressure on Bonn from Washington to initiate a detente process with, in the first case, France and, in the second case, the Soviet Union and its allies. However, the role of the United States should not be overstated. The Cold War was not the primary factor in the Franco–West German detente of the 1950s, and American pressure for east-west detente in the late 1960s, although important, was not the principal reason for the new West German Ostpolitik after 1969. As with the Frankreichpolitik, the policy would have taken shape in any case, but the interests of the United States determined some of the specific forms it took, including the linkage of the Ostpolitik to the 1972 Quadripartite Agreement on Berlin and the 1975 Conference on Security and Cooperation in Europe (CSCE).

In 1970 the Federal Republic gambled on the initiation of a detente process with governments that were far from ready to encourage a Locarno from below among their citizens, as France had been in 1950. The gamble was that the process itself would eventually provide Bonn—and its western allies—with means to encourage the capillarization desired. By focusing on the establishment of ongoing multilateral and bilateral relationships with its eastern neighbors, West Germany sought to create a pattern of asymmetrical linkage similar to that of the Frankreichpolitik. Its goals were somewhat different than they had been in the 1950s, the political and economic conditions of life in the Warsaw Pact countries having replaced Bonn's political and economic status as a foreign policy priority. However, one goal had not changed for the Federal Republic: its need to reevaluate and redefine the West German role in Europe in light of the German past. The preeminence of this goal made the Cold War and the American interest in detente important, but not determining, factors in Bonn's foreign policy decisions of 1950 and 1970.

West Germany's economic strength was initially its principal asset in the pursuit of a process that sought to link creation of a climate conducive to the development of a Locarno from below to the trade and infrastructure required by the countries of the Warsaw Pact. The impact of technology, both positive and negative, also worked in Bonn's favor in the 1970s and 1980s, as the rhetoric of international interdependence, despite its cliches, clearly came to describe a technological and environmental reality that was increasingly difficult to deny. The explosion at the Soviet nuclear power plant at Chernobyl in April 1986 became both the focal point and the confirmation of that interdependence to the practitioners of West German foreign policy.[12]

If the postwar Franco–West German commitment to a Locarno from below enabled Paris's and Bonn's asymmetrical linkage of their foreign policy goals to flourish, then the Ost- and Deutschlandpolitik reversed the process: asymmetrical linkage of Bonn's and its eastern neighbors' foreign policy goals enabled a Locarno from below to take shape. Their need to preserve cultural and historical monuments, train technical elites, build transportation and industrial infrastructures, and protect the lives and health of their citizens were a few of the factors that combined to make the governments of eastern Europe inclined to accept the human contacts and mobility inherent in a grassroots Locarno, whether they wished to or not.

The first open acknowledgment of this development, which had been taking shape for some time, came from Moscow and its Warsaw Pact allies in the months after Chernobyl. Bonn's success in establishing political, economic, and cultural relations with Albania in 1987 and 1988; Erich Honecker's 1987 visit to the Federal Republic; the transformation of East and West German sister cities from a curiosity (two in 1986) to a movement (fifty by the end of 1988); the 1987 boom in travel by East Germans to the Federal Republic that continued in 1988; progress in the work of the West German–Polish textbook commission; Chancellor Kohl's 1988 visits to Poland and the Soviet Union; the establishment of formal relations between COMECON and the European Community, under Bonn's chairmanship, in early 1988; and the flood of ethnic Germans allowed to migrate from the countries of eastern Europe to West Germany in 1988 were all signs of the broadening and deepening of detente sought by Bonn.[13] Only with such developments could West Germans and their allies begin to have confidence in the east-west detente process and the possibility of entente and cooperation with the nations of eastern Europe.

Even so, the Federal Republic and the United States had major differences of opinion on whether the Frankreichpolitik could be replicated in the east. In the early 1980s, the two allies had disagreed sharply on the possibility and desirability of pursuing east-west detente. In the face of Soviet adventurism outside Europe in the last Brezhnev years, they did different cost-benefit calculations. By the late 1980s, after four Soviet-American summits, ratification of the treaty limiting intermediate-range nuclear forces (INF) in Europe, and the election of Mikhail Gorbachev as president of the USSR, both Bonn and Washington appeared to share, once again, a positive assessment of east-west detente. This outlook did not mean, however, that the 1990s would be trouble-free. As that decade approached, the United States's attitude toward entente and cooperation with the countries of the Warsaw Pact was far from clear; however, Bonn, in the person of Free Democratic Foreign Minister Hans-Dietrich Genscher, made no secret of its enthusiasm for the evolution of detente into east-west entente as soon as possible.[14]

In the west, the Frankreichpolitik had formally marked its transition from a policy of detente to one of entente in January 1963, when Konrad Adenauer and Charles DeGaulle signed the Elysée Treaty. A dozen years after Monnet, Schuman, and Adenauer had staked their political future on the ECSC, their countries were committed—from the foreign offices to hundreds of city halls—to the friendship and cooperation the treaty affirmed. In the east, the first hopeful signs of entente had only begun to appear in the late 1980s, nearly two decades after Willy Brandt's wager at Moscow and Warsaw.

Nevertheless, for the Federal Republic, the pursuit of detente with its eastern neighbors was as important as it had once been with France. The principal reason was neither West Germany's vulnerability to nuclear and conventional attack nor its interest in economic growth and foreign trade. On the contrary, Bonn's foreign policy was motivated by twin goals, irrevocably linked: a resolution of German *responsibility* for the division of pre-1945 Europe; and a dialogue among Germans themselves, within the Federal Republic and between West Germans and their neighbors in the GDR, on their *identity* as Germans and Europeans. In an article published in conjunction with Chancellor Kohl's October 1988 visit to Moscow, Foreign Minister Genscher discussed identity and responsibility as the twin themes of West German foreign policy since 1949.[15] As a result of their history, wrote Genscher, Germans recognized that they had a "special responsibility for confidence-building between East and West."[16]

The foreign policy, and specifically the detente policy, of the United States toward the Soviet Union and its Warsaw Pact allies has never had to deal with the "historical task" that Genscher and his constituents accept as theirs alone. "We will not shirk our responsibility," the foreign minister wrote, "and no one can relieve us of it."[17] Washington, Paris, and London need not define their interest in east-west detente with regard to the history that weighs on Bonn. In the 1990s, however, the four NATO allies will be the principal shapers of western policies toward Mikhail Gorbachev's Soviet Union and its Warsaw Pact allies. They will all have economic, political, and military interests to defend. Only one of them, the Federal Republic, will have a negative historical balance to redress. Whatever the results of the 1990 federal election, the West German government will continue to take an activist approach to redressing that balance. The challenge for American foreign policy is not only to tolerate but also to encourage the construction of Bonn's "bridge of confidence" between east and west.[18]

By the 1980s, the keystone of Bonn's foreign policy had become the extension throughout the continent of the European Community's neo-Gaullist concept of economic integration and interstate political cooperation. Its Frankreichpolitik enabled that concept to become the hallmark of postwar western Europe, in which borders delineated, but no longer divided.[19] Bonn's Ost- and Deutschlandpolitik, in the pursuit of changes in the nature of the borders between eastern and western Europe, aim to remove the barriers to human contacts and to political, economic, and cultural cooperation that fell nearly four decades ago along the Rhine.

In the 1980s, the pursuit of this goal led West Germans to a new and, in the postwar period, unprecedented discussion among themselves of the historic German role as a bridge across the continent. The rediscovery of Königsberg and Prague as German cities contrasted sharply with the emphasis in the 1950s on Bonn's legacy from Carolingian Europe, its common heritage with France in the Roman-Catholic Rhineland. Not surprisingly, the West German "historians' debate" on the uniqueness (or lack of it) of the crimes of the Third Reich and the public discussion of German identity as Europeans of the center (*Mitteleuropa*), not the west, struck more than a few raw nerves at home and abroad.[20] Especially unwelcome to Bonn's neighbors and to many West Germans was an observable tendency to relativize and excuse by comparison the unique crimes of National Socialist Germany. At the end of 1988, the government took an unequivocal stand against minimizing the genocide perpetrated by Germans on Europe.[21]

As the Federal Republic turned forty, the eastern policies modeled on the Frankreichpolitik, their predecessor in the west, had begun to offer hopeful signs of developing a genuine Locarno from below. Much depended on whether the reforms begun by Mikhail Gorbachev's Soviet Union, economic restructuring and freedom to publish and criticize at home, continued to be coupled with new programs of educational and cultural exchange abroad and political-military confidence-building measures between NATO and the Warsaw Pact. In the aftermath of Chancellor Kohl's visit to Moscow in October 1988, West Germany's faith was secure in the applicability to eastern Europe of the process of detente-entente-cooperation it had developed with France forty years before.[22]

German interest in the success of that process will remain constant in the 1990s, or, as West German President Richard von Weizsäcker has often said, "as long as the Brandenburg Gate is closed."[23] His words emphasized the importance the Federal Republic attaches to German responsibility for the Europe of divisive borders, which was one of the Third Reich's legacies to generations unborn in 1945. Bonn's contribution to a positive change in the nature of those borders would have a profound effect on the Germans' discussion of their role and identity as Europeans; it could be their new legacy of freedom and stability to the entire continent.

In Bonn, the debates over the wisdom of pursuing a dialogue with the Soviet Union take place in a different historical context than they do in Foggy Bottom. Along the Rhine, it is easier to remember what Washington may sometimes forget, that the issues between France and Germany once seemed as intractable as those dividing east and west today. Those issues turned out to be manageable when both countries were able to define together a common interest in Europe's future. The Federal Republic's uncharacteristically optimistic assessment of the prospects for east-west entente and cooperation in the 1990s may turn out to be the height of realism, after all.

Notes

1. Felix Gilbert, *A European Past* (New York: W. W. Norton and Co., 1988), pp. 128–129.
2. Ibid., p. 136.
3. Ibid., p. 153.
4. "Auf Kohls Rat hören wir nicht wieder," *Der Spiegel*, no. 18 (April 19, 1985): 17–29.
5. Jenninger's attempt to analyze the Germans' "fascination" with Hitler in a speech condemning the organized brutality against German Jews on Kristallnacht, November 9–10, 1938, miscarried, but there was no question of his intentions. As Hans-Jochen Vogel, leader of the opposition SPD, said of him, "No neo-Nazi spoke here—someone failed in carrying out a great task." *The Week in Germany* (New York: German Information Center), November 18, 1988. See also: "Mit Knobelbechern durch die Geschichte," *Der Spiegel*, no. 46 (November 14, 1988):22–28.
6. An abridged version of which appeared as "The Ideals and Origins of the Franco-German Sister Cities Movement, 1945–70," *Journal of the History of European Ideas* 8, no. 1 (1987):77–95.
7. The phrase is Jean-François Revel's, in *The Totalitarian Temptation* (Garden City, NY: Doubleday, 1977).
8. Ernest R. May, "The Nature of Foreign Policy: The Calculated versus the Axiomatic," *Daedalus* 91 (Fall 1962): 653–667.

9. Ibid., 667–668.
10. The phrase is Henri Cravatte's, in "La conférence européenne des pouvoirs locaux," *L'Annuaire européen* (The Hague: Martinus Nijhoff, 1963), pp. 43–44.
11. Helga Haftendorn, "Wurzeln der Ost- und Entspannungspolitik der Sozial-Liberalen Koalition," in Horst Ehmke, Karlheinz Koppe, and Herbert Wehner, eds., *Zwanzig Jahre Ostpolitik* (Bonn: Verlag Neue Gesellschaft, 1986), pp. 19–20.
12. Discussions in Vienna and Bonn, 1986. Numerous West German political leaders have addressed the issues raised by Chernobyl, among them, former president Walter Scheel, in his June 17, 1986, speech to the West German parliament, found in *Bulletin* 73 (June 19, 1986): 613–619.
13. Jackson Diehl, "Bonn Official Sees Progress in Polish Ties," *Washington Post*, January 1, 1988; Marion Gräfin Dönhoff, "Der Wind des Wandels aus dem Osten," *Die Zeit*, May 15, 1987; Hans-Adolf Jacobsen, "Der Dialog war offener und konstruktiver," *General Anzeiger* (Bonn), May 16–17, 1987; *Deutschland-Nachrichten*, September 14, 1988; and *The Week in Germany*, November 18, 1988, and July 1, 1988.
14. See, for example, the summary of Genscher's September 12, 1988, radio interview in *Deutschland-Nachrichten*, September 14, 1988.
15. Hans-Dietrich Genscher, "Ein Plan für das ganze Europa," *Die Zeit*, October 28, 1988.
16. Ibid.
17. Ibid.
18. Ibid.
19. The phrase is Theo Sommer's, in his *Die Zeit* editorial, "Jenseits von Potsdam," June 24, 1988.
20. Gordon A. Craig, "The War of the German Historians," *New York Review of Books* (January 15, 1987): 16–19. The debate largely took place in the pages of *Frankfurter Allgemeine* and *Die Zeit* from 1986 to 1988. Three of the key *Die Zeit* articles were: Martin Broszat and Saul Friedländer, "Historisierung des Nationalsozialismus?" (April 29, 1988); Joachim H. Knoll, "Die Vergesslichkeit sollte uns Angst machen (May 1, 1987); and Jürgen Habermas, "Vom öffentlichen Gebrauch der Historie" (November 14, 1986).
21. Richard von Weizsäcker, "Germans and History: Give It to Us Straight" (excerpts from a speech to the Bamberg historians' conference, October 12, 1988), *International Herald Tribune*, October 29–30, 1988; and Helmut Kohl's November 14, 1988, speech in New York, quoted in *The Week in Germany*, November 18, 1988.
22. Theo Sommer, "Unterwegs zu neuen Ufern," *Die Zeit*, November 4, 1988.
23. Among other times, in discussion with the 1985–86 American fellows of the Robert Bosch Foundation, Bonn, September 18, 1985.

part one

DEFINING THE POSTWAR
FOREIGN POLICY PROBLEM

1

ADENAUER AND THE WESTPOLITIK

Defeated Germany

As the forces of the Soviet Union and the three western allies converged on the heart of Germany in the spring of 1945, they did so with a plan of military occupation and severance of German territory approved by Churchill, Roosevelt, and Stalin at Yalta in February 1945. Germans to whom the provisions of the Versailles Treaty had seemed intolerable had produced in World War II a situation far worse: the Allies refused to deal with any German government, proclaimed that the German state had ceased to exist, and declared their exercise of sovereignty over the territory of the former Reich as its occupying powers. The Yalta "Communiqué on the Occupation and Control of Germany" left no doubt as to the Allies' "inflexible purpose to destroy German militarism and Nazism and to ensure that Germany will never again be able to disturb the peace of the world." Only then would "there be hope for a decent life for Germans, and a place for them in the comity of nations."[1] The unwillingness to negotiate with Germans of any political background manifested itself initially at every level of contact between the occupying powers and the occupied.

This unwillingness stemmed from the assumption that a moral vacuum existed in the German body politic. The Allies simply did not expect to find Germans uncompromised by association with the policies of the Third Reich, and they were not prepared to listen to Germans who had their own ideas about the political future of their country. The political differences of opinion that existed below the surface of the wartime military alliance against Berlin had begun to take shape at Yalta, but one area was never a subject of interallied dispute: the common determination to destroy once and for all Berlin's ability to launch a new campaign for hegemony in Europe. In early 1945, the victorious powers understood this to mean the destruction of the economic, political, and military capacity of the German state—not simply restrictions on its armed forces, reminiscent of Versailles. The Big Three and France each had their own ideas regarding the optimal future German state, but for the moment they could agree on the need to eliminate Germany, as it had existed geographically and politically since 1871, as a factor in the European system.

Their determination to do so was reflected in the decisions made at Yalta and confirmed six months later at the last allied wartime conference at Potsdam. Three of these had far-reaching impact on postwar Germany: (1) the territorial reduction of the Reich, not only by reestablishing an independent Austria and returning the Sudetenland to Czechoslovakia and Alsace-Lorraine to France, but also by the annexation by the Soviet Union and Poland of historic German lands east of the Oder and Neisse rivers; (2) the division of the remaining territory of the Reich, west of the Oder-Neisse, into four zones and of Berlin into four sectors, each to be administered for the duration of the occupation by one of the four allied powers, with decisions affecting this reduced Germany as a whole to be taken by them collectively and unanimously in the Berlin-based Allied Control Council; and (3) the resettlement of ethnic Germans out of the territories returned to Czechoslovakia or annexed by Poland and the USSR into the four occupation zones.

Clearly, the allies shared the concept of a *Stunde Null*, a zero hour, in the political history of Germany. This realization came as a shock to many Germans, chief among them those political leaders who had spent the preceding decade in exile, underground, or in the prisons of the Third Reich. Few of them had understood the extent to which their country was to be an object of the policies of the other powers, no longer an actor itself in the politics of Europe. The nationalism that had led many of them to resistance in the labor unions, the army, and the churches was as unacceptable as any other form of German nationalism to the frustrated victors, who were determined never to hear again myths of a "stab in the back" on the homefront to a German army undefeated in the field.[2]

How the Allies' antipathy to German political action would have manifested itself through the years of occupation, had allied unity prevailed, will never be known. What can be said with certainty is that the disunity that soon became the Cold War, and the years in which a "hot war" seemed possible, brought to Germans west of the Oder-Neisse, and certainly to those west of the Elbe, advantages as well as disadvantages. Perhaps *only* two German states exist today because of the Cold War; arguably, had the wartime consensus not broken down, the end of occupation might have meant the end of any significantly sized

German state in Europe. The German assumption that, without the Cold War, no Iron Curtain would divide Europe is undoubtedly correct; that no division of Germany would have occurred is far less certain.

In the four short years that divided the allied victory in May 1945 from the establishment of the Federal Republic in May 1949, however, the Cold War did determine the course of the western allies' policies toward Germany. Five years after V-E Day, the new government in Bonn was playing an active role in shaping its own future. Germany's geographic location and the Federal Republic's economic potential combined to make the new state the linchpin in the strategy of the Atlantic Alliance for the defense of western Europe. A month older than the West German state, and still a treaty without an organization in 1949, the North Atlantic Alliance had an interest in defending itself on the Elbe, not the Rhine, and an even greater interest in creating a prosperous western Europe as a deterrent to Soviet aggression. In either case, Germany's recent enemies required the cooperation of an economically and politically viable West German state.

The events that led to that cooperation between the victors and the vanquished took place both in Europe, in Prague, Berlin, and Warsaw, and on the other side of the world from 1945 to 1949, as the tide turned against the Nationalists in the Chinese civil war. The process accelerated in 1948, and over the next seven years, Bonn became an indispensable partner in the reconstruction and defense of western Europe. By the tenth anniversary of the end of World War II, the Federal Republic was the fifteenth member of the North Atlantic Treaty Organization (NATO), the permanent political and military body of the Atlantic Alliance, then taking shape in Paris. What took place in that decade to establish the Federal Republic's role in western Europe?

The answers must be sought in the unique constellation of people and events that came together in the years from 1948 to 1952, both in Europe and abroad, and in the interpretation by both the western allies and the founders of the new republic of where they had all failed in dealing with National Socialism. The allied and German analysis focused on three factors: the weaknesses, structural and otherwise, of the Weimar Republic; the failure of Britain and France to respond to the foreign policy challenge of Nazi Germany in the five years from 1933 to 1938 ("appeasement"); and the importance of the Franco-German relationship to peace and prosperity, as well as to defense and deterrence, in western Europe. By 1950, the analysis of these factors, combined with the deteriorating east-west climate, had produced radical departures in the attitudes of Paris, London, and Washington toward Bonn, where the first West German government was receptive to the development of western European and Atlantic cooperation.

The analysis of the failures of the 1920s and the 1930s had three principal results for Germany in the late 1940s. First, the critique of Anglo-French appeasement policy was an essential element in the containment policy evolving in the U.S. diplomatic-military establishment. The result of the lack of resolution shown by London and Paris in countering Berlin's attacks on the interwar European order was, as Robert Bowie wrote, the "decisive development" in the thinking of those decision-makers who argued for a firm stand against Soviet expansionism in the years after 1945:

> The historical experience common to all [the western leaders was] the rise of Hitler to power and its consequences. . . . As Stalin seemed to pose such a threat, he brought to mind fresh memories of the failure to deal with Hitler when there was still a chance to do so. . . . Parallels to the 1930's determined the assessment of the situation as well as the reaction to it.[3]

By 1948, not much of a stretch of the imagination was required to see in Stalin another Hitler, and in Soviet policies in eastern Europe a sequence of events analogous to the dictators' challenge to the West ten years before.

When the February 1948 Communist coup in Czechoslovakia again drove the same president, Edouard Beneš, and the same foreign minister, Jan Masaryk, from office less than ten years after Munich—costing the latter his life—the Hitler-Stalin analogy grew more compelling. Britain, France, and the Benelux countries signed a mutual defense treaty in Brussels and, after months of delay, the Truman Administration won Congressional approval of the Marshall Plan. The Soviet blockade of the western allies' road and rail links to Berlin in June 1948, in response to the currency reform they had instituted in their zones, confirmed the U.S. conviction that Moscow was testing its commitment to the security of western Europe and the three allies' determination to remain in Germany.[4]

The development of containment as the principal doctrine of American foreign policy provided the opportunity for Bonn to elaborate policies resulting from analysis of the other two factors: the collapse of Weimar and the Franco-German relationship. From the West German perspective, the Cold War was not the crucial element in the enunciation of policies designed to avoid the failures of their country in the past. It was crucial, however, in determining the willingness of the three allies to support the establishment of the Federal Republic and to tolerate the articulation of an independent (West) German foreign policy so soon after the war. The Cold War made possible both the West German state and its pursuit of equal partnership in decisions affecting Germany.

Long before 1948, however, the commitment to a democratic

Germany and to rapprochement with France had characterized the thinking of opponents of Nazi Germany about the postwar world.[5] The reason was not the Cold War, but the two world wars. In thirty years, Europe had destroyed the cultural legacy of a millennium, the peace and prosperity of a century, and the lives of two generations. The wars had toppled monarchies, fomented revolution at home and in colonies abroad, and placed the fate of the continent in the hands of states on its periphery for the first time in three hundred years, since the Turkish invasion had been stopped at the gates of Vienna in 1683.

As a result, in the late 1940s, the east-west conflict was not the principal driving force behind the support for Franco-German reconciliation; rather, it was revulsion at what years of their mutual hostility had done to Europe. The Soviet threat was one danger, but so was the threat of war brought about by the western Europeans themselves. As they had three centuries earlier at the close of the Thirty Years' War, Europeans, including Germans disillusioned by their own recent history, saw clearly how close they had come to total self-destruction.[6]

Divided Germany

The focus on a viable democracy and a new relationship with France took on added meaning as any prospect of a peace treaty, a withdrawal of the occupying powers, and a definitive territorial settlement faded in 1947 and 1948. Nevertheless, major differences of opinion existed between the political parties authorized by the allies to operate at first locally and then at the state level within their respective zones. The new Christian Democratic Union (CDU) and the reestablished Social Democrats (SPD) had alternative visions of the role of Germany in Europe. By the early 1950s, the CDU's concept had prevailed. Abroad, the party and its leader, Konrad Adenauer, became virtually synonymous with the foreign policy of the Federal Republic in its first decade.

The CDU concept was one of a West German federal state anchored in a developing western European community. Its secondary features were a security relationship between this community and the United States and the renunciation of unilateral West German diplomatic overtures toward the Soviet Union. Although both features were made necessary by the Cold War, understanding them as solely a product of deteriorating east-west relations in 1947 and 1948 would be a mistake. They were far more a product of Adenauer's interpretation of the failures of twentieth-century German foreign policy, an interpretation shared by influential members of the SPD, although not officially by their party, and certainly not by Kurt Schumacher, its leader until his death in 1952.

Before examining the elements of Adenauer's federal state and its foreign policies, considering the alternatives to them proposed by Schumacher's SPD is necessary. Two decades ago, these alternatives would have seemed of historical interest but of little relevance to the course of actual West German foreign policy since 1949. That judgment clearly was premature. The differences between the SPD and the CDU reflected Germany's multifaceted historic role in Europe and the identity crisis of the Germans, bereft of their national state after only seventy-four years. The basic elements of the debate between Schumacher and Adenauer, which seemed to have lost significance for West German foreign policy by 1960, have reemerged with a vengeance since the mid-1970s.

The three major points of disagreement were: the priority given to reestablishing a German national state encompassing at least the four occupation zones, if not the boundaries of 1937; the necessity of securing withdrawal of the forces of the four occupying powers from German territory; and the demilitarization of the new German national state, if that were necessary for its acceptance by the four powers in a peace treaty. Schumacher's support of these three components of a postwar settlement earned him a reputation with the three western powers that rendered him, and his party for many years to come, suspect in their eyes as a German nationalist who was at best naive and at worst criminal in his assessment of the intentions of Soviet foreign policy.[7] Schumacher was not so much naive in his assessment of the Soviet Union, however, as in his appreciation of the *western* limits within which Germans had to operate in the late 1940s.

The reasons for this naiveté are not hard to identify: Schumacher's age, personal history, and commitment to his party all contributed to his failure to assess accurately the realities of the period. The year in which Schumacher was born, 1895, was significant in his duel with Adenauer. The SPD leader was a German nationalist who believed that his countrymen had the same right to self-determination as the other peoples of Europe and who sought to establish the patriotism of his party, much maligned for its internationalism in the years before 1914. In this, he was a perfect example of both the later Wilhelmine Empire in which he had grown up and the frustrations of 1919, when Germans failed to benefit from Woodrow Wilson's Fourteen Points. Germany, for Schumacher, was the national state of his youth, and its reestablishment the goal of his final years.

Given the experiences of his lifetime, he could not understand the impatience of the western allies with his type of nationalism. He misjudged completely their tolerance for the rebirth of a state that had been the economic and political, as well as military, foundation for

National Socialism's bid for European hegemony. Schumacher's political credo blinded him to the west's mistrust of his country; as a German Social Democrat, he saw the origins of National Socialism in the economic and social conditions of the twentieth century and deplored its racist ideology. A veteran of World War I, in which he had lost an arm, and a survivor of ten years in Nazi concentration camps, as a result of which he eventually lost a leg in 1948, Schumacher could not conceive of objections to a reunited, democratic, socialist Germany. His political opponent was far more realistic about the extent to which Germany and all Germans had used up their nationalist capital over the past half-century. Adenauer had no illusions about the acceptability of the rhetoric of Wilhelmine nationalism in 1949.

The question was not only of political rhetoric and tactics. Adenauer knew how to fit his policies into the maneuvering room available for them in 1949, as Schumacher clearly did not. However, the two men also had philosophical differences growing out of the question critical to German foreign policy until 1945: the appropriate role for Germany in Europe, given its geographical location and its interests from the Baltic to the North Sea. The CDU leader was a Catholic Rhinelander; his principal objection to German foreign policy in the 1920s had been its failure to give rapprochement with the west clear priority over relations with the Soviet Union.[8] Twenty years later, as chancellor, Adenauer seized the opportunity given him by Hitler and Stalin to do just that.

By early 1948, the three western allies, led by the United States, were increasingly frustrated with Soviet policies in the Allied Control Council (ACC) and in eastern Europe. They had come to the conclusion that Moscow was not prepared to reach any compromise acceptable to them on the future status of occupied Germany.[9] The destruction of coalition governments in Warsaw and Prague by their Communist members and the forced merger of the SPD with the German Communist Party in the Soviet zone were both ominous outcomes of compromises made with indigenous political parties supported by Moscow. At the same time, the economic situation in the three western zones was bordering on collapse; the currency reform required to stabilize the economy was blocked in the ACC by the Soviet Union.

The western allies were faced with two unpalatable prospects in the spring of 1948: on the one hand, continued Soviet intransigence on the currency reform, economic chaos in their occupation zones, and probable political turmoil, which they suspected was Moscow's aim; on the other, a possible compromise in the ACC, with the same results two or three years down the road that they were seeing in Prague, Budapest, and Warsaw.[10] The alternatives were not attractive, and on June 20, 1948, without ACC authorization, the three allies introduced the currency reform in their "Trizonia" and in the western sectors of Berlin. The Soviet Union responded with a blockade of the land and rail access routes to Berlin through its occupation zone, the use of which had been guaranteed to the three western allies in 1945 at Potsdam.

Had Washington and its allies responded to this blockade by sending a tank-escorted convoy through to Berlin, as the American commandant in Germany, General Clay, recommended at the time, the history of the past four decades would almost surely have been quite different. Despite the American monopoly of atomic weapons, however, the United States chose to utilize its economic and technological supremacy in another way: by mounting the Berlin Airlift. The Soviet Union chose not to attempt a blockade of the air corridors to the city; for eleven months, from June 1948 through May 1949, the allied planes—which had meant terror and destruction only four years before—took on a new meaning for the people of Berlin and Germany.

On the ground, as the crisis stretched on through 1948, two decisions reflected the accumulating fears of a Soviet military challenge to western Europe. In Washington, negotiations on a mutual defense treaty began between the United States, Canada, and ten western European nations. The North Atlantic Treaty was signed in the American capital on April 4, 1949, both symbol of the revolution in American foreign policy that had taken place since 1939 and herald of further changes to come. Thirty years after American repudiation of membership in a universal security organization and a peacetime alliance with France and Britain, a Democratic administration and a bipartisan majority in Congress had agreed to both.

The other decision of 1948 and 1949 was made by Germans, sixty-five representatives of the eleven states of Trizonia, meeting in a hastily converted natural history museum in Bonn. In the uncertain atmosphere of a potential Soviet-American confrontation in the air over Berlin, they drafted a constitution, the *Grundgesetz* (Basic Law), for a new federal West German state. The work of the Parliamentary Council, chaired by Konrad Adenauer, laid the basis for the foreign policy initiatives of the next decade. The executive, legislative, and judicial structures of the Federal Republic represented a commitment to the building of new relationships of mutual trust and prosperity with France and the other countries of western Europe.

By authorizing the reestablishment of political parties and reinstituting the electoral process from the ground up, from the local level to the states, the allied occupation authorities had predetermined the strength the individual *Länder* (states) were to have in shaping the Basic Law. This was no accident. Although the initial decisions on local and state political activity were made before the authorities knew that the four-power regime would break down, both the Americans and the French had strong reasons for favoring a decentralized Germany: the Americans because they believed in the strength of a federal system, the French because they believed in its weaknesses. Washington's "reeducators" saw in federalism the foundation of an enduring democracy; for Paris's strategists, it meant a safeguard against the channeling of Germany's economic potential toward war by a strong central government.

The federal idea had a long historical tradition in Germany, from the hundreds of small states of the Holy Roman Empire through the Weimar Republic. Only after 1933, for twelve short years, did Germans live in a centralized state in which even local authority was delegated from Berlin. France hoped, not without reason, that regionalism could be encouraged in post-1945 Germany and that French influence would be strong over the individual states, particularly in the Catholic southwest and Rhineland, as it had been before 1870. The historical precedent for such expectations was the Confederation of the Rhine, established by Napoleon in 1806. By no means did initial French plans foresee the establishment of any state, federal or otherwise, the size of the Federal Republic, and the French remained the most skeptical of the three western allies in 1949.[11]

Economic rationalization and the Cold War had combined, however, to convince the French to add their occupation zone to the Anglo-American "Bizonia" in early 1948. As a result, the economic integration of the three zones, especially after the currency reform, was already well underway when the Länder representatives gathered at Bonn to draft the Basic Law. The republic they established was one in which the constituent states retained broad areas of competence; as such, it was a more congenial neighbor for France than any state across the Rhine since 1871. The Basic Law delegated foreign policy to the federal government but gave the states control over education, cultural affairs, and economic development. It provided for no defense establishment because the Parliamentary Council had no plans to raise West German armed forces in 1948 and 1949.

For the purposes of Adenauer's foreign policy, the form chosen for the West German state established on May 9, 1949, signaled three things to France and its other western European neighbors: its willingness to forgo the goal of German reunification, in the short term, in the interest of the security and prosperity of western Europe; its commitment to a republican form of government and to rectifying the structural defects of Weimar and its antagonistic political parties; and its acceptance of further allied control over its external relations and military security. Adenauer's pursuit of sovereignty and international recognition for the Federal Republic was based on an accurate perception of how far and how fast the allies were willing to go. Step by step, he believed, a great deal could be achieved but not by intransigent demands for dramatic change; in this also, he was far more astute than Schumacher. Adenauer projected the combination of sobriety and gratitude that the western allies expected and conveyed the Federal Republic's "modest determination to serve its apprenticeship in democracy."[12]

The Federal Republic's Western Strategy

The first federal election in August 1949, after a year of economic growth and the success of the Berlin Airlift, brought the Christian Democrats a plurality that enabled Adenauer's party to form the first of its many coalitions with the Free Democrats (FDP). At age seventy-three, the former mayor of Cologne became the first chancellor of the new West German state; he was to remain in office for fourteen years. In that decade and a half, Adenauer took his party and the Federal Republic down the path to western European cooperation that all of his successors in the chancellery followed. His government also developed, in its Frankreichpolitik, a multifaceted policy of reconciliation with France that served as the model for his successors' Deutschland- and Ostpolitik after 1969.

This model had three components. First, recognizing the appalling reputation and continuing mistrust of Germany abroad, Bonn saw the advantages of pursuing its bilateral relations in a *multilateral framework*. One such framework was a given in the early years, as the three Allied High Commissioners looked down at Adenauer's new government from the Petersberg across the Rhine from Bonn. Replacing the military governors of the three zones in 1949, the civilian representatives of Paris, London, and Washington still had the final word on the Federal Republic's external relations, as well as on many domestic questions. In its first years in office, the government—for all practical purposes, Konrad Adenauer—had to walk a line of cooperating with as well as challenging the three western allies in the defense of West German interests.

Despite the angry remark by Kurt Schumacher in the Bundestag that Adenauer failed to defend those interests, that he was the "chancellor of the allies,"[13] the Federal Republic had established itself in their councils so successfully by the mid-1950s that the three western powers sometimes seemed to be the allies of the chancellor. The reason for Bonn's success lay in its support for a network of multilateral relationships with its western European neighbors in which the great political-military problem of the preceding seventy-five years, the Franco-German rivalry, could find a solution. Beginning in 1950 with the European Coal and Steel Community (ECSC), through the ill-fated European Defense Community (EDC), the 1954 Paris Agreements bringing West Germany into NATO, and the establishment of the European Economic Community (EEC) and Atomic Energy Agency (EURATOM) in the 1957 Treaties of Rome, the economic and political position of a significant German state in Europe was restored to the Federal Republic with the full cooperation of those neighbors that, in 1945, had most feared a rebirth of German power on the continent.

The second component of Adenauer's foreign policy, as he entered step by step into these multilateral commitments, was his willingness to confront the foreign policy implications of recent German history and to implement *confidence-building measures* (CBMs), not yet known as such, to counter the effects of that history. A quarter-century before the 1975 Helsinki Conference on Security and Cooperation in Europe (CSCE), no umbrella term yet existed for this aspect of Bonn's strategy, but by whatever name, CBMs played a major role in it. In many respects, West Germany itself, with its federal structure and emphasis on justice and freedom for the three western zones rather than on reunification, was the foremost confidence-building measure of all. Others followed: economic restitution to the victims of the Third Reich, including the new state of Israel, willingness to accept the results of the 1955 plebiscite in the Saarland, and NATO-dedication of the Bundeswehr's field army, among them.

Finally, a major component of this strategy of recognition and reconciliation was its emphasis on what was called in the 1950s, reminiscent of the hopeful but abortive rapprochement between Paris and Berlin in the 1920s, a *Locarno from below*.[14] While Bonn concentrated on the pursuit of detente with Paris in the developing multilateral institutions of western European and Atlantic cooperation, it encouraged individuals, private groups, and local governments to establish student exchange programs, summer language camps, sister cities and universities, and other frameworks of mutual contact for the citizens of the two countries. Seeing these programs between France and West Germany as they developed in the 1950s as "cultural" exchange in a narrow sense would be quite wrong. They were, largely, cultural exchange programs, and they were carried out by nongovernmental organizations, but both their local organizers and their supporters in Bonn had clear foreign policy goals in mind. Throughout the decade, a bilateral network of cooperation between the two countries developed at a level below that of "high" policy. The Locarno from below was evidence to other western Europeans that the Federal Republic paid more than lip service to democracy at home and reconciliation abroad.

In retrospect, the three components of Bonn's strategy were insep-
arable; the link between them was the burden of German history. The
three European wars launched by Germany since 1870, Berlin's annexation of Alsace-Lorraine in 1871, the 1914 occupation of Belgium, and
the Third Reich's racist assault on European civilization were the legacy
with which the Federal Republic had to live. Unlike many of his
countrymen, Adenauer had no illusions about the depth of anti-German
feeling abroad, no matter how much the Federal Republic was needed as
a player on the western side of the Cold War.[15] This clarity distinguished
him from other politicians in his own party and in the opposition parties.
From the point of view of his counterparts abroad, Adenauer's apparently
instinctive appreciation of their own skepticism—and that of their
domestic constituencies—made him the ideal first chancellor of the
Federal Republic.[16]

Adenauer's strategy of reconciliation with France through multilateral
cooperation, confidence-building measures, and grassroots diplomacy
was implemented in the 1950s and 1960s. Before examining this strategy,
however, we must consider the other side of the coin of this positive
concept: the renunciation by the Federal Republic of the same strategy
vis-à-vis the Soviet Union and eastern Europe. On the surface, such a
renunciation is puzzling. The burden of recent German history was, if
anything, greater in eastern Europe than in the west. The costs of that
history, for both Germans and their neighbors, had been higher east of
the Elbe than on the Rhine frontiers. In its first two decades, however,
the new West German state evolved no strategy of reconciliation with its
eastern neighbors comparable to the policy it pursued so vigorously in the
west. Why not?

The Cold War is a large part of the answer, but only part of it. The
breakdown in the wartime alliance made possible two things that were
essential to the success of Franco-(West) German reconciliation: an
American security commitment to France (through NATO) and the
foreclosure of a domestic debate in the Federal Republic comparable to
the Rapallo-Locarno debate that had plagued Weimar. Adenauer's
opposition to a German policy of "equidistance" in Europe had nothing
to do with the Cold War. In the 1920s, he had opposed a *Schaukelpolitik*
(pendulum policy) that brought Berlin few advantages in eastern Europe
but strengthened the new Communist government in Moscow and
antagonized London and Paris.[17] The Cold War confirmed his suspicions
of such a policy, but it did not create them.

For Adenauer, the appropriate path for Germans to travel in Europe
was one shared with the French, but until the late 1940s his viewpoint
was not the dominant one in the German foreign policy debate. In the
1920s, both late-nineteenth-century concepts of conflictual international

relations, in which economic and political rivalries were zero-sum games, and the domestic influence of the "east Elbians" within the German state prevented the elaboration of a clear policy of cooperation with France and Weimar's self-affirmation as a *west* European country. Stresemann came as close as he could at Locarno and Geneva, but both out of personal conviction and an appreciation of his domestic constituency he could not forgo either Berlin's dialogue with the Soviet Union or its demand for territorial revisions in eastern Europe.[18] When the Cold War more or less required that the Federal Republic forgo both, at least in the short run, Adenauer had no personal objections to doing so.

He rightly saw that the prospects for reconciliation with France depended, in the immediate postwar period, on the *lack* of prospects for reconciliation with the Soviet Union. Berlin had had too many options in the years before 1941; from Bismarck's alliances through the 1922 German-Soviet Rapallo Treaty and the 1939 Molotov-Ribbentrop Pact, it had had no pressing need to pursue detente with Paris. Bonn had no such options. Its restoration as a European power depended on the willingness of Paris to integrate a German state into the councils of Europe, and that willingness depended on the extent to which France could be convinced that such a state posed no security risk to it or its allies. Bonn's *inability* to maneuver between east and west was an asset, not a liability, but few of Adenauer's domestic political opponents recognized it at the time.

As Adenauer's policies took shape, Paris gradually came to believe that the economic and political strength of the Federal Republic did not detract from, but enhanced, its own security. This simple statement of the course of Franco–West German relations in the 1950s, however, disguises a revolution in French thinking, a revolution that would not have been possible had Bonn attempted to pursue the same policies in eastern Europe that it was pursuing in western Europe. Had the Federal Republic sought a dialogue in the east, the suspicions of decades past would never have died in Paris. Adenauer recognized that French policy aimed at a double containment: of Soviet ambitions, but also of any renascent German ambitions to hegemony in Europe.[19] He also knew that recent German history made London and Washington sympathetic to French concerns—and that they had a few of their own. Their double containment policy required that Moscow and Bonn not be able to turn to each other, as Moscow and Berlin had done in the early 1920s, against the will of the western victors.

It also required peacetime allies, specifically the Anglo-Saxons, as the French liked to say, and in 1949 Paris got the alliance that had been denied it in 1920. The North Atlantic Treaty and, in 1954, London's commitment to maintain the British Army of the Rhine in the Federal Republic changed the nature of the French domestic debate on the wisdom of encouraging a growing economic and military role for West Germany in Europe. No longer would France have to face Germany alone across their common frontier; the Low Countries, as well as the United States, Britain, and Canada, were members of NATO, and West Germany was neither in territory nor in population the state of 1937. These factors, combined with Bonn's lack of diplomatic options in the east, provided Paris with the confidence to pursue a relationship with its rearmed neighbor across the Rhine. These conditions were lacking a quarter-century before, when Weimar's pendulum policy had unsettled the Third Republic.

Bonn's Eastern Strategy: A New Pendulum?

For twenty years, the relationship between France and West Germany was at the heart of Bonn's foreign policy. By the mid-1960s, the strategy Adenauer had pursued in the West had brought about virtually all the results that could be expected of it. It had been a striking success. The Westpolitik alone, however, could not provide an answer to the question posed by a divided Germany. For that matter, twenty years after the end of the war, Germans were no longer sure what that question was: Open borders? Territorial revision? Political reunification? After the Saar plebiscite in 1955, no such troubling ambiguity had surrounded Bonn's aims in western Europe. Moreover, by 1965, West German expectations were higher: the days when one of Bonn's principal goals had been public acknowledgment by the western allies of its voice in their councils were long gone.

The 1960s in West Germany was a decade in which the results of the economic and political decisions of the early 1950s were clearly visible. To the generations old enough to remember the years before 1945, the economic miracle of reconstruction was more than matched by the political miracle of rapprochement with France. A new postwar generation, however, which had grown up with the institutions of western European cooperation, found nothing unusual in their existence. Taking the benefits for granted, that generation began to analyze the costs of its country's membership in the Atlantic Alliance and the European Community. It found, as an older generation of political leaders had already begun to recognize, that one of the expectations of the 1950s had remained, and was likely to remain, unfulfilled: that western integration would destabilize Soviet-dominated eastern Europe and contribute to a reunification of Germany on western terms.[20]

Twenty years after Konrad Adenauer presented his first cabinet to the Allied High Commissioners on the Petersberg, the first Social

Democratic chancellor of West Germany, Willy Brandt, submitted the program of his government to the Bundestag. After three years in the foreign office, Brandt came to the chancellery in 1969 with a mandate to redefine the Federal Republic's relationship with the Soviet Union, eastern Europe, and the German Democratic Republic. The years when Bonn's dialogue with the west required a blackout toward the east had passed; Adenauer's unhesitating choice for western Europe had changed the climate of the foreign policy debate. West Germany was now recognized by its allies as being *within* the West and, with them, a partner in the developing east-west dialogue.[21]

Consequently, those who set a new foreign policy agenda for the Federal Republic in the late 1960s turned to the western strategy of the 1950s for their model. The Social Democratic leaders of 1969 built a new Ost- and Deutschlandpolitik by following a course charted by the Christian Democratic West- and Frankreichpolitik of the preceding two decades. The three components of the eastern strategy of the 1970s remained those of its western predecessor: multilateral institutions, confidence-building measures, and grassroots diplomacy and detente from below. Adenauer in 1949 and Brandt in 1969 faced fundamentally similar situations, but by the latter date the very success of the detente policies of the 1950s had disguised the fact that that is what they were and that Adenauer's task in the west had been at least as daunting as Brandt's in the east.

Not surprisingly, Brandt's government did not call attention to similarities between its proposals and Adenauer's western detente. In 1969 the new government had political reasons to avoid drawing parallels between its pursuit of an eastern dialogue and its predecessors' pursuit of a western one. Drawing attention to how bad Franco-German relations had been only a generation before was not on Bonn's list of priorities. The politics of the hour required distinctions, not similarities: partnership *in* the west, dialogue *with* the east. As a result, the existence of the western partnership was taken for granted, which obscured the great achievement of the 1950s: the establishment of the Federal Republic's first dialogue, with the west. Before it became a partner, Bonn had been a supplicant, and before that, an enemy state. In its first decade, the position and role of the Federal Republic in western Europe had changed because it successfully implemented a concept of dialogue leading to partnership.

Nevertheless, whenever West Germans discussed dialogue and partnership with the GDR, the Soviet Union, and the countries of eastern Europe, uneasy warnings of trading Locarno for Rapallo and of "special paths" for Germany inevitably appeared in the capitals of western Europe and the United States. How recently a western dialogue with

Germany, much less partnership, seemed neither desirable nor likely had virtually faded from memory.

Certainly, the speed with which that partnership developed in the 1950s depended on the Cold War—more precisely, on the Soviet threat and the American response—for much of its dynamic. It also depended, however, to an extent which has been forgotten in the past quarter-century, on the recognition of a common threat *within* western Europe, if the hostility between France and Germany were allowed to continue. Not all the supporters of the western strategy in the 1950s were enthusiastic about it—far from it. The western option—the only one at the time—was near to Adenauer's heart, but it was a marriage of convenience for many of his constituents, as it was for other Europeans with fresh memories of war and occupation. It was not a love match but concern for the economic and political survival of their countries and of western Europe that took Paris and Bonn down a path that led to new destinations.

At the start of the journey in 1950, the direction it would take was anything but certain. Adenauer had been chancellor for less than a year when the trip began, with the proposal of the French foreign minister, Robert Schuman, to create a European Coal and Steel Community (ECSC). The Schuman Plan was offered to the Federal Republic on the fifth anniversary of the end of World War II in Europe. Paris's offer of cooperation was a far cry from the fifth anniversary of the end of World War I, when its troops had been in the Ruhr for ten months, and the Weimar Republic despairingly ended passive resistance to the French occupation.

That Schuman's proposal was meant to be the beginning of a new era in Franco-German relations was clear; that it would succeed was less so. Once before, in the Locarno years from 1925 to 1929, Europe had had expectations of better days to come between Berlin and Paris, but the seeds of the new relationship had never taken root. Ample reason for skepticism existed in 1950. Still, given an unexpected opportunity, after all that had happened in the intervening years, to build on the foundation laid by Gustav Stresemann and Aristide Briand a quarter-century before, the Federal Republic responded favorably to the French proposal. Adenauer's answer to Schuman began Bonn's long march through the institutions of Europe.

Notes

1. "Communiqué Issued at the End of the [Yalta] Conference," *Foreign Relations of the United States: The Conferences at Malta and Yalta 1945* (Washington: U.S. Government Printing Office, 1955), pp. 970–971. One of

the best concise treatments of the Allies' wartime diplomacy is still William L. Neumann, *After Victory: Churchill, Roosevelt, Stalin, and the Making of the Peace* (New York: Harper & Row, 1966).

2. This manifested itself not only in the occupation regime but also in the deliberations of the International Military Tribunal at Nuremberg, where, as Willy Brandt said forty years later, "the 'other Germany' had neither say nor influence." See: " . . . *wir sind nicht zu Helden geboren": Ein Gespräch über Deutschland mit Birgit Kraatz* (Zurich: Diogenes, 1986), p. 106.

3. Robert R. Bowie, "Die Zusammenarbeit der politischen Führungsgruppen," in Karl Kaiser and Hans-Peter Schwarz, eds., *Amerika und Westeuropa*, (Stuttgart: Belser Verlag, 1977), pp. 46–47.

4. The Ambassador to the USSR to the Secretary of State: "Such concessions as we might be willing to make would . . . only postpone the day when Soviet pressure to force us out of Berlin will be reapplied." *Foreign Relations of the United States, 1948*, vol. II: *Germany and Austria* (Washington: U.S. Government Printing Office, 1973), pp. 984–985.

5. See, for example, the documents reproduced in: Günter Buchstab, Brigitte Kaff, and Hans-Otto Kleinmann, eds., *Verfolgung und Widerstand: 1933–1945—Christliche Demokraten gegen Hitler* (Düsseldorf: Droste, 1986), especially the founding appeal of the Berlin CDU, pp. 270–271. On the French side, these ideas grew in the resistance movement itself. See, for examples, Henri Michel and Boris Mirkine-Guetzevitch, *Les idées politiques et sociales de la Résistance* (Paris: Presses Universitaires de France, 1954), especially, "Résistance. . . Espoir de l'Europe," pp. 396–397.

6. One of them was SPD leader Carlo Schmid. Born in France in 1896, son of a German father and French mother, Schmid became one of the most eloquent architects of the Federal Republic and the postwar Franco–West German relationship. In his *Erinnerungen* (Bern: Scherz, 1979), p. 217, he analyzed the failure of his generation to stop the rise of Nazism after World War I. Deciding in 1945 that he would have to find his "way out of the ivory tower," Schmid wrote that, "I and people like me [were] guilty, because we thought we were too good" for politics. He decided, because he did "not want to be guilty again," that he would "go into politics, with the knowledge that a goal cannot be reached through belief in its necessity alone."

7. Schumacher infuriated all three of the western occupying powers, his comments "almost invariably reflect[ing] a deep suspicion of their motives and intense irritation with their actions. . . . He denounced scathingly what he termed their insistence that they always knew better than Germany's 'legitimate' leaders what was best for German and world interests." French High Commissioner André François-Poncet was said to have called him a "Faustian schizophrenic," and a British official in 1949 reportedly found him a "dogmatic, doctrinaire, distorted old man with a twisted mind." As for the Americans, "Schumacher's relations with General Clay . . . were exceptionally bad." See Lewis J. Edinger, *Kurt Schumacher* (Stanford: Stanford University Press, 1965), pp. 160, 176, 179, 183.

8. See Hans-Peter Schwarz, *Adenauer* (Stuttgart: Deutsche Verlags-Anstalt, 1986), pp. 306–307 for a discussion of whether Adenauer objected to the

content or the style of Berlin's foreign policy in the 1920s. See also Wolfgang Stresemann, *Mein Vater Gustav Stresemann* (Berlin: Ullstein, 1985), pp. 262–263, where Adenauer is described as "a Rhinelander, to whom Bismarck's Reich was no noli me tangere, a man of the West, to whom—in contrast to my father—Königsberg seemed very far away."

9. Memorandum by the Deputy Assistant Secretary of State for Occupied Areas to the Under Secretary of State, March 10, 1948, *Foreign Relations of the United States, 1948*, vol. II: *Germany and Austria*, pp. 879–880.

10. Ibid., p. 880. In his reply to the joint State Department and Army instructions, General Clay "indicated that he had felt for some time that quadripartite agreement could not be reached."

11. As Alfred Grosser wrote, the French thesis was that "Prussia must be destroyed and Germany divided." *Affaires Extérieures*, (Paris: Flammarion, 1984), p. 35.

12. F. Roy Willis, *France, Germany, and the New Europe, 1945–1961* (London: Oxford University Press, 1968), p. 60.

13. Schmid, *Erinnerungen*, pp. 455–456.

14. The phrase was apparently first used in September 1951, when the International Mayors Union for Franco-German Understanding (IBU), founded in Switzerland in June 1948, held its fourth annual congress in Locarno. Emphasizing the link between the goals of its work and that of Aristide Briand and Gustav Stresemann a quarter-century before, the IBU began to develop a work program of cooperation at the local level, including sister cities, student exchanges, and other forms of people-to-people diplomacy. See Heinz Engelhardt, "Deutsch-französische Städtepartnerschaften," *Kulturarbeit* (1963): 5.

15. Schwarz, *Adenauer*, p. 719. Jean Monnet recalled in his *Memoirs* (Garden City, NY: Doubleday, 1978), p. 309, the "degree of mistrust" that Adenauer was "unable completely to conceal" at their first meeting, the effect of "long years of hard negotiation and wounded pride" on the chancellor. Adenauer's demeanor reflected, as Schumacher's did not, his awareness of how little sympathy existed abroad for Germany.

16. A fact not lost on Kurt Schumacher, who "never visited France, and seem[ed] entirely unable to understand the French point of view," which was, indeed, that "almost any other German leader, but particularly the Francophile Adenauer" was preferable to Schumacher as chancellor of the new West German state. The SPD leader was an eloquent spokesman for German interests, but Adenauer was able to accomplish more, precisely because he talked about the Allies with circumspection in public and to them with candor in private. See Edinger, *Kurt Schumacher*, p. 175.

17. Schwarz, *Adenauer*, pp. 306–307.

18. See, for a discussion of Gustav Stresemann's policy, Stresemann, *Mein Vater*, pp. 373–379.

19. Despite the fact that, as Grosser wrote (*Affaires Extérieures*, p. 79), "The possible division of Germany [was] no longer a way to prevent the rebirth of German unity, but the expression of the [east-west] division" of Europe. As Raymond Aron recognized at the time, the Cold War meant that "the

rapprochement of France with the western part of Germany was inevitable." As early as 1945, Aron had noted that Hitler had punished his own country more cruelly than the Allies ever could; by 1947, he was calling for a "positive and constructive French doctrine" aimed at the reconstruction of Germany, which "will be carried out against us, if we refuse to participate in it." Raymond Aron, *Mémoires* (Paris: Julliard, 1983), pp. 202, 213.

20. "The Russians, like the Americans, had begun to adjust to the status quo in Europe," while the Germans "were confronted daily . . . with the grim results of their division." Helga Haftendorn, "Wurzeln der Ost- und Entspannungspolitik der Sozial-Liberalen Koalition," in Horst Ehmke, Karlheinz Koppe, and Herbert Wehner, eds., *Zwanzig Jahre Ostpolitik: Bilanz und Perspektiven* (Bonn: Verlag Neue Gesellschaft, 1986), pp. 17–18.

21. And in the *west-west* dialogue. In his *Begegnungen und Einsichten* (Hamburg: Hoffmann und Campe, 1976), pp. 130–162, Willy Brandt described a decade of "conversations with DeGaulle" on the future of Europe and the Franco-German relationship. The French nationalist understood the motives underlying West Germany's search for a post-Adenauer Ostpolitik, provided, as Brandt noted (p. 153), that Germans recognized that "what was lost in the war, after their attack on Poland and Czechoslovakia," the borders of the Reich, could not be recovered.

2

GRAPPLING WITH THE PAST AND A GERMAN IDENTITY

May 8, 1945

Germans born in the second half of the twentieth century, whatever their personal history, are confronted early in life with their country's "difficult" recent past. Discussing that past is not getting any easier for them, in the short term, as the unspoken consensus on proper German behavior that existed for a quarter-century after World War II has largely eroded. In its place is a lively, even shrill, debate on the need to remember. But to remember what? Auschwitz and Dachau? The courage and fortitude of the average German soldier? The destruction of Rotterdam and Sevastopol? Of Hamburg and Dresden? Germans have a difficult history, but is it really more difficult than that of other nations? The answer once seemed so obvious that no one posed the question. Today, German historians trying to place the Third Reich in a broader historical context and individuals hoping to understand what they or their families did a half-century ago argue over both the question and the answer.[1]

Vergangenheitsbewältigung—coming to terms with the past—is the German expression used to describe the process. The English translation does not convey the multidimensional nature of the concept: the necessity to confront the past, to deal with it, to learn to live with it, to understand it—in order to come to grips with the present and the future. The German word describes a never-ending process, not a completed action, and a task facing all Germans born before or after 1945. That a people whose language requires such a word spends a good deal of time discussing its responsibility for what Friedrich Meinecke called the "German catastrophe"[2] is not surprising.

One of the best-known and most eloquent contributions to this discussion was Federal President Richard von Weizsäcker's speech to the

22

West German parliament on May 8, 1985, to commemorate the fortieth anniversary of the end of World War II in Europe. To commemorate, not to celebrate, as Weizsäcker said:

> For us Germans, May 8 is no day of celebration. Those who remember May 8, 1945 think of their own, often quite different experiences. Some came home, others became homeless. Some were freed, while for others, their captivity had only begun. Many were simply thankful that the nights of bombs and fear were over, and that they had survived. Others were saddened by the complete defeat of their own country. Embittered Germans faced shattered illusions, while others were grateful for the opportunity that had been given them to begin again. . . . Most Germans had believed that they were fighting in a good cause for their own country. And now they learned: it was all not only senseless and in vain, but in the service of the inhuman goals of a criminal leadership.[3]

This knowledge meant that Germans were not free to mourn their own defeat; the Allied victory had liberated Germans as well as the rest of German-occupied Europe from Nazism, something that became clear in the cold light of historical hindsight. Yet what use was that knowledge to German veterans, widows, and orphans in 1945? Given the recent past, the world had no interest in German self-pity.

Many Germans felt the same way. Unlike their neighbors, Germans had to learn to separate their individual grief from their national defeat and to mourn the dead and the lost while recognizing that Europe was well-spared the German victory for which they had died and sacrificed. Not hypocrisy but a clearer vision of their own past and future allowed many Germans to recognize that, as Europeans, they too had a stake in the victory over Nazi Germany. Among them were Social Democrats in exile abroad and in concentration camps at home; the founders of the Christian Democratic Union in Berlin, many of whom lived underground in the closing days of the war; the student protesters of the White Rose in Munich; and the Wehrmacht officers and Foreign Office members who plotted to kill Hitler on July 20, 1944.[4]

Recognizing that fact and, in the immediate postwar period, rebuilding public and private lives on it was one thing; integrating the dichotomies of defeat and liberation into a historical memory that would have meaning for generations of Germans too young to remember the war was another. The failure to accomplish this is one of the most glaring characteristics of postwar Germany, and time is running out. The generation old enough to have political responsibility in the 1930s and 1940s has already passed from the political stage. When Weizsäcker's generation, which fought the war as young men and women, departs, those who can speak from personal experience of guilt and responsibility will be gone, but the questions regarding guilt, responsibility, and German identity will remain.

These questions make the Federal Republic and the German Democratic Republic (GDR), heirs to the legacy of the Third Reich, unique allies within, respectively, NATO and the Warsaw Pact. The division of their country that resulted from the war has added to the German identity crisis. Indeed, facing their own responsibility for the division of Europe is another problem for Germans. Weizsäcker said:

> The meeting of Soviet and American troops on the Elbe became a symbol of the end of a European era. . . . The division of Europe into two different political systems ran its course. Postwar developments hardened that division, but without the war begun by Hitler it would not have happened. The . . . origins of the flight and expulsion and loss of freedom were not in the end of the war, but in its beginnings, and in the beginnings of that despotism which led to war. We may not separate May 8, 1945 from January 30, 1933.[5]

Germans live not only with questions of their responsibility for what they, or their parents or grandparents, did to Europe a half-century ago but also with the consequences of those German policies for Europeans today.

One of those consequences is the existence of the two German states. Their relationship to each other is the third component of the German identity crisis. After only seventy-four years of political unity, Germany as a national state ceased to exist in 1945. Many Germans lived through the entire life cycle of that state, from its unification under the king of Prussia in 1871 to the founding of the Federal Republic and the GDR in 1949. The second, and last, president of the Weimar Republic, Field Marshal von Hindenburg, fought as a young Prussian officer against the Austrians at Königgrätz in 1866, in the war that established the North German Confederation. Konrad Adenauer was already thirty-eight years old in the summer of 1914, when Europe plunged itself into World War I. In his speech to the Bundestag, Weizsäcker recalled that:

> a common past unites [us]. It can be a cause for happiness or a problem— may it always be a source of hope. We Germans feel ourselves bound to each other by our common history. On May 8, 1945, we experienced together a fate which unites us. . . . We have the confidence to believe that May 8 will not be the last date in our history which all Germans will share together.[6]

The final component of the German identity crisis is the symbiotic role that Germans have played historically between eastern and western Europe.[7] The Third Reich definitively rejected the legacy of cultural diversity and tolerance that Germany had inherited from its Prussian and

Austrian ancestors. In the late nineteenth century, Wilhelmine Germany had already begun to abandon that legacy to its own concepts of "Germanness," in a social Darwinian age; but, despite the political developments of the last hundred years, the consequences of German settlement in eastern Europe and the cross-fertilization of the German, Polish, and Slavic cultures over seven centuries remain. Nazi ideology and the Cold War both fostered an atypical and antihistorical relationship between Germans and their eastern neighbors. Weizsäcker took special care to consider this relationship:

> When we remember the suffering inflicted on our eastern neighbors in the war, we will better understand that detente and peaceful relations with these countries remains the central task of German foreign policy. Both sides must remember and respect each other. They have human, cultural, and historical reasons to do so. We want friendship with the peoples of the Soviet Union. . . . [A]ssuring people a lasting, secure future in the homes where fate brought them after May 8, 1945, and where they have now lived for decades, . . . is the real, human contribution that we can make to a European peace order.[8]

In the last years of the twentieth century, after a hiatus of three decades, Germans began again to face the reality of their own identity crisis and the foreign policy implications of their ambiguous history. Their failure to do so earlier led to a conscious effort on the part of some West German historians to do so now, among them, Michael Stürmer. Stürmer's contention that he who shapes a country's shared historical memory also shapes its political future may seem commonplace in nations with less difficult histories; in a country with Germany's experience of attempts to shape its collective consciousness, it can seem a sinister idea.[9]

Despite their wariness, however, even critics of the concept of "historicizing" Germany's past by comparing it with the totalitarian experience in other countries and eras recognize that the German identity crisis makes a new historical memory necessary. On the other side of the political spectrum from Stürmer, West German diplomat and journalist Günter Gaus attacked "those who proclaim that the raison d'être of the Federal Republic is its membership in the Atlantic Alliance." After World War II, Gaus maintained, West Germans deprived of their own national identity "adopted aspects of the identity of the Federal Republic's ally, the United States." Gaus concluded:

> NATO is the bridge to America for the West German majority: more than that, it is . . . the opportunity for an exchange of identity with the United States. . . . West Germany is like a man who lost his sense of balance a long time ago, but who has forgotten his injury because he has been able to lean

on someone else. If I were a rationally-thinking American, such an ally would bring me no comfort.[10]

In addition to its dependence on the United States, the majority of West Germans, wrote Gaus, "is oriented only to the present, having carefully directed both the past and the future into manageable channels."[11] Like many of his countrymen in the late 1980s, Gaus asked, "If Europe remains at peace and the two German states survive for another forty years: what consciousness of [our] own identity will prevail on this side of and across the Elbe?"[12] Bonn's allies were asking the same question.

The Other German State

Before turning to the impact of the German identity crisis on the Federal Republic, specifically, on its foreign policy, a word or two is required about the German Democratic Republic. In Western, particularly American, studies of east-west relations in Europe, East Germany barely existed at all until very recently. To a great extent, this gap reflected the success with which West Germany in the late 1950s advanced its claim to be the only legitimate German state, while the GDR remained the "Soviet-occupied zone." (The nature of the GDR's closed society clearly played a role but is not a sufficient explanation, as the other closed societies of eastern Europe and the USSR did not suffer from a similar blackout of American scholarship.) Several aftereffects of those years are relevant to the identity crisis and Bonn's foreign policy.

First, nuances of language are used by combatants in the West German political wars. The "zone" has passed out of fashion, except on the right-wing fringe, but a leading daily newspaper still writes "DDR," in quotation marks, when referring to the German Democratic Republic.[13] Sometime in the 1970s, Bonn developed a sensitivity to the use of initials to describe itself; since then, West German officialdom and anyone who does not wish to alienate that officialdom have avoided using FRG to describe the Federal Republic. (Its own antipathy to initials has had no impact on official Bonn's use of DDR.) Americans seem to have been the most accommodating; the British still use FRG, and the French use of RFA for the Federal Republic is as common as RDA for East Germany. For their part, the East Germans are the most consistent. They use DDR for themselves and BRD for the Federal Republic—with no quotation marks.

Moreover, Bonn's fixation with initials apparently applies only to the Federal Republic itself. West Germans happily refer to the two superpowers as USA and USSR, leaving mystified foreigners to wonder what all the fuss over FRG and BRD is about. As the latest development in the nuance wars, West German television commentators recently began referring to the Federal Republic as "the republic," a phrase that, consciously or not, they share with their East German counterparts, who use it to describe the GDR. (That West German television is available virtually everywhere in East Germany may or may not be relevant.)

To non-German speakers, what does all this mean? Does it matter at all? In many respects, the Bonn language wars are reminiscent of those fought in the United States in the 1960s between partisans of the Republic of China and the People's Republic of China. Whether one said "Taiwan" or "Red China" was very much a political question, and the extent to which the PRC is now referred to simply as "China" is indicative of the state of political relations between Washington and Beijing (Peking?). Similarly, in the years of the Cold War, Bonn succeeded, especially in the United States, in presenting itself as "Germany," excluding the GDR both linguistically and politically from the American consciousness. Ironically, now the Federal Republic itself, despite the word games it still plays, would like to see greater American awareness of the German Democratic Republic. Bonn is paying the price of its own past success.

By whatever name the GDR is known, however, the legacy of German history was clearly not left to West Germans alone. A study of the past forty years in East Germany would doubtless reveal an identity crisis different from that in the Federal Republic, but a crisis nonetheless. Compared to Bonn, however, East Berlin had two major advantages: the ideology of a Communist state and the flight of large numbers of the upper and middle classes to the western occupation zones.[14] In sheer numbers, Bonn inherited more people likely to have held politically and economically responsible positions before 1945.

To those who did bear responsibility for the crimes of the Third Reich, the GDR offered a much simpler answer than pluralist West Germany: embracing the new Communist system and working for its success were deemed a sufficient break from Nazi Germany. The west in general and the Federal Republic specifically were not always scrupulous in examining past political activities, particularly when a leading scientist or intelligence expert—witness Klaus Barbie—appeared crucial to Cold War competition with the Soviet Union, but neither the consciences of western decision-makers nor the voices of intellectuals opposing such political opportunism could be easily silenced. The all-embracing worldview by which the East German Communists could excuse service to the all-embracing worldview of National Socialism was not available to the west, not even in the heyday of McCarthyism.

East Berlin offered individual Germans more than a path away from responsibility for the Third Reich, however. Communism provided an interpretation of a millennium of German history in which National Socialism became the inevitable outcome of the betrayal of the working classes by a Prussian aristocracy and a property-owning bourgeoisie. For a quarter-century, East Berlin clung to a historical interpretation that rejected Luther, the kings of Prussia, and Bismarck, as well as Hitler, as part of a relevant—to the new socialist state—German tradition. Only in the last decade has historical scholarship in East Germany begun to move away from this centrally decreed interpretation of the German past, while restoration of historic buildings and statues has reached levels unimaginable in the early 1970s. (To say nothing of the 1950s, when historic buildings that had survived World War II virtually intact, including the palace of the Hohenzollerns on Unter den Linden, were deliberately destroyed.)

External factors help explain the GDR's new policies towards the interpretation of German history. Abroad, much East German historical scholarship was dismissed as trapped in a Stalinist time warp and vocabulary. More importantly, the growing accessibility of West German television in the 1970s prevented the GDR from filtering out alternative views of the German past, as it could much more successfully twenty years before. Finally, as West German tourism became a critical factor in the East German economy, the state of the GDR's historic cities—Weimar, Dresden, East Berlin itself—became not only an embarrassment but also an economic liability. West Germans without relatives there were not going to spend their money in the GDR, certainly not more than once, to see concrete slabs of Stalinist architecture, fallen-down monuments, and museums filled with ideological tracts.

As critical as all these factors were, however, to the economically pragmatic decision-makers in East Berlin, something even more important seemed to be taking place within the GDR with the view East Germans began to have of themselves. In 1945, many West Germans saw themselves at a zero hour, a *Stunde Null*, at which point the history of their country up to then came to an end. Such views have become increasingly rare in the Federal Republic. Much of the West German debate on identity and foreign policy over the past decade has grown from the realization that no people, no matter how wrenching a turning point it experiences, can put down the burden, or the glory, of its own history.

The concept of the zero hour, however, widespread as it was in the West German consciousness, reached its height in the GDR. Nevertheless, after thirty years of propagating that concept, the political leaders of East Germany over the past decade apparently concluded, as did their counterparts in the Federal Republic, that it was simply not true. More importantly, from their point of view, it would not meet the needs of East Germans for a more nuanced view of their own past. The new socialist citizen of the GDR was also the old German citizen, descended from Martin Luther and Frederick the Great, whether the East Berlin government would admit it or not.[15]

The German Democratic Republic's new receptivity to the idea of a common, bourgeois history its people share with citizens of the Federal Republic opens up new possibilities for West German foreign policy initiatives. The identity crisis of Germans in the GDR, possibly the major factor contributing to this receptivity, is beyond the scope of this study. The identity crisis of West Germans, however, is a critical component of their support for Bonn's foreign policy initiatives. What are two postwar generations searching for east of the Elbe that they did not find in western Europe? Are they likely to find it?

Prussians and Germans

The search for answers to these questions leads back into the long history of Germans in Europe before the establishment of a German national state. A German identity crisis is nothing new in modern European history; arguably, its existence is the normal state of affairs. Also arguably, Europe has been much better able to live with Germans and their identity crisis than with Germany in the brief decades, 1890 to 1914 and 1933 to 1945, when the country appeared to have defined an identity to its own satisfaction. The modern identity crisis has two components that have remained remarkably similar over the years.

The first component is the reality of the geographic position of the German-speaking peoples of Europe. Since the thirteenth century, when missionaries of the German Order brought Christianity to the Baltic borderlands, Germans have been the dominant political and economic force over a vast stretch of European territory. In fact, describing the area of German influence as central Europe, as is frequently done, is inaccurate unless *central* is so broadly defined as to rob the word of virtually all meaning. From Tallinn and Riga in the east to the Low Countries in the west, southwest into Switzerland and southeast to the Hungarian plain, German merchants and craftsmen were in the cities and towns of Europe, and German landowners and peasants were in the countryside. These people had no national identity crisis: they were German.

One of the ironies of the modern German dilemma, and one of the causes of it, is that Germans knew who they were at a time when other Europeans did not. Both for centuries of certainty and for succeeding centuries of uncertainty regarding their identity, Germans have the Holy Roman Empire to thank, more specifically, the Holy Roman Empire of the German Nation. In the years after the fall of Rome and the establishment of its two successor states, at Constantinople in the east and under the elected German emperor, with no permanent seat of government, in the west, German-speaking Europe was the one part of the former Roman continent in which civil and religious authority maintained a political system mutually acceptable to pope and emperor and to the local authorities, religious or secular, under them. The political system of pre-seventeenth-century "Germany" was decentralized, but it was a system, nonetheless.

The end of the German medieval and renaissance success story came with the birth of the modern nation-state. The Holy Roman Empire lingered, in name, under the Hapsburg emperors until Napoleon abolished it in 1806, but for all practical purposes it had ceased to exist a century and a half before, at the end of the Thirty Years' War in 1648. The Protestant Reformation, the strength of the individual German states that had begun to flourish under the Empire (the "first" Reich), the economic interests of the German bourgeoisie, and the Europe-wide role of the Hapsburg dynasty all militated against the parallel development in "Germany" of a national state to rival England, Spain, and France. Because of this, the second component of the German identity crisis was the triumph of the idea of the national state throughout Europe and its realization west of the Rhine, a development that began in the seventeenth century but did not reach its culmination for another 250 years, and that passed the Germans by.

The phrase is misleading but revealing. Not until the Napoleonic Wars of the nineteenth century did a majority of Germans begin to feel that anything had "passed them by." Until that time, Germany had an alternative form of political organization; clearly, it was different from what had evolved in France and Britain, but most Germans did not regard it as inferior. They had no reason to do so. The Protestant and Catholic German states, in the century after the 1648 Peace of Westphalia, devoted themselves to economic and social reconstruction and to the avoidance of another conflict like the Thirty Years' War. The destruction of central Europe in that war remained unparalleled for three hundred years, in part because of Europe's collective recollection of its devastation.

The major political development of that century in German-speaking Europe was the emergence of one of the smaller German states as a rival to Austria within the Empire and, by 1763, as the fifth recognized great power of the eighteenth-century European concert. More precisely, given the nature of both the state and the century, the Hohenzollern dynasty emerged as rival to the Hapsburgs and as sometime ally, sometime adversary of the Romanovs, Bourbons, and Hanoverians. The process by which the Hohenzollern electors of Brandenburg became kings of Prussia, beginning in 1701, and the evolution of the Prussian state over the next hundred years are both indicative of how little sentiment existed among Germans at the time that the nation-state was the ultimate form of political organization and that it was "passing them by."

From the nationalist perspective of the twentieth century, discussing the history of Prussia is difficult without falling into the trap of regarding it as the pre-history of the German national state established in 1871. However, the Prussian kings of the eighteenth century—and arguably of the nineteenth century, until the very last—did not regard either their state or their dynasty in this way. West German journalist and historian Sebastian Haffner warned against the tendency to think of Germany in 1900, or 1937, as the predetermined end of the rise of Prussia—itself not inevitable—when he wrote, "Centuries passed, and between the critical events, generations lived and died with no idea of what would come next; . . . the German knights and Electors Brandenburg would have been astounded, had anyone told them they were preparing the way for a future Prussian state."[16] Haffner rejected "the golden Prussian legend" of the German nationalists after the Franco-Prussian War:

> according to which, the unification of Germany had always been Prussia's mission, toward which its kings and even the Electors Brandenburg had consciously worked. . . . Prussia had no German mission; on the contrary, it let itself be talked into a German mission [in the nineteenth century, which] . . . ended in its own triumphant suicide.[17]

However, the nationalistic Wilhelmine interpretation of Prussian history that triumphed after 1871 was precisely the point because it effectively dealt with the identity crisis of Germans and their latecomer nation-state. Geographically dispersed throughout the continent, Germans, like other Europeans, had come to regard the nation-state as the logical outcome of European history. Linked with the demand for liberal revolution in the decades after the 1815 Congress of Vienna restored the Bourbons to the throne of France, nationalism initially frightened the ruling houses of the continent; the great irony is that the Hollenzollerns, the dynasty with fewer roots than any of the others in a particular national tradition, became the instrument of German unification. To German historians after 1871, however, that was the only possibility; if Prussia had not had a "German mission," in their eyes, its existence would have had no justification at all.[18]

The wars of Napoleonic France were the beginning of the end of

Prussia and of a Europe still not wholly given over to the idea of the national state. The success with which Napoleon made a fighting machine of the nation-state established by the Bourbons, now imbued with the zeal to spread the principles of the French Revolution throughout Europe, struck at both pillars of the Prussian state: its army and its multinational society. The formidable reputation that Frederick the Great's army had established in the Seven Years' War was destroyed on the battlefields of Jena and Auerstadt, and the French occupation of Prussia and the other German states, especially the cost of Napoleon's wars, provoked resistance to his rule. Because the strength of France was its nationalism, that resistance found its philosophical justification in German nationalism, which was anti-French, not pro-Prussian.[19]

Despite their willingness to use this nationalism against Napoleon in the decade from Jena to Waterloo, the leaders of Prussia were no more enamored of its implications than were the other allies and the defeated French at Vienna in 1815. The German national movement developed in the years before 1848 without Prussian support, indeed, despite vigorous repression by Berlin in the 1820s. As Haffner wrote:

> The European state system of 1815 was in reality an alliance . . . against the national, democratic, and liberal forces awakened by the French Revolution and unleashed by Napoleon. . . . Peace between the states was bought at the cost of an underground war between the states and their peoples. . . . [T]he story of the Restoration years, which seem so quiet on the surface, is the story of the slowly developing, increasingly powerful national and liberal revolutions which finally brought an end to the era.[20]

Despite Berlin's repression, the intellectuals who began to articulate a concept of German nationalism in this period looked to Prussia; for them, it had two advantages over Austria as potential founder of a German nation-state. First, after the Congress of Vienna, Prussia was a more purely "German" state than it had been in the last years of the eighteenth century, after the final partition of Poland. Indeed, in that period, its Polish- and German-speaking populations had been roughly equal in size, and its territory and interests centered east of the Elbe. After the Congress of Vienna, which reestablished a Polish state and "compensated" Prussia for the rejection of its claims to Saxony with territory in the Rhineland, Prussia became more "German" than Austria. The Hapsburgs ruled, as they would until the end in 1918, a multinational state, which they were never willing to abandon for the leadership of a German national state in central Europe.

Secondly, the developing Industrial Revolution gave both Prussia and the smaller German states an interest in each other that Austria did not share. The very size of the Hapsburg empire, as well as the feudal economic system that prevailed in large parts of it, meant that Austria had a large internal market already at hand to absorb the products of its own relatively limited industrialization, as well as a source of agricultural goods and raw materials. Prussia, however, needed a larger market, which it found in a customs union with the other German states, as well as a transportation network linking the ports of northern Germany with the new industrial cities in the Ruhr and Rhineland and the centers of agricultural production east of the Elbe. Whatever the lack of interest among the Prussian ruling classes in the idea of German nationalism, the economic interest of their state increasingly lay in its development of closer ties with the rest of "Germany." Their commitment to the Congress system and their disinterest in the nationalists was genuine, but, as Haffner wrote, Prussia, "against its will, always had a foot in the other camp."[21]

Looked at from the perspective of the late nineteenth century, the inevitable had resulted in 1871: the establishment of a German national state (the "second" Reich) under Prussian leadership. From any other perspective except that of the nationalist decades after 1871, however, the idea of Prussia as the leader of a new German empire was "about as implausible as Luther as pope."[22] This very implausibility contributed to the need of the Wilhelmine nationalists to create a new mythology of Germanness, extolling the virtues and uniqueness of the German people and culture.

The new state had no centuries-long national history with which to inspire its people, no Spanish Armada or Joan of Arc. The music of Wagner, the worship of the "German" Middle Ages by the historians, and the search for national symbols in such projects as the completion of Cologne Cathedral filled a void that was felt acutely in a nationalistic age.[23] Had Austria accepted a "German mission," it would have had no such problem; the Hapsburgs' inheritance from the Holy Roman Empire was legitimate. Under the Hohenzollerns, the new nation-state needed a mythology that the history of Prussia did not fully provide.

The Myth of Encirclement

The story of the corruption of late-nineteenth-century German nationalism in the twentieth century became the story of two world wars. Germany was not the only country that indulged in an orgy of national deification and social Darwinism in the years before World War I, but it was the only major European power that combined this self-glorification with an equally dangerous myth of encirclement by the other powers. The myth was based on fact: Germany's geographic position at the heart of Europe, a position aggravated by the cold war with France that was the principal effect of Berlin's annexation of Alsace and Lorraine in 1871.

Even today, the encirclement theme is alive and well as an explanation for Germany's bombastic and provocative foreign policy in the decade before World War I—and beyond. American historian David Calleo called it "one of the more remarkable accomplishments of modern historiography that the Germans, who never had a serious formal empire, should come to be seen as the most virulent carriers of the imperialist disease." He argued, instead, that

> Germany's "aggressiveness" against international order may be explained as plausibly by the nature of that order as by any peculiar characteristics of the Germans. Even Germany's Nazi episode may be seen as less the consequence of some inherent flaw in German civilization, some autonomous national cancer developing according to its own inner rhythm, than of the intense pressures put upon Germany from the outside. Geography and history conspired to make Germany's rise late, rapid, vulnerable, and aggressive. The rest of the world reacted by crushing the upstart. If, in the process, the German state lost its bearings and was possessed by an evil demon, perhaps the proper conclusion is not so much that civilization was uniquely weak in Germany, but that it is fragile everywhere. And perhaps the proper lesson is not so much the need for vigilance against aggressors, but the ruinous consequences of refusing reasonable accommodation to upstarts.[24]

The apologia will not stand up to scrutiny.

The German name became associated with imperialism, not because of the extent of the German overseas empire, but because of the ruthlessness with which Berlin, like Tokyo on the other side of the globe, pursued its "place in the sun." Like Japan, Germany was indeed a latecomer to the imperial club, but what is remarkable in the years before World War I is the extent to which France and Britain went to accommodate the desires of these countries to get into the game. Their recognition of Japan's conquests on the Asian mainland, Germany's economic role in the declining Ottoman Empire, the outcome of the Russo-Japanese War, and German participation in the scramble for colonies in Africa and concessions in China all testify to the readiness of Paris and London to "accommodate the upstarts."

The principal enemies of Berlin's imperialist policies at the time were in the new imperial capital on the Spree, not in London, but they were a decreasing minority after 1880. Chief among them, as long as he lived, was the founder of the new state, Chancellor Bismarck. Bismarck knew, better than anyone else, that in establishing the empire, Prussia-Germany had, as Michael Stürmer wrote, "overdrawn its European bank account" for many years to come.[25] Britain and Russia had tolerated three Prussian wars—with Denmark, Austria, and France—within six years and had acquiesced in the establishment of a new great power in the heart of Europe. Bismarck, as a Prussian statesman, saw no need for an overseas German empire, but more than that, he recognized that Berlin's reckless pursuit of further territorial claims, in or outside Europe, would demand more from the other powers than they could reasonably be expected to give.

In the years after Bismarck's departure from office in 1890, under the leadership of the young emperor, Wilhelm II, Germany began to make such claims. Stürmer wrote:

> What happened after that, the determined and aggressive construction of a battle fleet against England was a break from the Prussian continental tradition and its association with the British world power, a rebellion against Germany's position in the heart of Europe, and the departure from the principles of Bismarck's statecraft. It was forgotten that the German Empire would threaten its own existence by ignoring its position on the continent and by adding to the antagonism with France and the conflict with Russia a test of strength with England.[26]

London's response to Berlin's ambitions was outlined in a 1907 memorandum, made public only after World War I, by the permanent undersecretary of the Foreign Office, Sir Eyre Crowe. Far from confirming the apologists' contention that Germany was encircled and refused recognition of its great power status by England, the Crowe memorandum demonstrates the opposite:

> it would be neither just nor politic to ignore the claims to a healthy expansion [of] a vigorous and growing country like Germany. . . . It cannot be good policy for England to thwart such a process of development where it does not directly conflict either with British interests or with those of other nations to which England is bound by solemn treaty obligations. If Germany, within the limits imposed by these two conditions, finds the means peacefully and honourably to increase her trade and shipping, to gain coaling stations or other harbours, to acquire landing rights for cables, or to secure concessions for the employment of German capital or industries, she should never find England in her way.[27]

Indeed, despite Berlin's overtures to the Boers during the South African War and its naval building program, London recognized the advantages of having more than two or three powers in the game. British interests, as Crowe wrote, "would not be served by Germany being reduced to the rank of a weak Power, as this might easily lead to a Franco-Russian predominance equally, if not more, formidable, to the British Empire."[28] Fifteen years later, when the passions of World War I had cooled, with the threat from the German Navy eliminated and Lenin's government established in Moscow, London's *lack* of interest in a weak Germany again became clear. It found its first expression after World War I in John Maynard Keynes's attack on the 1919 Paris peace treaties, *The Economic Consequences of the Peace*.[29]

The reality of British policy, however, both before and after the war, was not as relevant to the development of Germany's identity crisis as were Germans' perceptions of their country's treatment by the other powers. Without a doubt, the fatal mistake in this regard was the nature of the 1919 peace treaties ending World War I, "dictated" to the new republic in Berlin by the victorious allies. The (in)famous clause of the Versailles Treaty in which Germany accepted its guilt for the outbreak of the war, the open-ended reparations demanded of Berlin, and the restrictions placed on the German armed forces all gave credibility to those who argued that this peace was encirclement by another name, an attempt to eliminate their country as a European great power. Berlin's exclusion from the League of Nations confirmed Germany's pariah status, while tainting that organization as a victors' club in the eyes of German nationalists. After the interpretation given to the Fourteen Points at Paris in 1919, Woodrow Wilson's concepts of international compromise and conciliation were regarded as the height of hypocrisy, and the League its tangible expression.[30]

The Weimar Republic began its life with handicaps not of its own making. Underlying the divisive foreign policy climate of the 1920s was the continued resonance of the encirclement–German mission mentality of the Wilhelmine years. The German army and nationalist politicians encouraged the belief that the defeat of 1918 had been caused by a "stab in the back" on the homefront. This myth served the dual purpose of discrediting the socialists and the liberal republicans at home while preventing the mobilization of public opinion to support a foreign policy of compromise and cooperation with Germany's former enemies. For a brief time in middecade, Gustav Stresemann seemed likely to succeed in reaching a modus vivendi with France, but the hostile reaction of the German public to his Locarno policy and to membership in the League was indicative of the depth of support that was waiting underground for a government that would openly reject the implications of 1918 and give the country a sense of purpose and a new role in Europe.[31]

With hindsight, Stresemann's premature death a week before the stock market crash in October 1929 seemed to presage the fate of his republic three years later. Germans still believed that the nation-state (in Europe) and the overseas empire (for the European states) constituted the natural order of things, an order that the machinations of socialists at home and hostile powers abroad had denied their country. In what appeared to be the heyday of the European empires—although, in retrospect, it was clearly their twilight—ample fuel was available to fan the fires of the Versailles revanchists. Belgium, the Netherlands, Italy, Spain, Portugal, Japan, and the United States, as well as France and Britain, were all colonial powers, a role stripped from Germany by the hated treaty. Moreover, the Paris peace conference itself had enshrined the principle of national self-determination while denying it to the defeated Central Powers. The Polish Corridor and an Austria denied union with Germany were wounds no Berlin government could ignore and survive.

The impact of Stresemann's death on German foreign policy in the early 1930s has never been the subject of much speculation, and properly so; it was not a close thing.[32] The foreign minister had never had a large constituency, even in his own party, for his policies of modifying the Versailles system through negotiation with its creators. Honored with the Nobel Peace Prize and respected abroad, Stresemann spent much of his time fighting rearguard actions against domestic opponents for his political life in Berlin. In the end, these struggles cost him his health and his life, perhaps mercifully, before the onset of the Depression undermined what little success Weimar had had in developing a liberal center committed to the republic.

In the political and economic climate of the early 1930s, neither Stresemann nor any other politician was a figure whose personal commitment to the republic alone could have rallied sufficient support for it. The temptation to analogize to what may have been a genuine lost opportunity in the 1880s, when the convictions of one man, the hundred-days emperor, Frederick III, might have changed the direction of German history, is strong but futile.[33] No adequate constituency on the right or left was ready to rally to the Weimar Constitution after the crisis struck in 1929 and 1930.

Less than twenty years after Stresemann died, the elected members of the West German Parliamentary Council proclaimed the establishment of the Federal Republic of Germany. A measure of the shock dealt to the German system by the intervening two decades was evident in the new state's constitution, the Basic Law, which accepted a postwar situation incomparably worse for Germany than that of 1919 while enunciating foreign policy goals Stresemann would never have dreamed of articulating for Weimar. He would have been thrown out of office—or worse. By 1949, however, Germans had turned as fiercely on the old ideas of breaking their encirclement to pursue a German mission as they had once rejected those who questioned the validity of those ideas.

Zero Hour: Germans Out of Time and History?

From the perspective of forty years, the fervor with which Germans after 1945 rejected the aims and means of the preceding century did not eliminate their country's political dilemma in Europe. Their identity crisis was disguised by the enthusiasm with which both new German states after 1949 played the roles expected of them in Europe; it did not go away. National Socialism had discredited not only the nationalist and imperialist dreams of the past but also the idea of dreaming itself. Germans after World War II quoted Bertolt Brecht approvingly: lucky the country that has no need of heroes—history has passed it by. They flocked to Thornton Wilder's story of everyman's survival, who gets through the disasters of life by the "skin of his teeth." The play seemed to describe the narrow escape that Germans had just had; they weren't going to tempt fate again by dreaming dreams of a place in the sun for Germany.

The Nuremberg war crimes trials made clear to Germans the infamous place they had created for themselves among the nations of the world. Theories of a fatal flaw in the German nation, which made it congenitally incapable of democratic self-government and unreliable as an international partner, were not only the property of a radical fringe.[34] The Morgenthau Plan for the deindustrialization of the country was one manifestation of the idea that Germany was simply too dangerous for Europe to live with, but it was not the only one. The men of July 20, 1944, had they succeeded in assassinating Adolf Hitler, would have found to their chagrin that the world had no sympathy left for German nationalism, no matter what form it took.[35]

The theories of a congenital German inability to practice political compromise at home or abroad can be rejected, however, without accepting David Calleo's indictment of the international system as the source of the "German problem" in the twentieth century. Civilization is, no doubt, fragile everywhere, but faced with the global economic and political problems of the 1930s, it also proved to be uniquely weak in Germany. Thousands of pages have been devoted to an analysis of this weakness, of Auschwitz and Dachau and their relationship to Goethe, Beethoven, and the religious tolerance of Prussia's 1685 Edict of Potsdam. For our purposes, analyzing why modern Germany embraced the policies of National Socialism is not as important as recognizing the effect of that embrace on the Federal Republic's self-confidence and convictions. *How* it happened is important, but *that* it happened is the critical component of West Germans' attitude today toward foreign policy and their country's role in Europe. The questions of guilt and responsibility that have clung to the name of Germany for four decades have made them wary of the exercise of power, the use of force, and the definition of a concept of national interest.[36]

In the immediate postwar period, the concept of a zero hour expressed the conviction of many Germans that only by wiping the slate clean of their past history could they begin again. Allied programs of denazification and reeducation, designed to teach the Germans democracy, were, with the ruins of Hamburg, Cologne, and Berlin, part of the atmosphere of the time, in which believing that the preceding decades and centuries had no meaning for post-1945 Germany was possible.[37] The flood of refugees arriving from lands east of the Oder, where Germans had lived for six hundred years, symbolized the reversal of the tides of history: Germans moving westward, toward the Main and Rhine, instead of eastward, across the Oder and Vistula.[38]

Despite the surface impressions, however, German history had no zero hour. When the states of the three western occupation zones sent their representatives to Bonn, soon to be the capital of the new republic, to draft its constitution in 1948, they encountered head-on the legacy of the past, the trauma of the 1920s and the crimes of the 1930s and 1940s. The key provisions of the Basic Law reflect the issues with which they had to deal: the weakness of the Weimar parliament, the abuse of his emergency powers by the first republic's head of state, the relationship of the states to the central government, the role of the military, the integration of refugees, restitution and compensation for the victims of the Third Reich, and the choice of symbols for the new republic. The response of the Basic Law to these questions belied talk of a zero hour, even as such rhetoric was at its height.

The first foreign policy decisions of the Federal Republic also belied the concept of a zero hour. Within a year of its proclamation in May 1949, the West German state had begun to pursue with its western European neighbors the foreign policy course that has remained constant through four decades. Understanding that course is not possible without reference to the historical German identity crisis and the impact on that identity crisis of the first half of the twentieth century. Bonn inherited in 1949 a political and economic legacy that reflected both the best and the worst of the preceding half-century of German policies in Europe.

On the one hand, the long-term potential and underlying strength of the West German economy was not in doubt. Despite the destruction of its physical plant and transportation network, which seemed worse in 1945 than it actually was, the investment Germany had made in scientific and technological development for a hundred years, the skills of its industrial and agricultural workers (including the refugees arriving from east of the Elbe), and the diversity of its economy were both an economic asset and a political problem. The Morgenthau Plan of 1944 and 1945 had reflected the fears that economic strength, translated into war-making potential, provoked abroad; despite the reluctant recognition by Germany's neighbors that Europe needed a strong German economy, the implications of that recognition posed a foreign policy problem for all of them. The Federal Republic's response to the solution proposed by France, the European Coal and Steel Community (ECSC), set the tone of the years to come.

Politically, West Germany faced the innumerable problems posed by a divided Europe and a divided Germany, the results of the policies of the German Empire from 1871 to 1945. For the first time, a German state did not have to deal with the reality of German-speaking populations from the "Meuse to the Memel"; the Big Three at Potsdam had abandoned the concept of minority protection enshrined in the 1919 Paris peace treaties and destroyed by Sudeten German revanchists and National Socialist Germany in the 1930s.[39] The resettlement of the Germans of eastern Europe into the four occupation zones freed Poland and Czechoslovakia of a minority they no longer trusted. Coupled with the evolution of the four zones into two German states, it also freed the new West German government from two issues with which its predecessors had had to deal: the geographic dispersal of Germans throughout the heart of Europe and the struggle for influence within the German state between Protestant, agrarian Prussia east of the Elbe and the Catholic, industrial Rhineland. The Federal Republic was, indeed, a *west* German state, despite its refugees, and the foreign policies Konrad Adenauer was able to pursue were the clearest indication of how much the internal balance of forces had changed.

The nature of those policies in the 1950s gave the impression, lamented by some and welcomed by others, that the Federal Republic had left its eastern European legacy behind. The desire of the new state to be recognized and accepted as part of the western European and Atlantic world was recognizably the overriding theme of its foreign and domestic policies for fifteen years. Not until the 1960s did Bonn shift the focus of its foreign policy from the Rhine to the Elbe and beyond and admit that, although a long period of German history in the east had come to a criminal and tragic end, the legacy of that period lived on. There were still Germans in eastern Europe and the Soviet Union, neighboring states living with the human and political results of the war begun by Germany in 1939, and the German Democratic Republic. None of this was going to change simply because the Federal Republic chose to ignore it.

In the decade from 1961 to 1971, Bonn chose no longer to ignore this legacy of the German past. The West German government began to implement new policies of reconciliation and dialogue with its eastern neighbors. The supporters of this dialogue with the GDR and the other countries of the Warsaw Pact postulated that it could, and would, provoke changes in the political and economic climate of eastern Europe. However, they failed to appreciate the impact that a newly articulated German role in the east would have on the Federal Republic itself and on its relationship with the countries of western Europe and the United States. From the perspective of a quarter-century, clearly West Germany was ill prepared psychologically for the effects on itself of a successful Ostpolitik. The questions of identity that West Germans had suppressed for decades reemerged with a vengeance in the 1980s, and so did many of the themes of the Wilhelmine and Weimar political debates that had seemed buried for good.

In Search of a National Contribution

One of these themes was the central historical importance of the German-Russian relationship. In his speech to parliament on May 8, 1985, the West German President called Bonn's relations with the countries of eastern Europe and the Soviet Union the "central task of German foreign policy." Such a statement from one of his predecessors twenty or thirty years ago would have caused a sensation at home and abroad. By 1985, the statement was unexceptional, but its implications for the Germans' renewed search for a role in Europe were far-reaching. The search itself made Bonn's western allies nervous.

Compared to their NATO allies—not only France, Britain, and the United States, but all the countries of the alliance—West Germans continued to have difficulty in the 1980s defining a concept of patriotism and national interest. Critics of their "search for harmony" lamented the wariness with which Bonn approached the prospect of conflict, political as well as military, in its international relations.[40] Clearly, legitimate cause existed for concern that the Federal Republic not impute to less-scrupulous powers a readiness to compromise that they did not possess.

However, little legitimate cause existed for the fears expressed by Bonn's allies that West Germany was in the process of abandoning its commitment to the west in exchange for nebulous promises of better relations with the GDR—reunification?—and its Warsaw Pact allies. The foreign policy goals of the Federal Republic in the 1980s were far from nebulous, and those policies reflected the lessons learned from the Westpolitik in the 1950s. Bonn clearly saw the search for answers to the German question as a process of Europeans defining a better future for Europe, a broadening of the western European dialogue of the 1950s.

In the 1980s, West Germans still had a more difficult time than their neighbors in the east *and* the west answering who they were and defining their role in Europe. Their tragic experience with national unity and their daily existence on the border of a continent divided because of German policies had denied them the tranquility of a self-confident patriotism that required one thing to flourish: the conviction that the national contribution, over the millennia of European history, had been a positive one. Germans stood alone, in both eastern and western Europe, as the nation that doubted that it could say this about itself and its historic role on the continent.

Only by pursuing both a West- and an Ostpolitik did the people of the Federal Republic in the 1980s hope to find an answer to the question of the German identity. Only by doing so could they take the story of the German role in Europe into a future more productive than the immediate past. In a speech at the historic Reichstag in 1982, when he was governing mayor of West Berlin, President von Weizsäcker reminded Germans that "the question of [our] identity has never belonged to Germans alone." Historically, the only constant in the political organization of central Europe was change, and "the center [was] not cut out in the long run to be a border." Weizsäcker said

> It took a long time for postwar Germans to become receptive to history again, especially contemporary history. . . . But without insight into the historical origins of our situation, we cannot understand it. Our history . . . will not let us go . . . even if we try for a long time to live without it. . . . [T]he insights of history will help give us the strength to find hope across that border, and to promote peace for ourselves and our neighbors.[41]

The assumption that Germans must or should choose between eastern and western Europe creates a false dilemma; the reality is that the future of Europe, like the German past, lies on both sides of the Elbe.

Notes

1. In a speech to the Bamberg historians' conference on October 12, 1988, the West German president reminded his audience that Germans needed "the power of historical facts, . . . and not the exploitation of history for specific purposes." Even the facts, however, about the German past will not provide unambiguous answers to individuals' and foreign policy questions. Richard von Weizsäcker, "Germans and History: Give It to Us Straight," *International Herald Tribune*, October 29/30, 1988.
2. Friedrich Meinecke, *The German Catastrophe* (Boston: Beacon Press, 1972).
3. Richard von Weizsäcker, "Ansprache in der Gedenkstunde im Plenarsaal des Deutschen Bundestages am 8. Mai 1985," *Nachdenken über unsere Geschichte* (Bonn: Bundespresseamt, 1986), pp. 17–18.
4. See, for example, Ger van Roon, "Der Kreisauer Kreis und das Ausland," *Aus Politik und Zeitgeschichte*, December 13, 1986, p. 32:

It was the goal of the members of the Kreisau Circle [named after the estate of one of its leaders, Count von Moltke] to bring together representatives of the groups which could make a decisive contribution to the rebuilding of Germany after the war—especially the churches and the workers' movement—to develop a common political program. This program was discussed with groups and individuals in other countries; the Kreisau Circle members thought and planned as Europeans.

And further (p. 46):

[T]he Kreisau Circle members were caught between the fronts: they were patriots, and their country was at war, but the National Socialist Third Reich was not their fatherland; as a result, they saw themselves as allies of the Allies. "We hope," wrote Moltke to [a friend in England], "that you understand clearly that we are ready to help you win the war and the peace."

5. Weizsäcker, "Ansprache in der Gedenkstunde," pp. 18, 24, 26.
6. Ibid., pp. 33–34.
7. See, for the best discussion of the emotional and cultural ties binding Germans to eastern Europe, Karl Schlögel, *Die Mitte liegt ostwärts: Die Deutschen, der verlorene Osten und Mitteleuropa* (Berlin: Siedler, 1986), esp. pp. 72–88; and for two personal accounts of the end of centuries of German cultural and political history east of the Oder-Neisse: Marion Gräfin Dönhoff, *Namen die keiner mehr nennt* (München [Munich]: DTV, 1986), and Christian Graf von Krockow, *Die Stunde der Frauen* (Stuttgart: Deutsche Verlags-Anstalt, 1987).
8. Weizsäcker, "Ansprache in der Gedenstunde," pp. 28, 32.
9. See Stürmer's preface to his *Das ruhelose Reich: Deutschland 1866–1918*, vol. 3 of the six-volume series *Die Deutschen und ihre Nation* (Berlin: Severin und Siedler, 1983), pp. 9–12, and his preface and introduction to Michael Stürmer, ed., *Die Weimarer Republik: Belagerte Civitas* (Königstein: Verlags-gruppe Athenaeum, Hain, Scriptor, Hanstein, 1980), pp. 9–36.
10. Günter Gaus, *Die Welt der Westdeutschen* (Köln: Kiepenheuer & Witsch, 1986), pp. 217–218.
11. Ibid., pp. 177–178.
12. Ibid., p. 209.
13. *Die Welt*, published in Bonn by the Axel Springer Press. In early 1989, there were reports of a change in editorial policy that would eliminate the quotation marks. See "Trostreiche Tüttelchen," *Der Spiegel* no. 4 (Jan. 23, 1989): 47.
14. Günter Gaus, *Wo Deutschland liegt* (München: DTV, 1986), pp. 63–64. Gaus has a tendency to romanticize the "lack of class structure" in the GDR, but he is correct that the division of Germany created a unique situation in the GDR. Compared to the other countries of the Warsaw Pact in the early postwar period, East Germany alone needed to build a political and social elite to replace the property-owning, prewar upper and upper-middle classes east of the Elbe, most of whom, given a choice, had naturally enough fled

to the western zones. Because the Federal Republic existed, these classes had an alternative that did not exist for their counterparts in Poland or Czechoslovakia.

15. Haug von Künheim, "Friedrich und sein Erbe," *Die Zeit*, September 19, 1986. See also Karl Heinz Janssen, "Im Schatten der Vergangenheit," *Die Zeit*, March 27, 1987.
16. Sebastian Haffner, *Preussen ohne Legende* (Hamburg: Goldmann, 1981), p. 26.
17. Ibid., pp. 9–10.
18. Thomas Nipperdey, *Nachdenken über die deutsche Geschichte* (München: C.H. Beck, 1986), especially the essay "Die Deutsche Einheit in historischer Perspektive," p. 213.
19. Ibid., p. 208
20. Haffner, *Preussen*, pp. 124–125.
21. Ibid., p. 125.
22. Ibid., p. 165.
23. Nipperdey, "Der Kölner Dom als Nationaldenkmal," *Nachdenken*, p. 157.
24. David Calleo, *The German Problem Reconsidered: Germany and the World Order, 1870 to the Present* (Cambridge: Cambridge University Press, 1978), pp. 5–6.
25. Michael Stürmer, *Bismarck* (München: Piper, 1987), p. 71.
26. Ibid., pp. 101–102.
27. "Memorandum by Mr. Eyre Crowe on the Present State of Relations with France and Germany," January 1, 1907, in G.P. Gooch and Harold Temperley, eds., *British Documents on the Origins of the War 1898–1914*, vol. III: *The Testing of the Entente, 1904–6* (London: His Majesty's Government Stationery Office, 1928), pp. 417–418.
28. Ibid., p. 417.
29. John Maynard Keynes, *The Economic Consequences of the Peace* (New York: Harcourt, Brace, and Howe, 1920).
30. As John R.P. McKenzie, *Weimar Germany, 1918–1933* (Totowa, NJ: Rowman & Littlefield, 1971), wrote (p. 67): "It is a bitter irony that [the Allies'] ostracism of the [Weimar] Republic played into the hands of the opponents of democracy, those very sections of the population which had filled leading roles in the war." The 1926 dispute over whether Germany should have a permanent seat on the League Council also gave the foreign minister's opponents, as McKenzie wrote (pp. 186–187), "another rod with which to beat Stresemann . . . for endorsing a policy which implied voluntary recognition of Germany's war guilt." On the other hand, as Hagen Schulze, *Weimar Deutschland 1917–1933*, vol. 4 of the six-volume *Die Deutschen und ihre Nation* (Berlin: Severin und Siedler, 1982) pointed out (p. 15): "Miracles happen in history without anyone noticing," and the miracle of 1918–1919 was that the Allies had not tried to set the German clock back to 1870, dismembering Bismarck's Reich in the heart of Europe.
31. Sebastian Haffner, "Gustav Stresemann: ein deutscher Realist," in *Im Schatten der Geschichte* (Stuttgart: Deutsche Verlags-Anstalt, 1985), p. 282.
32. As Haffner noted (*Im Schatten*, p. 285), the idea that, had Stresemann lived longer, Hitler could have been avoided, was certainly "an overstatement of Stresemann's possibilities." The foreign minister's son, however, disagreed.

In *Mein Vater Gustav Stresemann* (Berlin: Ullstein, 1985), p. 614, Wolfgang Stresemann wrote, "a *healthy* Gustav Stresemann might have spared Germany the Third Reich."

33. Wilhelm I lived to be ninety, and his son Friedrich III, the hope of constitutional monarchists and supporters of good relations with England—his wife was the eldest and favorite daughter of Queen Victoria—died after only three months on the throne in 1888. He was succeeded in the "year of the three emperors" by his twenty-eight-year-old son, Wilhelm II. The *Spectator* editorialized on June 17, 1888: "Germany mourned by the sickbed of an Emperor who might have inaugurated a better regime; but Europe mourned with her for the decay of the most effectual barrier to war." Quoted in the *International Herald Tribune*, June 17, 1988.

34. Karl Dietrich Bracher, *Die deutsche Diktatur* (Köln: Kiepenheuer & Witsch, 1969), p. 22, discussed the mirror image of the "fatal flaw" idea: the Germans' own "special national consciousness" of their role in Europe and its corruption in the twentieth century.

35. In her *Berlin Diaries, 1940–1945* (New York: Alfred A. Knopf, 1987), Marie Vassiltchikov, a white Russian emigré to Berlin, recalled her conversations with her boss at the German Foreign Office and friend, Adam von Trott zu Solz. Trott, who was deeply involved in the July 20 plot against Hitler, was executed on August 26, 1944. In September 1945, from notes made in July 1944, Vassiltchikov wrote (pp. 189–190):

> The truth is that there is a fundamental difference in outlook between all of *them* and me: not being German, I am concerned only with the elimination of [Hitler]. I have never attached much importance to what happens afterwards. Being patriots, *they* want to save their country from complete destruction by setting up some interim government. I have never believed that even such an interim government would be acceptable to the Allies, who refuse to distinguish between "good" Germans and "bad." This, of course, is a fatal mistake on their part and we will probably all pay a heavy price for it.

> In a September 1945 comment on this diary entry (p. 202), she added that Trott "sincerely believed that when faced with a 'decent' German government, the Allies would be less uncompromising. I often sought to dispel these illusions and . . . I think that subsequent events proved me right."

See also van Roon, *Aus Politik*, p. 46.

36. A highly critical (and frequently scathingly accurate) discussion of the lack of understanding of power politics in postwar West Germany is that of Hans-Peter Schwarz, *Die gezähmten Deutschen: von der Machtbesessenheit zur Machtvergessenheit* (Stuttgart: Deutsche Verlags-Anstalt, 1986).

37. See Gaus, *Die Welt*, pp. 80–81, in which he describes his own and Germany's yearning for a "history-less epoch" in the first years after the war, to be "a happy land with no need of heroes," in the words of Bertolt Brecht.

38. Schlögel and Dönhoff both discuss the westward tide of 1944 and 1945,

before the advancing Red Army, "the path on foot back into the Reich, which would soon be nothing more than the grounds of the chancellery"; a movement that "ended where it had begun, in Saxony and Magdeburg, or even farther westward, in Bavaria, Swabia, or Lower Saxony, . . ." (Schlögel, *Die Mitte*, p. 86). " 'Arrival' was a word which had apparently vanished from our vocabulary. On and on we went, through Brandenburg, Mecklenburg, Lower Saxony to Westphalia. I had crossed the three great rivers of our eastern Germany: the Vistula, the Oder, and the Elbe. . . . My forefathers had left the Ruhr in the fourteenth century to settle the eastern wilderness. Six hundred years later, on horseback, as they had been, with millions of others who had lost their homes, I retraced their path westward" (Dönhoff, *Namen*, pp. 7, 33).

39. Alfred de Zayas, *Nemesis at Potsdam* (London: Routledge & Kegan Paul, 1977), is overly tolerant of the behavior of German minorities in the interwar period, but he correctly notes that their support of Hitler and German revanchism was largely responsible for Allied disenchantment, at the end of World War II, with the League of Nations minority treaties, and that that disenchantment led leaders like Czechoslovakia's Edouard Beneš and the British and American governments to accept the principle of population transfers.

40. Schwarz, *Die gezähmten Deutschen*, pp. 28–35, is especially caustic on the "yearning for harmony" that characterizes the foreign policy discussion in the Federal Republic.

41. Richard von Weizsäcker, "Berlin ist Treuhänderin der deutschen Geschichte," in *Die deutsche Geschichte geht weiter* (Berlin: Siedler, 1983), pp. 299, 302.

part two

DEVELOPING THE FRANKREICHPOLITIK MODEL

3

THE LOCARNO LEGACY

French Suspicions in "a World Transformed"

The climate of Franco-German relations in the first years after 1945 was characterized by the same chill that had hung over the relationship between Paris and Berlin a quarter-century before. On the surface, little had changed for the better between the two countries. France had again emerged victorious against Germany in a world war but with no illusions of who had produced that victory—its allies in east and west, not Paris. Much to General DeGaulle's resentment, his country had only narrowly escaped, with British support, American plans to establish an allied military government in liberated France in 1944.[1] The narrowness of the French victory and the reality that Paris's place at the side of the victorious Big Three was far more a credit to DeGaulle's and Jean Monnet's political skills than to the performance of France's armies boded ill for Germany in 1945. If the past were a reliable guide to the future, Paris wanted a German neighbor weaker than France; if the Fourth Republic were weaker than the Third, then Germany must be weaker still.

The possibility that France's lack of confidence in its ability to assure its own security would result in even harsher and more insistent demands on Germany than had been made in 1919 was far from remote. The French government was well aware of the economic and military potential that existed across the Rhine, despite the destruction of 1945, and in the first few years of four-power occupation, French demands on Germany centered on the same issues that had dominated the 1920s: reparations, control of the industries of the Ruhr and the coal mines of the Saar, the strategic importance of the Rhineland, and decentralization, if not dismemberment, of the Reich. In the Allied Control Council

(ACC), the American and British representatives found their French colleague in many ways more intransigent than their Soviet counterpart and initially even more annoying, especially to the Americans. The United States had little regard for France's contribution to the war effort and even less for DeGaulle's abrasive style.[2]

Not invited to the conferences at Yalta and Potsdam, France had been given its occupation zone in Germany and sector in Berlin, at the expense of the territory already assigned to the British and Americans, by the Big Three at Yalta. Britain, fearful of another American withdrawal from postwar Europe, saw in France a future continental ally, but this was not much of a compliment: London had no other comparably sized allies from which to choose. Although France was weak, it was still stronger than any other state in western Europe. Paris had also been offered a permanent seat on the Security Council of the new United Nations, but neither DeGaulle's provisional government nor its successor after 1946, the Fourth Republic, was in a position of strength vis-à-vis the other three powers. Still, this did not stop the French from exercising the veto in the ACC that had come with their zone of occupation in order to forestall any central management of the four zones.[3]

The French military government was equally determined to pursue a hard-line policy within its occupation zone, and Germans who found themselves in it faced formidable obstacles when they attempted to reestablish democratic political life for the first time since 1933. German requests to travel out of the zone were routinely denied, making participation in events held in the other three zones virtually impossible. The border with France itself was closed until 1949. Too great an interest in Germany's neighbor could prove dangerous: Carlo Schmid was placed under arrest in Stuttgart when he volunteered to translate for the arriving French forces, who were suspicious of his bilingualism. Alfred Grosser later called initial French occupation policy a sure way to reinforce the parochial nationalism that the French most feared.[4]

The breakdown of the east-west wartime coalition against Germany emerged in stages over a period of months. Paris was not the only capital to suffer from a time lag in recognizing the implications of the developing Cold War for its German policy, but it was especially tenacious in its belief that old remedies could deal with new diseases. Recognition of the fact that "a French presence in the Rhineland did not mean much in a world transformed . . . did not play much of a role in French foreign policy until well into 1947."[5] For three-quarters of a century, France and Germany had jockeyed for strategic advantage along their common border, control of which, as an aspect of their military security, had become superfluous. In the context of the Cold War, a weak and divided neighbor did not enhance French security but symbolized one outcome of World War II France had not wished to see: the division of Europe into ideological blocks.[6] Despite the surface similarities of the Franco-German issues of the late 1940s to those of the 1920s, French policy faced an entirely different strategic situation.

Whether Paris could free itself in time from the psychological restraints of the past, however, was another question. France's attempts to reach agreement with the Weimar Republic on a post–World War I status quo acceptable to both countries had failed. The memory of that failure, like the three Franco-German wars since 1870 and the Nazi occupation, did not bode well for another attempt. On both sides of the border, however, people were willing to try. Raymond Aron saw as early as 1945 that "the German danger, as the French had known it between 1870 and 1945, belonged to the past."[7] A second postwar period, in which "French and Germans inevitably would suffer or assume a common destiny," had given the two countries "another crack at the dream of my youth—Franco-German reconciliation."[8]

The Locarno Interlude

In the years after World War I, that dream had seemed to have a future for a short time in the mid-1920s. In 1925 at Locarno, Switzerland, the foreign ministers of Germany, France, and Britain undertook a process of negotiating a settlement to the issues that divided their countries. Arising out of the Versailles Treaty, these issues were economic, territorial, and, most acutely, psychological: the question of the status and role of Germany in Europe and the world. In order to understand the foreign policy choices made by West Germany in the 1950s, understanding both what happened in the 1920s and the way the first generation of political leadership in the Federal Republic interpreted that experience is necessary. The interpretation was more important than the reality of the interwar years from 1925 to 1929, collectively known as the Locarno period. For good reasons, the failure of the foreign ministers' efforts to usher in an enduring era of better relations gave their successors pause.

Germany's Gustav Stresemann, Aristide Briand of France, and British Foreign Minister Austen Chamberlain, with their Italian and Belgian counterparts, met at the Swiss town of Locarno in October 1925 to sign a group of treaties resulting from negotiations initiated by Berlin in January of that year. Chief among those treaties was the "Rhineland Pact," in which Germany accepted the border established after World War I between it and Belgium and France. Berlin also accepted the existence of a demilitarized zone on the west bank of the Rhine, a part of Germany still under Anglo-French occupation in 1925, as provided for by the 1919 peace treaty. London and Rome guaranteed the Franco-German and Belgian-German borders in a pledge of assistance to whichever state found itself the victim of future aggression across them. This pledge was one part of the symbolic importance of Locarno to Stresemann's foreign policy: it did not discriminate in favor of Brussels or Paris, the two World War I victors having given their former enemy the same guarantee as their former allies.

Other aspects of the Locarno agreements and the process they set in motion were equally important. Germany joined the League of Nations, with a permanent seat alongside France and Britain on the League Council. Britain withdrew its troops from its occupation zone around Cologne, and the three foreign ministers began a series of negotiations on complete evacuation of Anglo-French troops from the Rhineland, German payment of reparations, Allied war debts, disarmament, and the status of the Saarland (under League of Nations administration until 1935, the profits of its mines going to France). In 1928, the three states joined twelve others in renouncing war as an instrument of national policy in the Kellogg-Briand Pact, somewhat mitigating concern that the lack of an "eastern Locarno" guaranteeing Germany's borders with Czechoslovakia and Poland meant that Berlin would use force to advance its territorial claims there.[9]

The hallmark of the Locarno period were the trilateral meetings of the three statesmen that took place several times a year in Geneva, around meetings of the League of Nations. Before the decade was over, Briand, Chamberlain, and Stresemann formed a "brotherhood of foreign ministers," which Chamberlain explicitly compared to the nineteenth-century Concert of Europe. In addition to discussing the specific issues facing their countries at these "Geneva tea parties," they "also arbitrated the affairs of the rest of Europe and coordinated their policies on matters considered by the League Council." According to American historian Jon Jacobson:

> The unique qualities of the Locarno diplomatic method were the exclusiveness, secrecy, and informality of the meetings and their frequency and regularity; they were convened periodically and held even if there were no prospect of conclusive results. . . . From their frequent personal contact, there developed . . . a set of personal-political relationships to which they could appeal when there were issues to be resolved and favors to be asked.[10]

Historians of the interwar years have looked for the failure of Locarno in the issues dividing France, Britain, and Germany that were left unresolved by the three foreign ministers in the time they had. Chief among them was the evacuation of French troops from the Rhineland. Stresemann never received the "magnanimous gesture" he hoped for from his two colleagues, but without it, he could never claim the credit for the Locarno policy that it, and he, deserved. Like Alsace-Lorraine for France after 1871, the evacuation of the Rhineland as a foreign policy issue had taken on a life of its own:

> Occupation was a reminder of the disaster of 1918; it was a highly visible indication of the limitations of German sovereignty imposed by the peace of 1919; and as long as it continued, the distinction between victor and vanquished remained. . . . Evacuation, on the other hand, was a symbol of recovery from defeat, of respect regained, and of the restoration of Germany to a position of full equality among the great powers. As such, its desirability was assumed and not debated; throughout the German body politic, the freedom of the Rhineland was accepted as Germany's primary national goal with little question or dissent.[11]

The psychology of *being* occupied, not the physical effects of the occupation (its economic impact on the Rhineland was apparently positive, and civilian-military relations were generally quite good), was clearly the issue that Stresemann never successfully resolved, either by securing an end to the occupation itself or by changing his constituency's expectations.

By the late 1920s, the persistence of the evacuation issue was overtaken by two other events. In the failure of Locarno to endure, historians have seen two external and, at its inception, unpredictable factors at work: the premature death of Stresemann, at age fifty-one, in October 1929, and the event that followed two weeks later, the American economic collapse. Since 1923, when he had been chancellor briefly during the Ruhr occupation crisis, until his death, after six continuous years as foreign minister, Stresemann had personified a positive image of the Weimar Republic abroad. With hindsight, the timing of his death has taken on a poignant quality of tragedy foreshadowed, but substance as well as symbolism lies in seeing it as the end of an era of opportunities that would not come again. Like Bismarck before him, Stresemann left Germany with a foreign policy dependent on one man, himself. Unlike Bismarck, he probably had no choice; he was at the helm of German foreign policy for only six years, not thirty, and in the service, not of a popular monarchy, but of, as Weimar has aptly been called, a "republic without republicans."[12]

The stock market collapse in New York and its repercussions around the world were, indeed, more than the economies of the Locarno powers could bear. American loans to Germany made possible the payment of reparations to France and Britain and their repayment of war debts back to the United States. Without the loans, neither the prosperity of Weimar's middle years nor its reparation payments would have been possible; both support for the republic at home and its ability to accommodate Paris and London depended on the strength of the American economy.

By the early 1930s, Germany could find few political or economic advantages in Stresemann's legacy. The September 1930 elections, in which the National Opposition parties—one of which was the National Socialists—won 26 percent of the seats in the Reichstag, signaled growing German unwillingness to support (or even tolerate) the continuation of Stresemann's policies. The unilateral March 1931 attempt to establish an Austro-German customs union, without prior consultation with the other two Locarno powers, was a portent of methods that would become all too familiar after 1933. In fact, "those responsible for the formation of German policy [had] decided that there was more to be gained by abandoning the policy of understanding than by continuing it." The last of the Locarno ministers to leave office, in January 1932, Briand saw the 1930 election and the customs union issue "transform . . . chronic French reservations regarding the policy of understanding into a near rejection of [his] Locarno policy."[13]

The historical critique of Locarno is, of necessity, based on a knowledge of what came after, often coupled with the related question: could the rise of Nazism and World War II have been prevented? Two mutually exclusive policies have often been suggested as better alternatives to Locarno: a harder line on the part of the allies toward Germany— an Anglo-French determination to maintain the letter of the Versailles Treaty—and the opposite policy of the "magnanimous gesture," an accommodation of Berlin's discontent with Versailles that went further than Briand and Chamberlain were prepared to go. This historians' critique and the hypotheses related to it, interesting as they are, do not, however, address the questions of principal concern to the foreign policy of the Federal Republic after 1949. Bonn's task was not an investigation of the origins of World War II but the establishment of a new relationship with Paris. Its analysis focused on the strengths and weaknesses of Locarno that remained relevant, given the political, economic, and strategic positions of France and Germany in the years after 1945.

Viewed from this perspective, the Locarno period offered West German foreign policy (and its French counterpart) food for thought in four areas: the importance of building good personal relations between political leaders; establishing multilateral institutions; forgoing demands for immediate and parallel bilateral concessions; and creating broad public support for detente in both countries. In these four areas, the Federal Republic attempted to build on the strengths and to remedy the weaknesses of the foundation for Franco-German rapprochement laid by Briand and Stresemann. The rapid unraveling of their labors after 1930 was the most disturbing aspect of the story. Why had Locarno come apart so quickly? Why had no one tried to save it? Not the failure of the foreign ministers but the speed with which that failure occurred and the lack of interest on both sides of the Rhine in their work—except to attack it—haunted West Germans like Konrad Adenauer and Carlo Schmid, old enough to remember and committed to trying again.

Four Lessons of Locarno

The first lesson the leaders of the Federal Republic drew from Locarno was the importance of the individuals involved and the positive and negative aspects of their *personal relationships*. Stresemann had not proposed the negotiations that led to Locarno because of any prior friendship with Chamberlain or Briand; he had not even met them before 1925. The British foreign minister was openly a Francophile who would have given France a bilateral security guarantee, had he had support for such a policy in the Baldwin cabinet.[14] Briand, even after Locarno, was seeking greater security in an American connection—if France could not have an alliance—when he proposed what became the Kellogg-Briand Pact in 1928. None of the Locarno foreign ministers had any personal or emotional commitment to Franco-German rapprochement, as the Lorrainer Robert Schuman or the Württemberger Carlo Schmid, born in France to a French mother and a German father, would have thirty years later.

The first area in which Locarno offered a positive model to the architects of Bonn's relationship with Paris in the 1950s, then, was its demonstration of the friendship and respect between the three men that developed in the course of their work together. They had come to Locarno in 1925 to defend and advance the national interests of their respective countries; they did not cease to do so in the years that followed. In the course of doing so, however, they developed relationships with each other based on a consensus on the importance of the tripartite dialogue. Substantive differences and even crises could and did develop between their countries in the Locarno years, but they believed, rightly, in each other's good faith. The personal relationships among Briand, Stresemann, and Chamberlain contributed to their conviction that, in the long term, the interests entrusted to them were better served by dialogue than by confrontation, setbacks and frustration in the short term notwithstanding.

The extent to which such relationships, not "based on three similar personalities, even less . . . on three identical views of the future of Europe,"[15] had developed among the Locarno foreign ministers encouraged Bonn to believe that relationships of trust and understanding could be built between the leaders of the new Federal Republic and its western neighbors in the 1950s. At the same time, the extent to which the Locarno policies had depended on the presence of the three men who initiated them was a disturbing aspect of the legacy of the 1920s; it loomed before Bonn as a warning of what could happen to a foreign policy made too dependent on the strength of a personal relationship. At the culmination of the first phase of the Federal Republic's dialogue with France in 1963, instead of an agreement or declaration of intent on future cooperation, Konrad Adenauer insisted on a treaty of friendship and cooperation between the two countries, subject to ratification by the Bundestag. He did so, he wrote later, to give Franco–West German relations a more solid foundation than his personal relationship with Robert Schuman or Charles DeGaulle.[16]

The implications of the weakness of Locarno, its dependence on particular individuals, were even more far-reaching, however. Stresemann was the least dispensable of the three foreign ministers because he represented the state with the shallowest roots in both the Versailles international system and republican government. No other Weimar politician of any prominence was willing to risk "fulfillment" of the Versailles Treaty; nor, as it turned out, was there a sufficient number of them devoted to their own democracy. Germany's commitment to Locarno was, to a precarious degree, dependent on Stresemann's commitment to and personal involvement in the process.

Across the Channel and at the other end of the spectrum of political stability, Chamberlain and his Labour successor in the last few months of Stresemann's life, Arthur Henderson, were representatives of a democratically elected government with broad popular support; behind them was a consensus on both the domestic and international orders within which British foreign policy was conducted. For all the specific disputes of the period, from the India debate to the General Strike, compared to Weimar, the stability of the country and the form of government that Chamberlain and Henderson represented were never in any real question. Moreover, London had no great quarrel with the European system of 1919 but also little to lose if it were modified, as long as change was accomplished by common agreement of the powers concerned. In fact, the tripartisan consensus was that it would need to be modified over time; the question dividing the Labour, Liberal, and Tory parties was how, not if.

Somewhere between his two colleagues, Aristide Briand was foreign minister of a victorious country in which republicanism was more securely anchored than in the Third Republic's first four decades. France was also the state that seemed to have the greatest interest in the

Versailles status quo; although this was true in the short term, in the long run, that status quo was ominous for the Third Republic. France's place in the Versailles system depended, in a way that Britain's did not, on maintaining Germany in an inferior position. As a result, instead of a healthy commitment to it, Paris had a paranoid and morbid attachment to the system that symbolized its victory over Berlin in 1918. Briand had a problem that was the mirror image of Stresemann's: he could go only so far so fast in accepting the changes Germany wanted. Like Stresemann, Briand had to fight for his policies in a government and parliament that were at best skeptical and at worst hostile to the compromises with the former enemy that Locarno represented.[17]

Bonn's analysis of the positive and negative aspects of the personalized Locarno process led naturally to three other lessons of the 1920s for the Frankreichpolitik of the 1950s. If the first lesson was the value of good personal relations between leaders of the two countries, the second lesson was the need to establish an ongoing framework of cooperation. To keep their rapprochement in the 1950s from developing a comparable dependence on individuals, to facilitate cooperation between broad segments of the political elite in both countries, and to assure that their relationship developed in a way that was acceptable and reassuring to the other states of western Europe, Bonn (and Paris) stressed the institutionalization of Franco–West German cooperation. Anchoring the bilateral relationship in *multilateral institutions,* in a way that Locarno had not done, became the hallmark of the 1950s.

Not surprisingly, the three foreign ministers had not attempted to build such institutions thirty years before. In the first place, the Paris peace conference had already produced a revolutionary innovation with which the states were learning to live and even to work: the League of Nations. In the second place, as Chamberlain indicated, he and his colleagues had another institution in mind as their historical analogy, the Concert of Europe.[18] Unfortunately, the nineteenth-century institution was not adequate to the twentieth-century task. Konrad Adenauer, Robert Schuman, and their colleagues saw this all too clearly with the hindsight of a quarter-century. When Schuman proposed the European Coal and Steel Community in May 1950, it was, as Jean Monnet wrote, a "bombshell," because the establishment of such an institution was unprecedented in the history of Europe.[19]

Relations among the principal Locarno powers in the 1920s had been fragile; no one in power at the time thought of making them less fragile by submerging trilateral tensions—which grew out of bilateral suspicions—in a broader institutional framework. Wedded to trilateralism at the state level, the foreign ministers found the issue of giving substance to the British security guarantee in the Rhineland Pact a problem rather than an opportunity. London "could not plan with the Germans for a war against France while planning with the French for a war with Germany," so it "decided against any staff talks at all."[20] The possibility of going beyond staff talks and of creating a permanent institution in which all participants would share information with each other seems never to have occurred to the Locarno powers.

To dismiss such an institution as an impossibility in the 1920s because of their underlying mutual suspicion, however, fails to take into account the level of distrust twenty years later. The climate in which the Schuman Plan was proposed was not as favorable as it seems with rosy hindsight; what had changed was the perception that any alternative to cooperation existed, skeptical though many of its early practitioners might be that the "hereditary enemy" could be trusted. "Whether the French wished it or not," wrote Raymond Aron, Paris and Bonn found themselves in the same boat by the late 1940s.[21]

In addition to incorporating the first two lessons of Locarno, the importance of building personal relationships and permanent institutions, Schuman's ECSC proposal and Adenauer's response to it also reflected the third: the need to *forgo demands for an immediate quid pro quo for every concession* made. Neither Stresemann nor Briand had enjoyed the luxury of being able to do so. As a result, both Paris and Berlin were often frustrated with each other by the time they reached agreement; it seemed to their citizens that no gesture of conciliation was ever made and that the other country had merely been forced to give in to obstinacy in the end. Stresemann's frustration that the French would not offer concessions in the early evacuation of the Rhineland was matched by French uneasiness over the durability of the Weimar Republic and its support for the Locarno process. To a large extent, this uneasiness was justified; the anti-Locarno forces in Germany were also antirepublican. In the Reichstag election of September 1930, they came together "to discredit Stresemann's foreign policy, to disgrace the Socialist-led Great Coalition government, and to rally the various right-wing organizations radically opposed to the Republic in a movement that would reach those voters disdainful of the Weimar system."[22]

The argument Stresemann made—that domestic support for the German republic would grow if it could demonstrate foreign policy successes to its constituents—was no doubt made in good faith. That a combination of passing time and allied concessions could free Weimar from the stigma of Versailles was not impossible, but that was not its only problem. French paranoia, especially its more hysterical variety, was unattractive to the British at the time and has not grown less so in the decades since. However, Paris's caution in making concessions to a government under virtually constant attack by communists, Nazis, die-hard monarchists, its own army, and various other political movements is hard to fault.

Raymond Aron recalled that "the menace of death hung over this republic without republicans and its left-wing, Marxist intelligentsia, who hated capitalism too much and did not fear Nazism enough to defend the Weimar regime."[23] Stresemann's personal good faith was not in question, but that of his colleagues, and their ability to carry out commitments made by their government, was. The leaders in Paris and Bonn thirty years later were critical of the Third Republic's unwillingness to make concessions in the 1920s, largely because of its eagerness to make them after 1935. They rightly saw that the combination had proved deadly. Fortunately, Bonn also saw that the foreign ministers in 1925 could not have predicted the policies of their successors and that the precariousness of the Weimar Republic had given Aristide Briand little choice at the time.

Adenauer was convinced that demands and counterdemands had proved the deathblow to Franco-German rapprochement in the past. He told the Bundestag in 1951, during the debate on the Schuman Plan, that an accountbook approach to the offer that had been made by Paris would "arouse the impression abroad, where there remains enough animosity towards us, that we Germans can never be satisfied with what we get, that we are only interested in again becoming what enough Germans once actually were."[24] For their part, Robert Schuman and Jean Monnet shared Adenauer's critique of the quid pro quo fixation of the 1920s. When asked by journalists if his plan were not a leap into the unknown, made by Bonn and Paris without negotiation of details or analysis of where it would lead, Schuman proudly replied that that was exactly what it was.[25]

He could do so because the commitment of the vast majority of West Germans to the new Federal Republic was not in doubt. Compared to his predecessor, Schuman had the advantage of dealing with a German government that enjoyed broad popular support. More important, however, was the fact that the republican *system* established in 1948 and 1949 reflected the will of virtually the entire political spectrum in the Federal Republic. Despite Kurt Schumacher's frequently vitriolic opposition to Adenauer's policies, the SPD was as responsible as the governing parties for the strength of the new democracy and its constitution. Much of the Basic Law reflected the efforts of the Parliamentary Council, in which the CDU and the SPD had been equally represented, to correct the weaknesses of the Weimar constitution: the powers allotted to the federal president, the requirement that a party receive 5 percent of the vote to be represented in parliament, the extensive powers maintained by the states, and the establishment of the constructive vote of no confidence as the opposition's only way to overturn a government.

With the German Communist party established in the Soviet occupation zone after 1945, Bonn had no significant antidemocratic opposition on the left; the antidemocratic right had discredited itself in the years after 1933. Moreover, in the Christian Democratic Union, Catholics and Protestants had finally constructed a nonsectarian republican party committed to "a new democratic order founded on the ethical and spiritual powers of Christianity."[26] From the far left of the SPD to the conservative right wing of the CDU, a consensus existed, after twelve years of Nazi dictatorship, that no partisan issue was more important than the maintenance of the new democratic system itself. At no time in his six years as foreign minister had Gustav Stresemann known the luxury of such a consensus.

The political institutions of the new Federal Republic, which enabled Paris to develop confidence in Bonn's good faith and ability to carry out international obligations, were the first of many confidence-building measures undertaken by the West German state. Without a doubt, Adenauer's government took two steps for every one taken by France; Germany was twice defeated, with a reputation as a warmonger before 1933 that had been made worse by the Third Reich's policies of aggression and extermination. Unless Bonn could "quiet French security fears and hinder a rebirth of German nationalism,"[27] it would not recover an independent voice in the councils of Europe. Bonn had strong reasons to go farther and faster down the road to rapprochement with France than Paris initially thought desirable. The critical factor in the establishment of the western dialogue in the 1950s was not that West Germany took two steps for France's one, but that France did take the one.

Schuman needed evidence from Adenauer that his belief in the possibility of cooperation with the Federal Republic was not misplaced. He was dealing at home with a situation familiar to Aristide Briand in which "an old-fashioned, more or less clearly anti-German security policy continued to set the tone at the Quai d'Orsay." The object of that policy remained "a long-term control of Germany"; its supporters had to be convinced that that control could be achieved "through a new concept of partnership and European federation."[28] Despite the rhetoric of a new era—which was in fact dawning—the fears of the past remained. Schuman could build a broad domestic coalition in support of the ECSC only by bringing together the heirs of both Raymond Poincaré and Aristide Briand, the skeptics and the partisans of Franco-German cooperation.

Adenauer's government was more than willing to undertake the confidence-building measures Paris required; it had little to lose and a great deal to gain. The chancellor succeeded in making the Christian Democratic Union "the great party of Europe. And what was originally the basic orientation of his own party became over the years the orientation of the whole state." The construction of "Europe," as West German historian Hans-Peter Schwarz wrote, promised "partnership with the western European democracies, equality, new responsibilities in the state community, a peaceful future, and a modern foreign policy."[29] Seen in its historical context, however, the advocacy of such a policy was not risk-free. The chancellor was old enough to know "how dangerous it was to be seen as a politician of fulfillment by the German public."[30] Walter Rathenau and Gustav Stresemann had lost their lives, the first murdered and the other's health broken, in an attempt to establish better relations between Berlin and the great powers of western Europe.

The chancellor, who as mayor of Cologne had lived under British occupation of the Rhineland from 1918 to 1926, needed to convince his countrymen that "ties to the West and nationalism were not opposites"; for Adenauer, "Europe" meant the abandonment of "a fixation on the nation-state," not the abandonment of German interests. The false dichotomy Germans had postulated between their own nationalism and the nationalism of their neighbors since 1815 must be rejected: "National interests would continue to play a role in the European context, but they could then be seen in proportion." Adenauer was convinced that "the almost unbridgeable differences between France and Germany could only be dealt with if the imagination of the governments and the people were moved by some fundamentally new idea."[31]

The author of the "fundamentally new idea" had never met Konrad Adenauer before May 1950, but Jean Monnet had come independently to virtually the same conclusion. The draft plan for the European Coal and Steel Community that he prepared for Robert Schuman on one Sunday, April 16, 1950, reflected his conviction that "a totally new situation must be created: the Franco-German problem must become a European problem." Heir to a cognac business with worldwide interests, architect of joint allied shipping arrangements in World War I, and father of the Fourth Republic's plan for economic recovery, Monnet "saw our policy towards Germany beginning to slip back into its old ways, [fighting a] diplomatic rearguard action against Germany's inevitable rehabilitation." Monnet believed that the recognition of the principle of equality in Franco-German relations was essential. He had told Schuman in January 1950 that "we failed in 1919 because we introduced discrimination and a sense of superiority. Now we are beginning to make the same mistakes again."[32]

The alternative Monnet and Schuman constructed was a revolution in French policy toward Germany. Although not losing sight of Paris's historic goals of "containing" German economic, political, and military potential, the ECSC proposal was the first European initiative in the creation of an institutional status quo *with* the Germans in which the latter would have a stake. (The United States was already trying to use the Marshall Plan institutions to promote economic cooperation in western Europe, including the three western zones of occupied Germany.) This had not been accomplished at Vienna in 1815, Paris in 1919, or Locarno in 1925. France's offer to place its own coal and steel industries under the control of an international authority, if West Germany would do the same, was explicitly designed as a first step toward breaking the cycle of past mistrust. The psychological impact of the proposal was immediate and immense, coming as it did from one of the four occupying powers, and the western power that until 1950 had seemed determined to maintain the "sense of superiority" that Monnet lamented, even at the expense of Paris's good relations with London and Washington.

Nevertheless, Monnet knew that "every step towards reconciliation caused an outcry in the German Bundestag as in the French National Assembly."[33] Opposition politicians in both Paris and Bonn wanted to know in advance what solutions to the problems of their respective countries were offered by the ECSC; Monnet saw in their cost-benefit calculations the same quid pro quo mentality that had doomed Locarno. "It was," he wrote later, "less a question of solving problems, which are mostly in the nature of things, than of putting them in a more rational and human perspective, and making use of them to serve the cause of international peace."[34] Unwilling to see Monnet's draft nitpicked to death in a demand-counterdemand cycle reminiscent of the 1920s, the French government insisted on an agreement in principle to the establishment of a supranational "high authority" before the negotiations on the ECSC treaty began.[35] This insistence meant that Britain declined the Schuman proposal, as France suspected it would, and West Germany accepted it immediately. The third lesson of Locarno had been learned and applied in Paris and Bonn. Schuman, Adenauer, and Monnet had begun the "revolution against the old order of policy objectives" that "none of the [Locarno] policy makers was inclined to conduct" a quarter-century before.[36]

As this revolution was taking shape in Bonn and Paris, the fourth and final lesson of Locarno had already begun to have an impact on relations between the two countries: the need for *broad public involvement in the process* of political rapprochement. Before the Federal Republic of Germany had even been established, private individuals in the three western occupation zones, France, and the other countries of western Europe began creating a network of contacts designed to give depth and breadth to a new German democracy and its relations with its neighbors. Their efforts, and the support they received later from the new federal government in Bonn, reflected an analysis of the failure of the democracies to involve their citizens in the rapprochement policies of the 1920s. In that decade, as in the centuries before, "international understanding was narrowly conceived of as applying to the concept of the 'state.' The citizen was either never considered, or was only considered as performing functions for the relations between states."[37]

The Locarno foreign ministers were not men given to the cultivation of public participation in the making of foreign policy. They knew how to utilize public opinion on specific occasions, but the nineteenth-century Concert, of which Chamberlain was so fond, depended on precisely the opposite approach—keeping private citizens uninvolved and public emotions out of foreign policy decisions. The American concept of open diplomacy seemed to be a recipe for disaster to most European statesmen of the period, who believed that the business of the state was best conducted when unaffected by the often jingoist sentiments of their own citizens. In an age of mass politics, however, whether democratic statesmen liked it or not, others had already begun to influence the public's attitude toward the conduct of *its* foreign policy and toward the statesmen who had now to be elected, not appointed by a monarch, to carry it out. As all the Locarno ministers, but especially Gustav Stresemann, found, the failure to create an informed public opinion in support of their goals left the field open to those manipulating the public to oppose them.[38]

In the first years after World War II, the lesson of the Locarno ministers' failure to create broad-based, democratic support for their policies was translated into action by private citizens. Instead of the embittered climate of the years after 1871 and 1919, in which revanche for Alsace-Lorraine and Versailles had been the watchword of the public's attitude toward Franco-German relations, citizens' groups began to foster an atmosphere in which mutual understanding could grow. The realization of the need for such a movement existed on both sides of the Rhine; it was particularly acute among Germans, who had to deal with the legacy of their country's attempts to subjugate and destroy the cultures of its neighbors, but it was also strong within the ranks of the French Resistance. In this respect, the armistice of 1940 and the establishment of the Vichy government had forced on those who joined the resistance the recognition that their war would not fit the mold of 1870 or 1914. It was not fundamentally a war between French and Germans, but a war between what France had once stood for and what Germany had come to stand for after 1933.

This spirit of European resistance to the destruction of a common civilization was captured in Albert Camus's "Letters to a German Friend," published clandestinely in 1943 and 1944. In his preface to a postwar edition of these essays, Camus wrote:

> When the author of these letters says "you," he means not "you Germans"
> but "you Nazis." When he says "we," this signifies not always "we
> Frenchmen" but sometimes "we free Europeans." I am contrasting two
> attitudes, not two nations, even if, at a certain moment in history, these
> nations personified two enemy attitudes. To repeat a remark that is not
> mine, I love my country too much to be a nationalist. . . . This is why I
> should be ashamed today if I implied that a French writer could be the
> enemy of a single nation. I loathe none but executioners.[39]

Fortunately for postwar West Germany, Camus was not alone in this
attitude. Considering the magnitude of the crimes of the Third Reich in
the occupied countries of Europe, their citizens might have been
expected to turn away en masse from those preaching reconciliation in
the years after 1945, but the opposite was true. Men and women like
Camus took a self-critical attitude to their own prejudices and to their
countries' past pursuit of narrowly defined national interests at the
expense of two millennia of European civilization.

In the French zone of occupation, however, official policy required
a quarantine of all Germans from the victors. Like the British and the
Americans, the French initially pursued an occupation policy that
postulated that "Hitler was the logical and virtually inevitable product of
Prussianism and a united Germany. To save Germany and the world
from another Hitler, it was necessary to destroy Prussia and to divide
Germany."[40] But then what? Did the German nation have a character
flaw that would lead inevitably to another cycle of militarization and
conquest? Did the security of their neighbors require the permanent
subjugation of the German people?

The questions themselves, once the war was over, sounded like ones
posed by Hitler and Goebbels; wartime propaganda notwithstanding,
such policies were not consistent with either the aims or the principles of
the western Allies. In the summer of 1947, coincident with the prepa-
ratory conference of the Marshall Plan in Paris, the American occupation
authorities had formally abandoned the more or less punitive doctrine of
denazification, decartelization, and decentralization contained in Joint
Chiefs of Staff Directive 1067 for the policy of political and economic
reconstruction enunciated in JCS-1779.[41] A year later, the blockade of
the western sectors of Berlin confirmed Washington's conviction that
rehabilitation of German political life and the developing east-west Cold
War both mitigated against the punitive plans made during the war years
for handling defeated Germany.

Paris held out longer, giving ground only gradually until the historic
offer of May 1950, when it became the "engine" rather than the "brake"
in the definition of a new European role for western Germany.[42] In the
event, individual French officials were more far-sighted. Long before the

outlines of the Cold War became clear, those who saw the need to sow the seeds of a new Franco-German relationship began to sabotage official policy, giving the occupation, as Alfred Grosser wrote, almost in spite of itself, "a creative originality that ran counter to its policies in general." They rebelled against "the incoherence of an attitude which consisted in reproaching the Germans . . . for being nationalist, while denying them all outside contact, notably with the French." The rebellion, at the grassroots of the occupation, "would not have succeeded had the [Resistance's concepts] not existed in France." Its success brought a new dimension to foreign policy. Such groups as the Offenburg Center, founded in 1945, and the French Committee for Exchanges with a New Germany, established three years later:

> Took a new approach to Franco-German rapprochement. Compared to traditional cultural contacts, the notion of culture was transformed and its clientele enlarged. . . . Focusing on youth movements, labor unions, political parties, and churches, . . . [they] developed a human infrastructure of Franco-German politics which proved invaluable when the reorientation took place at the national level.[43]

Nothing like this binational "human infrastructure" had existed in the 1920s. Stresemann and Briand had waged constant battles against their hostile domestic constituencies virtually alone. However, when he offered Monnet's concept of the ECSC to Bonn, Robert Schuman knew that in his own country and in the Federal Republic there was organized and vocal support for rapprochement, not revanche.[44] Despite the existence in France of opposition from the coal and steel industries, labor unions, die-hard nationalists on the right, and communists on the left, and, in Bonn, opposition from an SPD that feared perpetuating the division of Germany and distrusted French motives, a constituency also existed for the policy of the "magnanimous gesture," the "revolution against the old order of policy objectives" that had eluded the Locarno foreign ministers a quarter-century before. Schuman and Adenauer both had to wage a campaign for public opinion, but in an atmosphere light-years away from the hostile domestic environments in which Stresemann and Briand had tried to carry out their foreign policies.[45]

A New Process of Dialogue

In 1950, political leaders in both Bonn and Paris showed that they had learned the lessons of Locarno. Over the course of the next decade and a half, those lessons were put into practice. Leaders of the two countries began to establish a relationship based on regular consultations with each other, in which wide-ranging discussions of plans and policies rather than just negotiations on specific problems became the norm. The mutual trust that grew between French and West German politicians and diplomats in this process was in the best tradition of the Locarno "tea parties."

The lessons learned from what Locarno had not done, however, were even more important. The signing of the Franco-German (Elysée) Treaty of Friendship and Cooperation on January 25, 1963, marked the culmination of the first phase of postwar cooperation between Bonn and Paris. In little more than a decade, the new commitment to western European institutions had produced three major successes: the ECSC, Euratom, and the Common Market. The consensus on the importance of institutions had also made possible the eventual solution of the problems posed by the premature attempt to establish a European Defense Community (EDC): in the creation of the Western European Union (WEU) and West German membership in NATO. Finally, the treaty itself institutionalized the routines of bilateral consultation that had begun to take shape in the Adenauer years.[46]

The story of the creation of those institutions and practices is essentially the story of the application of the third lesson of Locarno, the abandonment of an unproductive cycle of bilateral demands and counterdemands, and the fourth lesson, the development of a grassroots constituency for rapprochement. The mobilization of support for the Locarno from below of the 1950s and Bonn's and Paris's willingness to follow Jean Monnet's injunction to make use of their problems in the cause of peace led to the evolution of a new concept of international relations in the Federal Republic. That concept found its first expression in the relationship with France and in the institutions of Western Europe. Beginning in 1969, Bonn began to test its applicability in an east-west context. Only a decade before, the development of such an Ostpolitik had seemed as unlikely as the possibility of rapprochement between France and a democratic Germany had seemed in 1940, a decade before the Schuman proposal.

In the 1920s, Berlin's Locarno policy had not foreclosed the maintenance of good relations with Moscow.[47] The new Locarno of the 1950s differed from its precursor and model in that respect. Rapprochement between Bonn and Paris developed in the climate of the Cold War, which determined, not the pursuit of their detente, but many of the specific paths it followed. The initial impetus to reconciliation, for the men and women of the early postwar years, had been the threat posed to European civilization by a new Franco-German war. As the threat from the Soviet Union began to overshadow that fear, the cultivation of a dialogue between Bonn and Paris took on a new urgency in those capitals and in Washington and London.

At the national level, by the early 1960s, it was easily forgotten that the Cold War had not been the primary motive behind the first proposals for Franco-German reconciliation after World War II. The legacy of their hereditary enmity seemed less urgent than the Soviet threat to French and West German diplomats and soldiers engaged in common economic and defense planning. At the grassroots, however, the Cold War never supplanted the historical memory of three Franco-German wars in the consciousness of those committed to rapprochement between the two nations.[48]

The existence of the Soviet threat had far-reaching consequences. It gave to Bonn's rapprochement policies of the 1950s an air of being directed against the USSR and eastern Europe. In the years before 1969, the chief characteristic of the new Locarno seemed to be the choice that Adenauer and the Federal Republic had made for the west, in sharp contrast to Stresemann and the Weimar Republic. *How* West Germany implemented its decision for western Europe was the story of Bonn's foreign policy in the 1950s; after the ECSC debate of 1950 and 1951, *whether* to implement it was never in question. Throughout the years of the Cold War, nevertheless, new patterns of foreign policy decision-making and constituency-building were evolving in western Europe. In the long run, they proved beneficial to the development of a new climate of relations between eastern and western Europe in the early 1970s.

The different nature of the two threats—the one of a fourth Franco-German war and the other from the Soviet Union—was best illustrated by the different responses each demanded. The end of the "happy period of Europe" came rather quickly, as Alfred Grosser wrote, when only six weeks after Paris's proposal of the Schuman Plan, "the war in Korea dramatized the explosive problem of German participation in western defense."[49] The fight over the European Defense Community and its aftermath were testimony to both the strengths and the weaknesses of the developing new Locarno. In hindsight, the Soviet threat alone, although important, was clearly not enough to encourage the kind of lasting rapprochement sought by the two "hereditary enemies."

The fear of a new European war *between French and Germans* was the stronger of the two motives bringing Bonn and Paris together in the 1950s. Consequently, when Adenauer's Social Democratic successors, facing the possibility of an east-west nuclear confrontation in Europe in the 1960s, began to apply the lessons of Locarno to east-west detente, their approach was a logical evolution of the new Locarno, not a reversal. By that time, however, the impression that Bonn's dialogue with Paris would always be accompanied by a lack of dialogue with Moscow had become common in the Federal Republic itself and in the capitals of Bonn's allies. The strength of that impression and the implication that rapprochement with France depended on West Germany's willingness to make a choice between eastern and western Europe were legacies of the double threat that shaped the nature of the Franco-West German dialogue after June 1950 and of the fears of a Soviet-German agreement symbolized by the Rapallo-Locarno duality of the 1920s.[50]

The search for an east-west detente—without jeopardizing detente with Paris—became the principal task of Bonn's foreign policy after 1969. That search has not always been welcomed in the French capital, and as the Federal Republic turned forty, neither two SPD chancellors nor their Christian Democratic successor had a definitive answer to the question of whether Paris genuinely believed that no "Rapallo" option was competing with "Locarno" in Bonn. Understood as a process of dialogue between states with a difficult common history but also a common interest in survival, Locarno, by the 1980s, had become the basis of West German foreign policy in both eastern and western Europe.

Notes

1. For a description of his successful efforts to prevent this, see Jean Monnet, *Memoirs* (Garden City, NY: Doubleday, 1978), pp. 211–220. DeGaulle himself later wrote: "That the failure of his policy in Africa had not been able to dispel Roosevelt's illusions was a situation I regretted for him and our relations. But I was certain that his intentions, venturing this time into metropolitan France, would not even begin to be applied in fact." See Charles DeGaulle, *The Complete War Memoirs*, Vol. II, *Unity, 1942–1944* (New York: Simon and Schuster, 1968), p. 545. With less bravado, Monnet admitted in his memoirs (p. 211) that "[DeGaulle] thought that I might have some influence on Roosevelt's decision. I was less certain. Clashes of character are impervious to reason. This one was to resist my efforts of persuasion for a very long time."
2. U.S. Secretary of State James Byrnes described Stalin's and FDR's common lack of regard for France's contribution to the war effort in *Speaking Frankly* (New York: Harper and Bros., 1947), pp. 24–28, and his own lack of success (pp. 169–171) in convincing Paris that there were better ways of assuring French security "than by slicing away sections of German territory."
3. A policy that contributed to the failure of the Moscow Foreign Ministers' Conference in 1947 and that made France, in F. Roy Willis's phrase, "the distasteful ally" of London and Washington during the "year of long, irritable, and often arid planning and negotiation" that followed. See *France, Germany, and the New Europe, 1945–1967* (London: Oxford University Press, 1968), pp. 19–24.
4. Alfred Grosser, *Affaires Extérieures* (Paris: Flammarion, 1984), p. 80. Schmid was finally released after French troops searched his house and concluded that "anyone who has translated Baudelaire is not a member of the SS." See Carlo Schmid, *Erinnerungen* (Bern: Scherz, 1979), pp. 220–222.

5. Grosser, *Affaires Extérieures*, p. 34.
6. Ibid., p. 79.
7. Raymond Aron, *Mémoires* (Paris: Julliard, 1983), p. 250.
8. Ibid., p. 251.
9. Robert H. Ferrell, in his *Peace in Their Time: The Origins of the Kellogg-Briand Pact* (New Haven: Yale University Press, 1952), p. 49, is critical of the Locarno Treaties precisely because "they had the effect of grading frontiers in Europe into those which were guaranteed (the western frontiers of Germany) and those which were not guaranteed (namely, Germany's eastern frontiers)." Ferrell is also skeptical of the Geneva Protocol and the resolution of the League of Nations' Eighth Assembly rejecting wars of aggression as a means of settling international disputes, commenting (p. 127) that "diplomats cared little for gestures." This cynicism is unfair to Stresemann, who had to search for means with which to pursue the Weimar Republic's goals in eastern Europe that were acceptable to its western neighbors; exactly the same problem later confronted Willy Brandt. There is no reason to believe, as Ferrell seems to imply (p. 177–178), that Stresemann's enthusiasm for the Kellogg-Briand Pact was purely tactical. He realized, as his son later wrote, that Briand had tried "to put an extra sausage on the fire" with the United States and had instead given Germany the occasion to make another favorable impression on Washington by being the first country to accept the proposed Pact of Paris. However, this does not lead to the conclusion that Stresemann's attempt to commit his country to renunciation of the use of force in pursuit of its foreign policy goals was less than sincere.

    In his eloquent May 5, 1928, address at Heidelberg (when he and U.S. Ambassador Jacob Schurman received honorary doctorates), on a day when his son "had seldom seen him happier, more free from care," Stresemann spoke of the " 'right of nations to life and freedom,' " a right that was not the opposite, but the companion of their " 'learning to understand each other and to come together in peace.' " The task of the statesman was " 'to help shape the future, by keeping the goal firmly in view, but by recognizing when new means are necessary to achieve that goal.' " He told the students of Heidelberg that his policies were aimed at establishing " 'a free, fully sovereign Germany, serving peace and the further development of mankind.' " In believing that territorial revisions would be possible without the use of force, Stresemann was not so much hypocritical as he was thirty years ahead of his time. See Wolfgang Stresemann, *Mein Vater Gustav Stresemann* (Frankfurt am Main: Ullstein, 1985), pp. 506–508 and 519–520.
10. Jon Jacobson, *Locarno Diplomacy: Germany and the West, 1925–1929* (Princeton: Princeton University Press, 1972), pp. 69–70. As a sympathetic but not uncritical study of the three Locarno foreign ministers, Jacobson's book remains unsurpassed, and I am indebted to it for much of the following discussion.
11. Ibid., pp. 363–364.
12. By, among others, Sebastian Haffner, in a short but evocative essay, "Gustav Stresemann: ein deutscher Realist," in *Im Schatten der Geschichte* (Stuttgart: DVA, 1985), p. 284: "By personal conviction a monarchist,"

Stresemann "became increasingly more impatient with the bitter and fruitless struggle between the monarchists and republicans" that eventually helped destroy both the Weimar Republic and Germany.

13. Jacobson, *Locarno Diplomacy*, pp. 355, 358–359.
14. Ibid., pp. 37–38.
15. Ibid., p. 75.
16. Konrad Adenauer, *Erinnerungen* (Stuttgart: DVA, 1968), p. 198; and Charles de Gaulle, *Memoirs of Hope: Renewal and Endeavor* (New York: Simon & Schuster, 1976), pp. 174–181.
17. The Locarno statesmen were themselves aware of the weakness of a foreign policy built on their personal relationship. Stresemann, Jacobson wrote (*Locarno Diplomacy*, pp. 387–388), once "sentimentally compared himself to Ibsen's Nora, always hoping for a change for the better, and always being disappointed"; and Briand in early 1928 "reminded Stresemann that neither of them was immortal and that one day a member of the right wing of the German Nationalist Party might become German Foreign Minister. Then, what good would trust placed in Stresemann do France?"
18. Ibid., pp. 68–69.
19. Monnet, *Memoirs*, p. 306.
20. Jacobson, *Locarno Diplomacy*, pp. 34–35.
21. Aron, *Mémoires*, p. 250.
22. Jacobson, *Locarno Diplomacy*, pp. 353–354.
23. Aron, *Mémoires*, p. 73.
24. In the May 31, 1951, Bundestag debate on the Schuman Plan. The text is in Roland Delcour, *Konrad Adenauer* (Paris: Seghers, 1966), pp. 148–160.
25. Monnet, *Memoirs*, p. 305.
26. From the founding call to action of the Berlin CDU, June 26, 1945, in Günter Buchstab, Brigitte Kaff, and Hans-Otto Kleinmann, eds., *Verfolgung und Widerstand, 1933–1945, Christliche Demokraten gegen Hitler* (Düsseldorf: Droste, 1986), pp. 270–271.
27. Hans-Peter Schwarz, *Adenauer, Der Aufstieg: 1876–1952* (Stuttgart: DVA, 1986), p. 701.
28. Ibid., p. 719.
29. Ibid., p. 651.
30. Ibid., p. 683.
31. Ibid., pp. 702, 708.
32. Monnet, *Memoirs*, pp. 284, 274, 294.
33. Ibid., p. 284.
34. Ibid., p. 297.
35. Ibid., pp. 311–312. See also Alan Bullock, *Ernest Bevin, Foreign Secretary* (New York: W.W. Norton, 1983), pp. 779–780.
36. Jacobson, *Locarno Diplomacy*, p. 373.
37. Hansjürgen Garstka, *Die Rolle der Gemeinde in der internationalen Verständigung nach dem zweiten Weltkrieg gezeigt am Beispiel der deutsch-französischen Verständigung* (Stuttgart: IBU, 1972), p. 2.
38. Although Ferrell described (*Peace in Their Time*, p. 14) "the 'intrusion' of public opinion into foreign policy" in the years after 1918, neither Strese-

mann nor Briand had been capable of mobilizing, at the local level, support for their policies. Because, as Jacobson noted (*Locarno Diplomacy*, p. 388), they both accepted the nineteenth-century concept of inter*state* relations, in which national governments alone made foreign policy decisions, they were unable to conceptualize the Locarno from below that became the hallmark of Franco–West German rapprochement after 1950.

39. Albert Camus, *Resistance, Rebellion, and Death* (New York: Vintage Books, 1974), p. 4.

40. Grosser, *Affaires Extérieures*, p. 35.

41. Alfred Grosser, *The Western Alliance* (New York: Vintage Books, 1982), p. 63.

42. Grosser, *Affaires Extérieures*, p. 81.

43. Ibid., p. 80.

44. Among them, the International Mayors Union for Franco-German Understanding and European Cooperation, the Council of European Communes, the Deutsch-französisches Institut, the Europa-Union, and numerous organizations of veterans and deportees. For a discussion of their role, see Edwina S. Campbell, "The Ideals and Origins of the Franco-German Sister Cities Movement, 1945–70," *Journal of the History of European Ideas*, 8, no. 1 (1987): 77–95.

45. The Ludwigsburg Franco-German Institute, for example, called its principal task the promotion of "understanding with France in all areas of intellectual and public life," based on the perception that "the world situation had changed so basically that neither France nor Germany would be able to survive alone." See Fritz Schenk, *Zwanzig Jahre Deutsch-französisches Institut Ludwigsburg* (Ludwigsburg: Satz und Druck Süddeutsche Verlags-Anstalt, 1968), p. 6. The "purely private initiative" of the Institute's founders (Carlo Schmid was its first president) signaled the beginning of a revolution; commonplace a quarter-century later, such initiatives had been virtually nonexistent a quarter-century before.

46. For the text of the treaty, see Delcour, *Konrad Adenauer*, pp. 177–183.

47. Stresemann, *Mein Vater*, pp. 367–369.

48. A speech typical of the sister cities movement was the one Freiburg's mayor gave in Besançon in 1959, in which he described their mutual goal as

liquidating definitively the unhappy differences between our two great peoples . . . and establishing an active and friendly cooperation. We remember with horror the August and September days twenty years ago when the Nazi government in Germany . . . unleashed a world war which brought much suffering and evil to nearly every nation, most especially the French, and which led the German people to the abyss. Today, in contrast, the two countries, up to and including their respective heads of government, are working together in a spirit of friendship. We must strengthen and expand this governmental cooperation by basing it on cooperation between our citizens at the local level.

Speech by Dr. Joseph Brandel, September 9, 1959, contained in the archives of the city of Freiburg im Breisgau, *Partnerschaft mit der Stadt Besançon*, vol. I, 1957–1960.

49. Grosser, *Affaires Extérieures*, p. 85.
50. As David Calleo noted in *The German Problem Reconsidered* (Cambridge: Cambridge University Press, 1978), p. 174, despite his attempt to loosen Bonn's ties with Washington, "DeGaulle had seen a collective European policy, with France the interlocutor between Germany and the East." Instead, "the Germans after Adenauer rejected French tutelage and seized the initiative for themselves."

4

FROM DETENTE TO ENTENTE WITH FRANCE

Institution Building in Western Europe

From 1949 until his resignation in 1963, Konrad Adenauer personified the Federal Republic of Germany abroad. To the countries of the western alliance, the chancellor represented the abandonment of the attempt to establish German hegemony over central Europe. Its commitment to a western European state system based on the values of Christianity, parliamentary democracy, and social responsibility united Adenauer's Christian Democratic Union (CDU) with the Italian Christian Democrats, led by Alcide de Gasperi, and with Robert Schuman's Popular Republicans (MRP) in France. For the first time, the democratic forces of the center right seemed to be in the vanguard not only of the rhetoric of internationalism but also of practical steps taken in the direction of a united Europe.

Kurt Schumacher's SPD, like Clement Attlee's Labour government in Britain, was hostile to the political and economic integration explicit in Jean Monnet's concept of the European Coal and Steel Community.[1] For different reasons but with the same effect, the wariness of the two parties of the left toward the Schuman Plan was shared by the Tories, who did little to implement their own opposition rhetoric in favor of "Europe" after they returned to government in 1951.[2] Nevertheless, Britain was a member of the victorious coalition of 1945, with a global empire and commonwealth; its skepticism toward European integration was understandable, if not acceptable, to its allies. The opposition of the SPD raised fears abroad that the nationalism historically associated with the German right had migrated to the left of the political spectrum.[3]

Schumacher's premature death in 1952 and the victory of the CDU-FDP coalition in the second federal election in 1953 left the Social

73

Democrats a divided party, with many of its most prominent members, like Carlo Schmid, actively involved in the government's pursuit of western integration and reconciliation with France. As Adenauer's foreign policy went from success to success, the SPD was involved in an internal debate that culminated in its adoption of a new domestic and foreign policy program in 1959 and 1960. The Godesberg-Hannover program abandoned the remnants of the party's opposition to West German membership in the European Communities and NATO and to the establishment of the Bundeswehr and military conscription. Ten years after the founding of the Federal Republic, opposition to Adenauer's foreign policies was a recipe for eternal political opposition. Recognition of this was the essential first step toward the chancellery for a party whose electoral support had remained nearly constant, at 30 percent, since 1949, while the CDU's support had climbed from virtual parity in the first election to 45 percent in 1953 and 50 percent in 1957, the only absolute majority ever achieved in a West German federal election.[4]

In his six remaining years in office, however, Adenauer had neither the domestic nor the foreign policy successes of his first two terms. When he stood again, at age eighty-five, as candidate for chancellor in 1961, the CDU was a divided party, anxious for new leadership and confronted by political, economic, and social issues produced by its own success. The price demanded by the Free Democrats for the government coalition they formed that year with the Christian Democrats was a guarantee that Adenauer would resign halfway through his term in 1963.[5] Before he kept that promise, the chancellor negotiated the agreement with France that marked the end of his foreign policy dominance and of detente with Paris. With the 1963 (Elysée) Treaty of Friendship and Cooperation, the pursuit of a Franco-West German detente was clearly over; an entente had been established between the two countries.

At the time, the positive aspects of the treaty were overshadowed by the dispute between Paris, on the one hand, and Washington and London, on the other, over the French role in NATO and the British application for membership in the Common Market. With the establishment of the Fifth Republic in 1958 and the election of General DeGaulle as its first president, Bonn had feared that the Schuman-Monnet concept of western integration through institution building would be abandoned; the rhetoric of DeGaulle and his supporters during his years in the "desert" after 1946 was hardly encouraging.[6] Surprisingly, the Fifth Republic did not disavow the Treaty of Rome signed by its predecessor; what DeGaulle did bring to bear, however, was a concept of a Franco-German "special relationship" within Europe and the Atlantic Alliance, which struck a responsive chord in Adenauer but divided the CDU into Atlanticist and Gaullist factions.[7]

Despite the new constellations that began to take shape in the early 1960s—within the SPD, in a France relieved for the first time since 1945 of the burden of a colonial war, and in the ranks of those who had been advocates of both western European and Atlantic cooperation in the years since 1949—the fundamental concepts of Adenauer's Frankreichpolitik were never called into question. The emphasis on personal relationships and permanent bilateral and multilateral institutions, the rejection of the demands and counterdemands of traditional diplomatic negotiation, and the cultivation of a public constituency all made relations between France and West Germany increasingly resemble those between interest groups and individuals within a democratic state who share a commitment to the system itself stronger than any specific disagreement they have on a given issue. In such a state, however, the system that commands their support is clearly defined by law and custom. What western European or Franco-German "system" existed by 1963? Did Bonn and Paris really share the same vision of the issues and options facing Europe?

Four issues explicitly or implicitly shaped the evolution of detente between the Federal Republic and its western neighbor in the 1950s: the Soviet threat, the cultural and economic "American challenge,"[8] the threat of war, and the reunification of Germany. The institutions the two countries established in the years from 1950 to 1957 were designed to enhance their options for dealing with these issues. The priorities of Bonn and Paris were not always the same, but neither were they mutually exclusive. They were elaborated in two frameworks, the Atlantic and the (western) European, and in the development of policies chiefly concerned with *economic growth*, *defense*, and *cultural exchange*.

These three areas of Franco–West German cooperation bear closer examination as an example of the detente process that culminated in 1963. In *economic decision-making* from 1950 to 1957, Bonn reached agreement with Paris on two questions that had seemed intractable only a few years before: the status of the Ruhr and Saarland. With the Benelux countries and Italy, France and West Germany established the European Economic Community (EEC). In the area of *defense* the Federal Republic accepted the plan of French Prime Minister René Pleven for what became the European Defense Community (EDC), but its constituent treaty failed to win approval from the French National Assembly in 1954. Instead, security cooperation between the two countries developed, through the mechanism of Western European Union (WEU), within the Atlantic Alliance. Finally, Bonn encouraged a lively and highly decentralized program of *cultural exchange* between private groups and citizens, including summer language camps, student exchanges, joint sport programs, and apprenticeship training. Many of these activities were conducted within the framework of sister cities relationships, which were encouraged and supported by private umbrella organizations in the two countries.

Bonn's policy toward each of these areas of Franco–West German cooperation reflected its assessment of the issues posed by the Soviet Union, the United States, and war in a nuclear age, as well as that of German reunification. Moreover, as the concept of detente with France developed in the 1950s, it took on a dynamic of its own in which these issues not only affected cooperation between the two countries but also were affected by it. The end of an era of "eternal enmity" between France and Germany was bound to have profound effects on the international relations of Europe. Ironically, Bonn's dilemma in the Franco-American quarrels of the 1960s was one of the first signs that it had.

The European Coal and Steel Community

Before that chapter in the history of the Atlantic Alliance could be written, however, the Federal Republic had before it a blank page on which to develop the western detente of the 1950s. In each area of cooperation, it sought to apply the lessons of Locarno, focusing on confidence-building measures (CBMs) and the development of permanent institutions. The first opportunity to put these lessons into practice was the Schuman Plan proposal, and its implementation set the tone and the methodology of the 1950s. The structure of the European Coal and Steel Community (ECSC) was the model for future cooperation between Bonn and Paris.

The treaty signed between France, the Netherlands, Belgium, Luxembourg, Italy, and the Federal Republic on April 18, 1951, established a community of member states to which each of them delegated decision-making authority in specific areas of what had been national policy affecting their coal and steel industries. The treaty set up a High Authority in Luxembourg. Although its members were appointed by the member states, it had independent authority over the production and distribution of their coal and steel; it was given the power to tax this production and to determine the use of those taxes. Representation on the High Authority was proportional to the size of the states, yet its decisions were by majority vote and immediately binding on all members when taken. It could resign only as a body, to prevent national influence from being exerted on individual members. The ECSC Treaty also established an advisory labor council, assembly, council of ministers, and court to adjudicate differences between the member states; the court's decisions were binding on them.[9]

The structure of the ECSC was a watershed in the evolution of both global and regional international organizations; for the Federal Republic, the chief importance of its structure was the role the ECSC played in detente with France. When Monnet left Paris for Luxembourg in August 1952 to become president of the High Authority, he and his negotiating partners had established a framework for dealing with bilateral economic issues of long standing between France and Germany. Indirectly, from the French perspective, these issues were also security issues because German economic potential had often enough, for Paris, translated into war-making potential in the past. Bonn's agreement to the treaty reflected its analysis of this French perspective in the aftermath of recent German history. How did the ECSC apply the lessons of Locarno and respond to the issues facing Bonn in the early 1950s?

First, it acknowledged the continuing relevance of the issues of the 1920s—"if only the French could lose their fear of German industrial domination, then the greatest obstacle to a united Europe would be removed"[10]—while recognizing that the inability of the Locarno statesmen to break out of their concept of the Concert of Europe had contributed to the failure of their efforts at rapprochement. Jean Monnet later recalled that both Winston Churchill's call for a United States of Europe in Zurich in 1946 and Aristide Briand's proposal of " 'a federal link' between the peoples in Europe" in Geneva in 1929 "had nothing to do with action." Briand had limited his proposal to ties that "should not affect the sovereign rights of nations." Monnet was convinced that only an institution that did limit these rights could be a new beginning in 1950, providing it did two things: assure France a measure of control over the economic potential of its former enemy; and acknowledge West Germany's sovereign equality by establishing this control *with* Bonn, instead of against it, and by agreeing to submit France's coal and steel production to the same controls.[11] The ECSC did both.

Monnet later praised the "two men who by themselves had dared to commit their countries' future" to the ECSC, inevitably calling to mind a comparison of the political courage of Robert Schuman and Konrad Adenauer to that of Aristide Briand and Gustav Stresemann. Monnet most clearly reflected the legacy of Locarno when he added that the commitment Schuman and Adenauer had made required "institutions to give shape to an agreement based on goodwill. Nothing is possible without men; nothing is lasting without institutions." The final text of the Schuman proposal contained praise for Paris's earlier efforts at Franco-German reconciliation, which, as Monnet wrote, was "a homage to Aristide Briand, but also a farewell to rhetoric."[12]

During the summer of 1950, the delegations from the Benelux countries and Italy, meeting at Paris to draft the text of the ECSC treaty, experienced what must have seemed at the time almost a violation of a law of nature: solidarity between their French and German colleagues. Bonn's conviction that "the importance of the Schuman Plan is above all political" was expressed in its call on "all members of this conference to subordinate their economic interests to this great political goal."[13] Monnet later recalled that Walter Hallstein's "firm and dignified statement" in response to economic objections from the smaller countries had "confirmed that France and Germany still saw eye to eye. That was the crux of the matter."[14] Indeed, it was.

In Bonn itself, however, Adenauer's parliamentary battle for the ECSC was less congenial than the work underway in Paris. Although Monnet "asked that the word 'negotiations' not be used to describe our meetings," because the six delegations were there "to undertake a common task—not to negotiate for our own national advantage,"[15] Adenauer's government was engaged in convincing both parliament and public of the wisdom of undertaking the confidence-building measures inherent in the Schuman Plan. Only a short time before, Bonn had reluctantly concluded that it would have to accept the membership of an autonomous Saarland in the Council of Europe and West German participation in the International Ruhr Authority (IAR). Adenauer had been willing to demonstrate his country's commitment to reconciliation with the western allies, even at the cost of a potentially permanent alienation of the Saar territory from Germany and the recognition of international restrictions on German industrial production without reciprocity.[16] Both proposals reflected a concept of controlling German economic potential that had characterized the 1920s and that was based on inequality between the victors and vanquished.

As an alternative to these two prospects, the Schuman Plan was far more advantageous to the Federal Republic, so much so that Monnet recalled of his first meeting with Adenauer that "clearly, he could not believe that we were really proposing full equality; and his attitude was still marked by long years of hard negotiation and wounded pride." They talked for an hour and a half, during which Monnet "saw the old man gradually relax and reveal the emotion that he had been holding back." Calling the French foreign minister's proposal "a matter of morality," the chancellor told him:

> I have waited twenty-five years for a move like this. In accepting it, my Government and my country have no secret hankerings after hegemony. History since 1933 has taught us the folly of such ideas. Germany knows that its fate is bound up with that of western Europe as a whole.[17]

Adenauer's political opposition did not agree that the fate of Germany should be linked to the Schuman Plan. The vitriolic opposition of Kurt Schumacher to the French proposal demonstrated once and for all his failure to understand the burden of recent German history that the Federal Republic inevitably bore. Schumacher attacked the ECSC as an institution based on "capitalism, cartels, conservatism, and clericalism" that would bring another fifty years of occupation and decrease the prospects of German reunification.[18] His criticism appeared both unintelligible and inflammatory to Washington and London, as well as to Paris, which correctly saw Monnet's concept as the antithesis of the artificial economic superiority, based on reparations and occupation, that France had sought in the 1920s. In all of the western allies, Schumacher inspired a "veritable repulsion"; his "intransigent attitude" and "passionate language" making any frustrations they had with Konrad Adenauer seem minor by comparison.[19] France's Socialist president, Vincent Auriol, called Schumacher a "madman" and a "National Socialist," both unfair characterizations but indicative of the reputation the German Social Democrat had created for himself and his party.[20]

With hindsight, and stripped of its political hyperbole, the criticism Schumacher leveled at the ECSC contained a measure of truth. The establishment of western European institutions did not mean the continuing occupation of Germany, but it did mean, in the context of the Cold War, a hardening of the division of his country and of eastern and western Europe. Not the Schuman Plan, however, but the refusal of Moscow three years earlier to allow the countries of eastern Europe to participate in the Marshall Plan had assured the separate economic development of the two parts of the continent. The principal problem with Schumacher's critique of Adenauer's foreign policy was that it postulated alternatives that did not exist.

The chancellor knew, as did Monnet, that the United States and Britain were no more likely to capitulate to French efforts to block the economic and political recovery of the Federal Republic in 1950 than they had been in the past two years.[21] Washington's economic leverage over Paris was considerable and grew greater in the next few years, as the United States became the principal source of financing for France's war in Indochina. Unlike Schumacher, however, Adenauer also saw that concessions forced from France in such a manner could never serve as the basis for a lasting rapprochement between the two countries; they would only reinforce the "French neuroses" of vulnerability to German economic strength with which Monnet's plan was attempting to deal.[22]

Moreover, American pressure on the Fourth Republic was not going to produce the option of a reunified, democratic Germany. The SPD knew as well as the CDU that the democratic state it had helped create in the Federal Republic was not acceptable to the Soviet Union.[23] The refusal of the Berlin Social Democrats, led by Ernst Reuter, to accept merger with the German Communist Party and the move of the SPD-led city government to the western sectors in 1948 had made Reuter a symbol of West Berlin's refusal to capitulate to Soviet pressure during the year-long blockade. Given the consensus that existed among all major political parties in the Federal Republic that German unity was not to be bought at the cost of justice and freedom, the only alternative to cooperation with France in the economic and political integration of western Europe was the perpetuation of a state-of-occupation limbo, acceptable neither to the western allies nor to West Germans.

Schumacher's criticism of the ECSC reflected historical German suspicions of France that were not regarded as legitimate in 1950. Despite the split in the east-west wartime coalition and the strategic importance of the Federal Republic to the western alliance, and despite the individual resistance of some Germans—Kurt Schumacher chief among them—to the policies of the Third Reich, in the eyes of the world, Germans had forfeited their right to be suspicious.[24] Adenauer's foreign policy demonstrated his recognition of the fact that they would have to win back the right to be skeptical, like equality, over time.

Finally, Schumacher's characterization of the Schuman Plan was wrong. Naturally, Paris's proposal was in France's interest, but the ECSC also served the interests of all the countries that created it. It was not a cartel; nor was it the instrument of conservative, Catholic capitalists to oppress the working class. Schumacher's rhetoric, in fact, was more in tune with the labor movement's struggles in Wilhelmine Germany than with the reality of Europe's postwar recovery. The SPD leader was a German patriot, but one who was out of touch with the economic and political environment in which the Federal Republic conducted its foreign policy. As a result, the SPD found itself opposing not only the government but also the German Labor Confederation (DGB) on the subject of the ECSC. The labor movement "welcomed the proposal on the grounds that it would remove Allied controls over German production and give organized labor as well as their country a greater voice in European affairs."[25]

Socialism's historic antipathy to private ownership, its skepticism of religion, particularly Roman Catholicism, and its tendency to see nationalization of basic industries as a panacea for poverty and inequality of opportunity manifested itself in the attitude of both the SPD and the British Labour Party to the Schuman Plan. Neither within the Federal Republic nor in the creation of the new institutions of western European cooperation, however, was the CDU a party interested in the exploitation of a large and growing part of its own constituency, West Germany's industrial workers. Moreover, as Alfred Grosser wrote:

Contrary to one of the popular themes of the era, the Schuman-Adenauer-de Gasperi trinity was not above all "papist." What the three had most in common were their birthplaces, in Lorraine, the Rhineland, and the South Tyrol, and their desire to free Europe from its tragic border conflicts.[26]

The Schuman Plan introduced an enduring element to the foreign policy of the Federal Republic: its commitment, not to the abolition of Europe's political borders, but to overcoming their divisive impact on economic prosperity and human contacts.

The treaty establishing the ECSC was signed in the Salle d'Horloge of the Quai d'Orsay, where Gustav Stresemann, Aristide Briand, and the representatives of thirteen other countries had signed the Kellogg-Briand Pact in August 1928. More than the Pact of Paris, however, the treaty signed in April 1951 represented the two countries' "renunciation of war as an instrument of national policy." France's acceptance of the Federal Republic's equality, in both the negotiation and the terms of the treaty, and Bonn's open acknowledgment of Germany's historic responsibility for Paris's fear of its industrial potential laid the foundation for the cooperation that followed in the years ahead. In its tenor and purpose, as well as in its substance, the Schuman Plan was a confidence-building measure par excellence.

Rearmament and the Status of the Saar

The success of the ECSC made possible an amicable compromise between Bonn and Paris on two issues that would have appeared hopelessly divisive only a short time before. The establishment of the ECSC in 1952 meant the end of the Ruhr Authority; three years later, France accepted the results of the Saar referendum, which demonstrated that the vast majority of the population wished neither autonomy nor annexation by France. The French had administered the Saar since the end of World War II and in the first postwar years had planned to annex it outright. Since the early 1950s, however, Paris had supported the Council of Europe's proposal to "Europeanize" the territory and had expected that this Europeanization would win approval from the Saarlanders. Instead, they voted overwhelmingly against it.

What was remarkable, however, was not their vote but the reaction of Paris. Three years after the establishment of the High Authority in Luxembourg, control of the Saar's coal resources did not have the same strategic significance for the Federal Republic. The old hysteria, which had characterized Paris's determination to keep as many industrial assets as possible out of German hands, was gone. Describing coal and steel as "the key to economic power and the raw materials for forging weapons of war," Monnet had predicted, "to pool them across frontiers would reduce their malign prestige and turn them instead into a guarantee of peace."[27] Paris's willingness to accept the results of the plebiscite proved him correct. The Fourth Republic reached an agreement with Bonn in June 1956, the technical details of which were agreed upon four months later, by which the Saarland joined the Federal Republic on January 1, 1957. France had consented to the peaceful expansion of the territory of the West German state.

The second compromise of the mid-1950s was, if anything, even more surprising: in the course of two years, France agreed not only to the territorial expansion of the Federal Republic but also to the establishment of a West German army. This settled the crisis between the two countries that had developed over the question of a West German contribution to the defense of western Europe. If the Schuman Plan and its elaboration had demonstrated the importance of institutions and confidence-building measures, the failure of the Pleven Plan for the European Defense Community demonstrated the psychological limits within which detente between the two countries had to operate. Unlike the proposal for the ECSC, the Pleven Plan had been a response to considerable and growing external pressure on France to consent to the establishment of a West German army, chiefly from the United States.[28] The outbreak of the war in Korea in June 1950 brought into the open a debate that had been going on behind closed doors since 1948. When the allied foreign ministers met at the United Nations General Assembly in the fall of 1950, the Americans formally requested that they initiate discussions on German rearmament. The European army proposed by Prime Minister Pleven in October was an attempt to meet the American demands while preventing the creation of independent West German armed forces.[29]

The nature of the Pleven Plan was, therefore, fundamentally different from that of its predecessor. Jean Monnet was the author of both, but his draft of the ECSC had been based on an assessment of France's long-term interest in rapprochement with Germany, while the military proposal was a response to a short-term situation perceived as acute by the leader of the western alliance.[30] The United States's conviction that the Soviet Union might attempt the military conquest of western Europe led it to demand the establishment of West German armed forces, despite the psychological, political, and economic misgivings that existed in Europe, notably in the Federal Republic itself.[31] Fear was the predominant motive behind the Pleven proposal: the Americans' fear of a Soviet attack and France's fear of the West German army Washington believed essential.

Because of this, the Pleven Plan, from the point of view of West German foreign policy, was a mixed blessing. Both West German and

French public opinion saw the EDC proposal, unlike the Schuman Plan, as the direct result of the pressure in favor of a West German military role in Europe emanating, with increasing insistency, from the United States.[32] The ECSC proposal had been, in many respects, a response to the same kind of pressure from Washington for the "restoration" of the Federal Republic on the western side in the Cold War and one that reflected French fears of the strength of the German economy. It was, nevertheless, a genuine French initiative that recognized the mutual economic dependence of the two countries. The Pleven proposal, its critics charged, was a reflection of France's economic dependence on the United States, and there was truth to the criticism.[33]

From Bonn's perspective in the early 1950s, however, the French proposal was one that could not be rejected.[34] The leaders of the Federal Republic saw the irony in the Pleven Plan, based on distrust of West German soldiers expected as members of a European army to give their lives for France, but the historical legacy of the past and the foreign policy issues of the present still made it attractive to the Adenauer government. Acceptance of the EDC was another occasion, as the ECSC had been, to demonstrate Bonn's commitment to western European cooperation and to renunciation of the hegemonic goals Berlin had pursued in the past. Should the Pleven proposal fail, the burden for that failure, Adenauer knew, must not rest with the Federal Republic.[35] In the event, after three difficult years, it did fail. Wherever the responsibility lay—with the intransigence of the French National Assembly, the unwillingness of the Benelux countries to accept the compromises in the constituent treaty desired by that assembly, or the lack of support given the EDC by the Mendès France government—it was not in Bonn.[36]

In retrospect, the significance of the EDC failure was only partially understood at the time. The initial negative French reaction to the prospect of West German (re)armament had evolved by 1954 to a disinclination to merge the French army into a European force.[37] The strength of this reaction reflected an attachment to the traditions and history of the national armed forces, which also prevailed in Britain and in the United States, not a reluctance to participate with Germans in the defense of western Europe. The compromise worked out between the members of NATO and the Federal Republic in 1954 and 1955, whereby the Bundeswehr was finally established in November 1955, was the best indication of the major foreign policy success the Adenauer government could claim: the evolution of French policy in less than ten years from demands for the dismemberment and demilitarization of Germany to support for the membership of the Federal Republic in the Atlantic Alliance. The fear that the failure of the EDC would set the clock of Franco–West German relations back to 1949 proved unfounded.

On the contrary, in the 1954 Paris Accords, the French government accepted what had been deemed an impossibility only a few years earlier: a West German army under West German command in peacetime. (In wartime, like the armed forces of all the NATO member states at that time, the Bundeswehr would be under the command of SACEUR, the American Supreme Allied Commander.) The restrictions Adenauer accepted on the new army were few, but they were significant in terms of their psychological impact on Paris: renunciation of atomic, biological, and chemical weapons, dedication of the Bundeswehr to NATO duty, and limitation of its deployment to the NATO area, as defined by the North Atlantic Treaty. In its internal organization, the new army, based on a three-tiered structure of career soldiers, conscripts, and long-term volunteers, developed a concept of the "citizen in uniform," and of the armed forces' responsibility to the democratic state.[38]

The effort the Bundeswehr put into analysis of the German Army's hostility toward the Weimar Republic and its culpability for the crimes of the Third Reich was far more than mere window dressing for foreign public opinion. The debate in the Federal Republic itself on the desirability of establishing a new army and the crisis of conscience among former soldiers considering service in it were real and difficult. Far from embracing their new military role with open arms, many West Germans only reluctantly accepted it; the enthusiasm that had accompanied Berlin's remilitarization programs in the 1930s was nowhere to be found.[39] This, too, however, was a sign to Paris that Bonn was not Weimar. Only a few years later, when the crisis over Algerian decolonization tested the French Army's loyalty to the elected government of the republic, the democratic consensus in West Germany seemed, for a time, far stronger than that in France.

For all of the Fourth Republic's problems, however, the conduct of its foreign policy had a remarkable degree of consistency. In Adenauer's critical first five years in office, when he was de facto West Germany's foreign minister, the chancellor dealt with only two French foreign ministers, Robert Schuman and Georges Bidault. After an interim period, this continuity was reestablished with the Fifth Republic, in the person of Charles DeGaulle, from 1958 until 1963, when Adenauer left office. Other West German politicians and diplomats were also continually involved with Paris in the Federal Republic's first two decades, notably Walter Hallstein and Carlo Schmid; by the early 1960s, the young leader of the post-Godesberg SPD, Willy Brandt, had begun to repair the damage done by his party's hostility toward the Schuman Plan. The early death of Kurt Schumacher, at age fifty-seven in 1952, was personally tragic but politically fortuitous in its impact on the SPD's relations with its sister parties in western Europe and on Bonn's image abroad. In the decade following Schumacher's death, as the Saar and rearmament questions demonstrated, Bonn and Paris made progress inconceivable thirty years before.

"Capillarization of the European Idea"

Below the "high" politics of the two capitals, local and regional officials and private citizens of both countries had also developed an extensive network of relations with each other by 1963. Economic and defense cooperation at the national level was paralleled by cultural cooperation at the local and regional levels. Like the 1954 and 1955 agreements on the status of the Saarland and West German membership in NATO, the breadth and depth of that cultural cooperation by the late 1950s seemed a miraculous achievement such a short time after the end of World War II.

In many ways, the commitment of the two countries to the development of cultural cooperation was the best indication of their determination to meet the four challenges facing them, from the United States, the Soviet Union, German reunification, and war itself. Because cultural relations were relatively free from the daily pressures of the Cold War and the demands of economic expansion, they most clearly revealed how France and West Germany conceived of their relationship over the long term. What Bonn and Paris might have to support in the short run, their constituents wished to support in the long run: the cultivation of a constructive relationship between the two countries and their participation in the development of economic and political cooperation among the countries of western Europe.[40]

By January 1963, when the Elysée Treaty was signed, the framework for cultural cooperation between West Germany and France was well established. Its principal institution was the sister city relationship, which embodied the pragmatic idealism of the postwar generation in western Europe. West German democracy and western European cooperation required a commitment to dealing with the practical tasks at hand while not losing sight of the aspirations of the individual citizen—a balancing act that the local governments of the continent had historically performed with far more success than the national politicians. That the chancellor of the new Federal Republic was a former mayor of Cologne was altogether fitting. The civic virtues Konrad Adenauer brought with him to Bonn were in great demand throughout postwar western Europe.

The sister cities movement had its origins in the occupation years, when the three western allies encouraged German political redevelopment from the ground up. In the French occupation zone in the German southwest, long-standing historical and cultural ties made that area the focal point of the movement. The founders of the sister cities movement saw in the independence of the local communities a safeguard of individual liberties and a bulwark against totalitarianism.[41] They were influenced by the American concept of town meeting democracy, which became known through its foremost European inter- preter, Alexis de Tocqueville, and by concepts of cantonal democracy, consciously offered by the Swiss founders of the two principal sister cities umbrella organizations, the Council of European Communes (CCE) and the International Mayors Union for Franco-German Under- standing (IBU), as the basis for a new era of democratic government in western Europe.[42]

The movement's founders had conceived of strong and autonomous local communities as the essential infrastructure of Franco–West German reconciliation, "a guarantee of long term understanding and of overcom- ing a pernicious nationalism." As early as 1947, they had begun to organize meetings of mayors of the two countries. By 1951, the CCE and the IBU were both actively promoting cooperation at the local level and the establishment of ongoing relationships between municipalities in both countries. At its conference in Innsbruck in 1952, the IBU first used the words *sister city* to describe such relationships. The guidelines adopted by the Mayors Union that year described its goal as the "continual development of closer relations between the two countries" through mobilization of the "creative power of the communities, . . . independent of the changing nature of high politics."[43] A decade later, the president of the European Conference of Local Authorities (CEPL) described the sister cities' role as one "of propagation, of 'capillarization' of the European idea from the summits of power and theory towards the people."[44] By that time, over five hundred communities in France and the Federal Republic had entered into a formal sister city relationship with each other.[45]

The reasons why two particular cities sought a relationship with each other were unique to them. The support of communities throughout the Federal Republic for the concept itself, however, like the other aspects of Bonn's Frankreichpolitik in the 1950s, derived from the local leaders' assessment of the failure of Locarno. That the 1951 conference of the IBU was held at Locarno was not coincidental, nor was the mayors' description of their goal as the construction of a Locarno from below more durable than the edifice of reconciliation begun by Briand and Stresemann.[46] The first postwar generation of West German local officials was highly self-critical of its own lack of support for the Weimar

Republic and for reconciliation with France after World War I. "We are just a band of idealists," one of them wrote, "but how else is the political impulse from below supposed to manifest itself?"[47]

It manifested itself in a movement for cultural cooperation between the two countries that, as Alfred Grosser wrote, created the "human infrastructure" of Franco-West German detente.[48] Former French prime minister and mayor of Lyon Edouard Herriot expressed the opinion of his French and German colleagues when he wrote:

> If I talk with an English mayor, or a German or Russian one, I discover that we have the same preoccupations. . . . Whether it is a matter of education, of help for the aged, of protection for the child, it is always the same, for all human beings, wherever they are, wherever they work, to whatever nation they belong. . . . The bringing together of the local communities is the best condition for the bringing together of men; it is the limited and precise ground where men naturally encounter each other.[49]

With the creation of the Franco-German Youth Office (DFJW/OFAJ) in the 1963 Elysée Treaty, Bonn and Paris gave formal recognition and encouragement to the work of the sister cities. Ten years later, the French government established a working group in the office of the prime minister to study the "effects on cultural, educational, technological, and economic life" of the cities' "decentralized cooperation," and by the 1980s, well over a thousand West German towns had signed sister cities charters with communities in France.[50]

The signing of the charter was a formality that normally followed several months, or even years, of contacts between two cities. Its purpose was to declare the focal points of their specific relationship—school exchanges, apprenticeship programs, municipal planning, as the case might be—but also to state their broader aims in establishing an ongoing relationship with each other. In the Adenauer years, these aims focused on the past and the future: overcoming the burden of recent Franco-German history on the relationship between France and the Federal Republic and defining a place for Europe in a postwar world dominated by the hostility between the two superpowers and the destructive capacity of nuclear power. With its emphasis on music, art, education, and other aspects of the cultural heritage of the two countries and of western Europe, the sister cities movement reflected the tensions inherent in the Atlantic relationship long before they manifested themselves on the national level in the late 1960s. The practitioners of detente from below between France and West Germany spoke frequently of a European "third way" between the superpowers in the 1950s, a decade before French Gaullist or West German Social Democratic concepts of a

European path between Moscow and Washington became critical parts of the continent's political vocabulary.[51]

The consciousness of a European identity required not only an external reference point—the threat of Soviet totalitarianism and the challenge of American economic and cultural hegemony—but also a common perception of the history shared by the two countries and their European neighbors. This aspect of their cultural relationship was not left principally to the sister cities. Instead, private institutes, encouraged by Paris and Bonn to bring together high school and university teachers, journalists, writers, and other shapers of public opinion, worked throughout the Adenauer years to write new textbooks, develop language programs for children and adults, and identify specific factors that had encouraged parochial interpretations of Europe's past. Chief among these initiatives was the Ludwigsburg Franco-German Institute (DFI), founded in 1948 with Carlo Schmid as its president.

The institute's premise was that "as a result of the Second World War and technological developments, the world situation had changed so fundamentally that neither France nor Germany would be able to survive alone."[52] In its first twenty years, the DFI worked with over one hundred private, semipublic, and public institutions in France, chief among them the French Committee on Exchanges with the New Germany, whose origins had been in the resistance movement. By 1967, over twenty thousand participants had taken part in the programs of the institute, and its published discussions of specific aspects of Franco-German relations, the *Ludwigsburger Beiträge*, were well respected in both countries. The DFI was able to commemorate its twentieth anniversary by noting, "despite the malaise of the Bonn-Paris relationship since 1963, cultural and personal relations have become still closer and more numerous. This positive development was accomplished apart from the occurrences of day to day politics."[53]

In Adenauer's bittersweet last years in office, the Federal Republic's detente policy culminated in the entente with France embodied in the Elysée Treaty. Ironically, that very entente, for which so many individuals in both countries had worked so long, was not welcomed unambiguously, but was lamented because it seemed to threaten the broader goals of western European and Atlantic cooperation. Moreover, the generation old enough to have experienced the failed attempts at rapprochement in the interwar years, as it left the political scene, began to wonder about the dedication of the "successor generation"—not yet called that—to cooperation between the two countries.

Reflecting on Goethe's comment that at a "stage in civilization" man "rises above the nations and senses that happiness or sorrow of his neighbor as if it were his own," one French professor wrote that those like himself who had "experienced war and its destruction" and who had committed themselves to creating a Locarno from below knew:

> more than others about inhumanity. But they also know that the sufferings experienced by one generation can rarely be appreciated by another generation which has not experienced them itself. They know . . . the questionable value of historical teaching in relation to personal experience. Still, they believe in the pedagogic, educational, infectious power of example.[54]

The example that the communities, organizations, and individuals involved in Franco–West German cultural exchange gave to Bonn and Paris was a reminder that the capillaries of detente between the two countries remained committed to a productive relationship between them, despite the hardening of the foreign policy arteries at the national level by the mid-1960s.

Entente Established

From the perspective of two decades, those arteries were never in as much danger as they seemed to be at the time. Against the historical background of the failure of Locarno and two world wars, the squabbles with Paris of the Erhard-Kiesinger years over British membership in the European Community and NATO nuclear policy appeared more ominous to Bonn than they were.[55] The Frankreichpolitik that Adenauer had pursued since 1949 was clearly one of the reasons why disagreements between the two countries remained manageable. The institutionalization of their dialogue, multilaterally in the ECSC and bilaterally in the Elysée Treaty, the extent of personal contacts not only between the heads of government and foreign ministers but also between virtually all cabinet members in both countries with similar responsibilities, and the detente achieved below the level of national politics all mitigated against any long-term rupture of the relationship. The evidence of a mutual willingness to compromise, which had first manifested itself in the Saar agreement and in West German NATO membership ten years before, reasserted itself in the 1960s. Marriage of convenience for many and love match for only a few in the 1950s, by 1969 the relationship between Bonn and Paris was strong enough to survive the political changing of the guard in both capitals—from the CDU to the SPD in Bonn, and *l'après de Gaulle*, the Fifth Republic without the General, in Paris.

Nevertheless, the arrival of the Social Democratic party in the chancellery and the departure of Charles DeGaulle from the Elysée

Palace had a more profound impact on the Franco–West German relationship than had Adenauer's retirement in 1963 or the demise of the Fourth Republic in 1958. With the changing of the guard in 1969, the political leadership of West Germany and France passed definitively to the generation that had fought World War II and out of the hands of those who had already held political or military decision-making positions in the years before 1939. Not only the personalities involved, however, but also Bonn's changing relationship with its eastern neighbors gave a new context to the Frankreichpolitik after 1969.

As foreign minister of the Grand Coalition from 1966 until he became chancellor in 1969, Willy Brandt had already begun to explore the possibilities of a detente between the Federal Republic and the countries of the Warsaw Pact. The diplomatic approaches made by the Kiesinger government to eastern Europe, however, still lagged behind those of Paris. DeGaulle's conception of France's historic role there and of a community of European states "from the Atlantic to the Urals" had seemed like anti-American adventurism to many partisans of western European and Atlantic cooperation in the Federal Republic in the early 1960s; his Ostpolitik appeared simultaneously directed at a historic German threat that no longer existed and destructive of western Europe's security relationship with the United States.[56]

With the 1967 Harmel Report, however, the Atlantic Alliance itself had identified the pursuit of detente, as well as the assurance of deterrence and defense, as an appropriate task for NATO's third decade.[57] Two years later, despite the intervening crisis precipitated by the Soviet invasion of Czechoslovakia, the first SPD-FDP coalition moved rapidly to develop a new Ostpolitik for the Federal Republic. Almost overnight, Bonn took the lead from Paris and the new Pompidou government in attempts to identify mutually beneficial changes in the east-west status quo that had prevailed in Europe since the Second World War and to negotiate those changes with Moscow and its Warsaw Pact allies. The impact of this Ostpolitik on the relationship between the Federal Republic and France, which had developed from 1949 to 1969 in a climate of limited options for Paris but of even more limited ones for Bonn, was uncertain. Their detente had survived the Saar referendum and the EDC; their entente had weathered France's withdrawal from the NATO military command and its vetoes of British entry into the Common Market. Whether Bonn's efforts to revise the Yalta status quo would be more constructive than Berlin's attempts to change Versailles, only time would tell. The Federal Republic's first task was the enunciation of a concept of Ostpolitik that would neither dislodge—nor appear to dislodge—the Frankreichpolitik from its place in Bonn's foreign policy commitments.

Notes

1. Monnet "realized that the British phantom had to be exorcised once and for all," and Adenauer had to deal with "the violent intransigence of Schumacher, who demanded independence for Germany more loudly than anyone," if the Schuman Plan were to become reality. With the magnanimity of one whose ideas triumphed in the end, Monnet later wrote: "All in all, the [ECSC] debates vindicated the Community countries' parliamentary systems: they bore witness to the scruples of men who were called upon to delegate part of that very national sovereignty which was their own *raison d'être*." Jean Monnet, *Memoirs* (Garden City, NY: Doubleday, 1978), pp. 335, 362.
2. Kenneth Harris, *Attlee* (London: Weidenfeld and Nicolson, 1982), p. 315; and Alan Bullock, *Ernest Bevin, Foreign Secretary* (New York: W.W. Norton, 1983), pp. 783–790. Bullock notes that "reading between the lines of Monnet's memoirs strongly suggests" that he did not desire Britain to be a founding member of the ECSC. Although that may be going a bit too far, Monnet made no secret, in 1950 and 1951 and in his book, of his conviction that British membership was less important to the success of the ECSC than were the principles embodied in the Schuman Plan *and* that Britain, in any case, would "come in" later. He was right, in both cases.
3. "It soon became clear," wrote F. Roy Willis, "that Schumacher's attack on the Schuman Plan was inspired by deep suspicion of France." Willis quotes from a series of articles by the SPD leader in the French Socialist newspaper *Le Populaire* in 1951; Schumacher's comments help explain why he inspired such loathing abroad: "The French cannot claim the smallest original success for their actions in several decades. Behind their activity to give the world a new shape there is not a single great idea, European or humanitarian." F. Roy Willis, *France, Germany, and the New Europe, 1945–1967* (London: Oxford University Press, 1968), p. 128.
4. *Federal Republic of Germany: Elections, Parliaments and Political Parties* (New York: German Information Center, 1986), pp. 14–15.
5. Marion Gräfin Dönhoff, *Von Gestern nach Übermorgen* (München: DTV, 1986), p. 97.
6. Jean LaCouture, *DeGaulle: Le Politique, 1944–1959* (Paris: Seuil, 1985), pp. 635–639.
7. Willis, *France, Germany*, pp. 328–331.
8. The phrase is Jean-Jacques Servan-Schreiber's in *The American Challenge* (New York: Atheneum, 1968).
9. Monnet, *Memoirs*, p. 333. The institutional structure of the ECSC was laid out in an August 5, 1950, memorandum, less than three months after Schuman's original proposal.
10. Ibid., p. 292.
11. Ibid., p. 283.
12. Ibid., pp. 300, 304–305.
13. Ibid., p. 328.
14. Ibid.
15. Ibid., p. 323.

16. Hans-Peter Schwarz, *Adenauer: Der Aufstieg, 1876–1952* (Stuttgart: DVA, 1986), pp. 690–699. This is not to imply that Adenauer was pleased with either the IAR or, particularly, the separation of the Saarland from Germany, but as he said in the Bundestag on June 13, 1950, he had "come to the conclusion that under no circumstances should the Saar question be allowed to disturb relations between France and Germany or to make more difficult the construction of western Europe." The text of the speech is in Roland Delcour, *Adenauer* (Paris: Seghers, 1966), pp. 101–131.
17. Monnet, *Memoirs*, pp. 309–310.
18. Ibid., p. 319. See also the text of Adenauer's May 31, 1951, speech to the Bundestag in Delcour, *Adenauer*, pp. 147–160, and Willis, *France, Germany*, pp. 128–129.
19. Lewis Edinger, *Kurt Schumacher* (Stanford: Stanford University Press, 1965), pp. 186–187. Edinger does an excellent job of discussing Schumacher as "the patriotic leader" (pp. 144–189) and the impact of his intransigence on the foreign policy role of the SPD.
20. In his memoirs, *Journal du Septénnat*, quoted in Alfred Grosser, *Affaires Extérieures* (Paris: Flammarion, 1984), p. 38.
21. Schwarz, *Adenauer*, pp. 719–720.
22. Grosser, *Affaires Extérieures*, pp. 80–81; Monnet, *Memoirs*, p. 291.
23. Edinger, *Kurt Schumacher*, p. 157: "Neither building West Germany into a forward bastion of Western capitalism nor accepting reunification on Soviet terms" was acceptable to Schumacher. He "refused to buy Soviet agreement to the reunification of Germany at the expense of inalienable German rights, above all of individual and national freedom."
24. Alan Bullock describes (*Ernest Bevin*, pp. 268–269) the difficulty Labour Foreign Secretary Ernest Bevin found in "accepting the Germans as allies and reconciling himself to the risk of recreating German industrial-military power, the destruction of which in two wars had cost British, French, and Russians so dear." Bevin was not alone in revolutionizing his country's policies toward Germany after 1946, whatever his personal opinions, but as Willis noted (*France, Germany*, p. 61), even among Bonn's friends, "there was a tendency to treat the Germans like naughty children" and to expect a level of repentance of which Kurt Schumacher was wholly incapable. Other SPD leaders, like Carlo Schmid, shared Adenauer's greater sensitivity to the historical burden inherited by the Federal Republic and *all* its citizens, whatever their own experience under the Nazis. See Carlo Schmid, *Erinnerungen* (Bern: Scherz, 1979), pp. 304–305, 519.
25. Edinger, *Kurt Schumacher*, p. 255.
26. Grosser, *Affaires Extérieures*, p. 83.
27. Monnet, *Memoirs*, p. 293.
28. Schwarz, *Adenauer*, pp. 750–752; Grosser, *Affairs Extérieures*, pp. 85–86; Monnet described (*Memoirs*, p. 342) the "shock" Schuman received in September 1950, when he arrived in New York for the United Nations General Assembly and was confronted by Dean Acheson with American demands for a West German military contribution to the defense of western Europe.
29. Monnet, *Memoirs*, pp. 346–348.

30. "We had," wrote Monnet (*Memoirs*, p. 343), "no choice: so I wasted no time thinking about which course I preferred—a pointless question when events are in command."

31. Ibid., p. 350; Schwarz, *Adenauer*, pp. 766–774. As Schwarz noted (p. 771), "Rearmament had become the central theme of [West German] domestic policy," not only an issue between Bonn and the NATO allies. It led to the Federal Republic's first cabinet crisis, with the resignation of Interior Minister (later Federal President) Gustav Heinemann, threatened to split the CDU, and gave the SPD an issue with which to attack both Adenauer (for his heavy-handedness) and the allies (for their apparent interest in German soldiers without German equality). A detailed discussion of the entire process is Robert McGeehan's *The German Rearmament Question: American Diplomacy and European Defense After World War II* (Urbana: University of Illinois Press, 1971).

32. McGeehan, *German Rearmament*, pp. 62–67: "The French government sought some escape from the dilemma imposed by the U.S. ultimatum."

33. Ibid., p. 222; Jean Lacouture, *Pierre Mendès France* (Paris: Seuil, 1981), pp. 298–318. In the early 1950s, in addition to aid under the Marshall Plan, Washington was paying eighty percent of the cost of France's war in Indochina. See Grosser, *Affaires Extérieures*, pp. 95–96.

34. McGeehan, *German Rearmament*, pp. 141–143.

35. Schwarz, *Adenauer*, pp. 830–836. As Schwarz pointed out (pp. 833–834), Adenauer feared three things: American isolationism, the possibility of cooperation between Paris and Moscow, and his own countrymen's fascination with reunification through neutrality.

36. Willis, *France, Germany*, p. 184: "EDC was dead, but the German problem remained."

37. Ibid., p. 188.

38. Donald Abenheim's *Reforging the Iron Cross: The Search for Tradition in the West German Armed Forces* (Princeton: Princeton University Press, 1988) is an excellent study of the concepts on which the Bundeswehr was founded.

39. Willis, *France, Germany*, pp. 195–197.

40. Hans Speidel, *Aus unserer Zeit: Erinnerungen* (Berlin: Ullstein, 1977) pp. 257–258.

41. Adolph Gasser, *L'Autonomie communale at la réconstruction de l'Europe* (Neuchâtel: Editions de la Baconnière, 1946), pp. 29–30. See also Gasser's *Geschichte der Volksfreiheit und der Demokratie* (Aarau: H.R. Sauerländer, 1939).

42. Adolph Gasser founded the CCE; Eugen Wyler and Hans Zbinden were cofounders of the IBU. Zbinden's writings are contained in: *Im Strom der Zeit* (Bern: Francke, 1964), *Die Moralkrise des Abendlandes* (Bern: Herbert Lang, 1943), and *Europa Wohin?* (Bern: Francke, 1969). The Mayor of Berlin-Tempelhof Bernhard Hoffman summed up the premise of both organizations in his May 24, 1973, speech at the IBU's conference at Évian, France, "Die Gemeinde im Jahre 2000": "Democracy can only grow healthy on a large scale if it is put into practice every day in small things. The words of Alexis de Tocqueville are still true today: 'The strength of free peoples resides in the community.' Communal institutions are to liberty what

primary schools are to science. Without communal institutions, a nation may give itself a free government, but it will not have the spirit of liberty."

43. The text of the Innsbruck Guidelines is found in Hansjürgen Garstka, *Die Rolle der Gemeinde in der internationalen Verständigung nach dem Zweiten Weltkrieg, gezeigt am Beispiel der deutsch-französischen Verständigung* (Stuttgart: IBU, 1972).

44. Henri Cravatte, "La conférence européenne des pouvoirs locaux," *L'Annuaire européen* (The Hague: Martinus Nijhoff, 1963), pp. 43–44.

45. A. Chauvin, *France-Allemagne*, Information Bulletin of the Commission of Franco-German Affairs, No. 10 (Paris, 1972).

46. Heinz Engelhardt, "Deutsch-französische Städtepartnerschaften," *Kulturarbeit*, 1963.

47. Theodor Eggers, Christmas message to the members of the Europa-Union, Freiburg im Breisgau, 1960.

48. Grosser, *Affaires Extérieures*, p. 80.

49. Quoted in Carl J. Friedrich, "The Grassroots Base of the Unification of Europe," *Public Policy: A Yearbook of the Graduate School of Public Administration* (Cambridge, MA: Harvard University, 1963), Vol. XII, p. 33.

50. Communiqué of the Secretariat General of the French government, January 25, 1973, *Communes d'Europe*, April 1973.

51. The idea of Europe as a third force was present in many of the speeches and publications of the sister cities in the 1950s, and Hans Speidel comments in his memoirs (*Aus unserer Zeit*, p. 257) that it was the subject of Carlo Schmid's speech at the ceremony formally establishing the Franco-German Institute (DFI) at Ludwigsburg in 1949.

52. Fritz Schenk, *Zwanzig Jahre Deutsch-französisches Institut Ludwigsburg* (Ludwigsburg: Satz und Druck Süddeutsche Verlagsanstalt, 1968), p. 6.

53. Ibid. The "malaise" was a result of the problems caused by Paris's veto of British membership in the European Community and its withdrawal of French forces from the unified NATO command. At the DFI's fortieth anniversary celebration on October 6, 1988, the West German president called on both countries "not only to defend their freedom together with conviction, but to test the possibilities of cooperation with eastern Europe that would open up its political system." Representing President Mitterrand, Jean-Louis Bianco replied, "We have no fear of your Ostpolitik; we concur in it." *Deutschland-Nachrichten*, October 12, 1988.

54. Jean Petit, "Fribourg en Brisgau: Une Contribution à l'Europe Unie," *Besançon*, 1964 Yearbook.

55. Willis, *France, Germany*, p. 318, called the Erhard years (1963–1966) a period when Bonn faced an "unwanted choice: Washington or Paris?"; as the relationship between Adenauer's successor and DeGaulle worsened, the Franco–West German relationship also entered its chilliest period since 1950. See also Grosser, *Affaires Extérieures*, pp. 205–208.

56. Ernst Weisenfeld, *Welches Deutschland soll es sein?* (München: C.H. Beck, 1986), pp. 100–101.

57. "The Future Tasks of the Alliance," *NATO Final Communiqués, 1948–1974* (Brussels: NATO Information Service, n.d.), p. 198.

THE FASHIONING OF OSTPOLITIK

Different Issues in the East

In retrospect, the 1950s were a decade in which the foreign policy aims of the Federal Republic appeared clear and uncomplicated. Economic reconstruction and the building of a new domestic political framework preoccupied the West Germans. Their success at accomplishing both depended on the stability of western Europe, which in turn required a strong United States committed to the political and economic reconstruction of its allies. Bonn's devotion to the Atlantic Alliance was, in the short term, perfectly compatible with its interest in reconciliation with Paris and cooperation with its western neighbors.

The question of West Germany's relations and relationship with its eastern neighbors, however, remained ambiguous. In theory, the West-politik provided an answer to it by postulating the inevitable demise of Soviet control of eastern Europe, which would be drawn, as to a magnet, to cooperation with the free and prosperous states of the west.[1] Nothing was inherently illogical in the magnet theory, particularly in the years before 1953, when Stalin died. The Soviet Union had been under his control for most of its existence; the possibility that the death of its dictator might bring about profound changes in the country's economic and foreign policies, as it did in China twenty years later, was not farfetched.

By the early 1960s, however, it had become apparent that Moscow's willingness after Stalin's death to meet with the western leaders and to contribute to compromises on certain east-west issues—Korea in 1953, Indochina in 1954, and Austria in 1955—did not indicate a willingness to renounce control of the foreign and domestic policies of the Warsaw Pact states. In East Berlin in 1953, Hungary and Poland in 1956, and Berlin in 1961, the Brezhnev Doctrine, as yet unnamed, was put into practice; Moscow's policy was finally given a name with the Warsaw Pact invasion of Czechoslovakia in 1968.[2] The Soviet state and its eastern European empire would both survive Stalin.

The implications of this enduring Soviet power for Bonn's foreign policy were serious, as indeed they were serious for the containment policy that Washington had implemented since 1947. Leaders of both the United States and the Federal Republic had imagined the Cold War—despite their rhetoric—as a matter of several years, at most a decade or two.[3] The North Atlantic Treaty had an initial twenty-year term, the Alliance originally did not encompass the stationing of American troops in Europe, and, until the Korean War, the United States had no peacetime conscription.

Like containment's American architects, its early practitioners in the Federal Republic expected that, given a breathing space in which to rebuild, the west's economic and technological strength would ultimately prevail without a direct military confrontation with the Soviet Union.[4] It had, after all, in the Berlin Airlift. However, the maintenance of Soviet hegemony in eastern Europe after the death of Stalin and the West German realization that the rhetoric of rollback bore no resemblance to Washington's actual policy gradually changed Bonn's calculation. With the building of the Berlin Wall in August 1961 at the latest, it was clear that changes in eastern Europe were not going to come about through the internal collapse of the Soviet Union or external military pressure from the United States.[5]

That the Cold War status quo was a straitjacket for the Federal Republic's foreign policy was also increasingly clear to Bonn.[6] The Hallstein Doctrine, denying relations with Bonn to any state (except the Soviet Union) that recognized the GDR, was the most obvious example of that policy's increasing incompatibility with reality, but its failure to meet the needs of the 1960s was the symptom, not the cause, of a changing international environment. Adenauer had known what he had to accomplish when he entered the chancellery in 1949; the first problem for his successors was defining their own aims. Given the success of Bonn's diplomacy in western Europe, but its failure to produce changes east of the Elbe, what role did they see for the Federal Republic in a decade in which both the consolidation of the Yalta status quo and a new superpower dialogue became reality? Was reunification in fact the preeminent goal of West German diplomacy? What did Bonn want in eastern Europe, and why?

The problems West Germany faced in the east and those that had characterized the Frankreichpolitik of the 1950s were different in three ways. The first major distinction between the two was the Federal

Republic's *lack of territorial claims in western Europe.* This was such a self-evident part of Bonn's foreign policy that, whatever other criticism was leveled at Adenauer, he was not chastised for accepting the western borders—and was even prepared to face, had it come to that, internationalization of the Saar. In this, Bonn shared the perspective of Weimar, because guaranteeing those borders had been one of the few undisputed aspects of Gustav Stresemann's foreign policy. Both Locarno and Adenauer's successor to it were predicated on the absence of (West) German demands for changes in the territorial status quo in western Europe.[7] Such was not the case when Bonn looked eastward.

However, the existence of major territorial disputes was not the only distinction between the Federal Republic's pursuit of detente in the west in the 1950s and its search for detente in the east in the 1960s and 1970s. The *international political constellation within the eastern alliance* was quite different from that in the west a decade before, in which Bonn's and Paris's allies had all been supportive of their reconciliation. Indeed, in the early days of the Cold War, the principal allies of the two countries sometimes appeared more eager than they to have them move quickly down a path of western European cooperation.[8] The only hostility toward this cooperation in the 1950s came from Moscow and the Warsaw Pact, not from the United States, the only western country able to make Bonn pay an immediate price for policies not to its liking. Moreover, despite its opposition to West Germany's membership in the Atlantic Alliance, even Moscow was interested enough in good relations with Bonn to hand over to the Federal Republic thousands of German POWs in 1955 and to establish diplomatic relations with the new NATO member.[9]

Consequently, the Federal Republic's foreign policies in the 1950s met with little but applause internationally. The willingness to acquiesce in the Europeanization of the Saar, the acceptance of the restrictions on West German armed forces inherent in the EDC and later of the limitations on them contained in the Paris Accords, the support given throughout West Germany to rapprochement with France at the grassroots, and the seemingly ungrudging commitment of the benefits of the economic miracle to western European prosperity as a whole all made Bonn a model of cooperative international relations in that decade.[10] In sharp contrast to its predecessor only two decades before, the Federal Republic seemed to have banished the concepts of conflict and confrontation from its foreign policy vocabulary—much to the delight of its western allies in their own relations with the new state.

Its relationship with the states of eastern Europe and the Soviet Union was different. Their attitude toward Bonn was as ambiguous as the Federal Republic's attitude toward them, and this ambiguity reflected the third distinction between the Frankreichpolitik and its eastern counterpart. Not only did Bonn have territorial claims in eastern Europe that were nonexistent in the west, it also had a *historically ambivalent attitude toward the very existence of several of the Warsaw Pact states.* The refusal to accept the German Democratic Republic as anything but the "Soviet Occupied Zone" of Germany and the Hallstein Doctrine of refusing diplomatic relations with any third state recognizing the GDR were the most extreme examples of this attitude. Moreover, the Federal Republic had territorial disputes with the three other principal Warsaw Pact countries with which it most needed to deal: Czechoslovakia on its southeastern border, Poland, and the Soviet Union. Bonn refused to recognize as a part of Poland that part of 1937 Germany east of the Oder-Neisse Rivers "under Polish administration" since 1945 and, as a part of the USSR, the territory of East Prussia. Furthermore, it maintained the legal validity of the 1938 Munich Agreement, which had ceded Czechoslovakia's Sudetenland to Germany.[11]

These territorial questions were more than that, however. In the context of the historical role of Prussia and Germany in eastern Europe, they had a far more ominous character when seen from the capitals of the Warsaw Pact states. Prague and Warsaw had no love for Moscow, but the vast chunks of their territory disputed by Bonn would have made normal relations between them and the Federal Republic virtually impossible in any case.[12] The Soviet cries of German revanchism that accompanied the creation of the West German army and the Federal Republic's membership in NATO found, not surprisingly, an audience in eastern Europe.[13] Bonn's rearmament had been controversial *within* the west and no doubt would have been more so had territorial disputes of such significance existed between it and its western neighbors.[14] Whatever their attitude toward the Soviet Union, given their historical experience with Berlin, the countries of eastern Europe were virtually forced back into Moscow's shadow as long as Bonn remained intransigent on their existential territorial questions.

In addition to these three major distinctions—the territorial disputes that did not exist in the west, Moscow's lack of support for a detente between the Federal Republic and its eastern neighbors, and the fear of those countries for their existence as well as their territorial integrity— other factors complicated Bonn's development of a detente policy in the east comparable to its rapprochement with France in the years after 1950. The presence of German-speaking minorities in the countries of eastern Europe, notably in Poland and the Soviet Union, was a factor that had played no role in Adenauer's Frankreichpolitik. In the case of Poland, Czechoslovakia, and the GDR, Bonn had also to deal with a large and vocal segment of its domestic political constituency that had been expelled or had emigrated from those countries after 1945. Its votes and influence had a major impact for two decades on the Federal Republic's claims to former German territory in eastern Europe.[15] These interest groups had had no counterpart in the domestic political debate on reconciliation with France in the early 1950s.

Finally, any policy of reconciliation with the countries of eastern Europe would of necessity be more complex diplomatically than its western predecessor had been. Adenauer's instinct for the importance of the Federal Republic's relationship with France was correct. If Bonn and Paris could agree, both their smaller neighbors and their larger allies would feel more secure. This was not true in the east; unlike Bonn's western diplomacy, its initiatives in eastern Europe had to respond simultaneously to the interests of several countries, all of which were skeptical of improved bilateral relations between any one of them and the Federal Republic. Although this meant that the West- and Frankreich-politik could have no direct parallel in the east, however, the elements that had spelled success for them became even more important in a more complicated diplomatic constellation.

Stocktaking by the Grand Coalition

Adenauer left office in October 1963 as the developing dispute over nuclear policy between France and the United States within the Atlantic Alliance became the dominant concern of West German foreign policy.[16] In retrospect, the fear that the Federal Republic, for the first time in its history, would have to choose between good relations with Paris and its alliance with Washington was overstated. DeGaulle had no desire to see Bonn follow his own country's path away from integration of its armed forces in NATO.[17] That integration of the West German army in part made possible French withdrawal from the NATO command in 1967.[18] However, this was unclear to Bonn at the time, at a moment when any new initiatives toward eastern Europe required solidarity and cohesion within the western alliance. For three reasons, the need for these initiatives became increasingly obvious to Adenauer's successors in the chancellery as the decade progressed.

First, by the early 1960s, the German Democratic Republic was no longer a Soviet bargaining chip in negotiations on German reunification. With the construction of the Berlin Wall, East Berlin signified its intention to stem the tide of migration of its youngest and best educated to the Federal Republic, and Moscow clearly assented to this policy.[19] Bonn could continue for some time to deny the reality of a second German state, but by the mid-1960s those denials had begun to irritate its western allies and to appear as obstacles to their own early attempts at east-west detente.[20] Meanwhile, within the Warsaw Pact, the influence of the GDR was growing, and it was evolving "from satellite to partner" of the Soviet Union.[21]

Second, the Hallstein Doctrine was becoming a hindrance, not an asset, to Bonn's foreign policy, especially its attempt to establish good relations with the newly independent countries of the Third World.[22] Ironically freed from the economic burden of colonialism and the political burden of decolonization by the detested Versailles Treaty, West Germany should have had an advantage over its western allies in dealing with the new states.[23] However, this advantage was largely offset by Bonn's attempt to prevent those countries from establishing relations with the GDR. The Hallstein Doctrine applied to the members of the new nonaligned movement—more interested in good relations with Moscow than with Bonn—was both counterproductive and futile. The Federal Republic alone had neither the political nor the economic clout to make the lack of relations with it a major handicap for the proliferating new states, and its western allies were hardly willing to abandon to Moscow their own relationships with these states for the sake of Bonn's position on the GDR.[24]

Finally, the human cost of the eastern policies of the 1950s was mounting, both because physical contact between families and friends divided by the inner-German border and the Berlin Wall became more difficult after 1961 and because a generation that knew only the post-1945 European status quo began to reach maturity. In many respects, this generation seemed uninterested in the cities and landscapes east of the Elbe, but at the same time its disenchantment with the historical legacy of its parents and grandparents was made worse by the nature of West Germany's borders and by Bonn's relationship with its eastern neighbors.[25] The emigrés from the east, most of whom had begun to realize by the mid-1960s that they would not be returning to their families' former homes east of the Oder-Neisse, were not the only ones disoriented by the Yalta status quo. The cost paid by those who were born after 1945 or whose family origins were in the territory of the Federal Republic was more subtle: the divorce from centuries of their own history and from that part of the continent in which Germans had had an enduring, positive impact on the history of Europe.[26]

An older generation of Germans born in Bavaria or Bremen or the Rhineland shared with Germans from Königsberg, Prague, and Weimar a common political, economic, and cultural historical tradition. Although not a tradition of unity in a national state, it shaped the lives of millions of Europeans—Germans and non-Germans—for centuries. A Rhinelander of the older generation, who might never have set foot in Dresden, still had a living connection with that city—as the Dresdener had a tie to the personally unseen cities of Cologne and Nuremberg. Historian Felix Gilbert, a native Berliner returning to Germany as a member of the American army in May 1945, gave free rein to the emotions that stemmed from Germany's cultural integrity when he "drove along the autobahn on the hills overlooking the Moselle Valley" and decided to make a detour:

> For anyone who has grown up in Germany the Moselle Valley—praised in poems and celebrated for its wines—has a romantic enchantment. I had never been there and I wanted to see it. . . . The sun was shining, the trees had fresh leaves, and bushes and flowers were beginning to bloom. The hills were still brown, but full of vines. . . . No reason why 1945 should not be a good wine year.[27]

After 1961, the last generation of political leaders in the Federal Republic old enough to have positive personal memories of this German central Europe, the young adults of the war years, came to power. Men like Willy Brandt and Richard von Weizsäcker saw more clearly than Carlo Schmid's Wilhelmine generation that the ties of language, culture, and history with which Germans had built a bridge between eastern and western Europe—until they themselves destroyed it— would not continue to exist of their own accord.[28] The postwar generation in the Federal Republic, disoriented by Germany's assault on European civilization in the 1930s and 1940s, was also being deprived of its birthright: not the territories east of the Oder-Neisse that had once been German, but a living knowledge of the German role in shaping that European civilization that had survived only by uniting to defeat the Third Reich.[29]

In December 1966, after three increasingly unproductive years of government by a CDU-FDP coalition under Ludwig Erhard, domestic economic and foreign policy issues led the two largest parties in the Federal Republic to a historic turning point in their relationship with each other: the establishment of the Grand Coalition between the CDU-CSU and the SPD that Adenauer and Schumacher had both sought to avoid in 1949.[30] The first chancellor lived long enough to see a Social Democratic vice chancellor and foreign minister, Willy Brandt, represent the Federal Republic at the NATO Council table and at the regular consultations with Paris established by the Elysée Treaty. In defining new policies toward eastern Europe, however, Brandt was not acting alone. His CDU chancellor, Kurt Georg Kiesinger, was equally convinced of the need to continue the efforts begun by Erhard's foreign minister, Gerhard Schröder, to move in "small steps" away from the eastern policies symbolized by the Hallstein Doctrine.[31]

As had been the case with France, however, small steps were not enough. When he proposed the coal and steel community to Robert Schuman, Jean Monnet had declared his conviction that only a major initiative, clearly recognized as such, could channel his country's relationship with its German neighbor in a new direction.[32] Bonn confronted the same reality when it looked to the Federal Republic's eastern neighbors in the 1960s: only large steps could produce the change in climate conducive to rebuilding the German bridge between eastern and western Europe that had once existed. With a mandate from the West German electorate to take those steps, Willy Brandt entered the chancellery and Walter Scheel became foreign minister in 1969. The Social Democrats and their Liberal coalition partner began to fashion a revolution in Bonn's eastern relations as far-reaching as the one that had taken place in the west after 1950.[33] They did so by using the model offered by Adenauer's Westpolitik.

Bonn's Assets and Liabilities in the East

Because the issues facing the Federal Republic in eastern Europe were not identical to those in the west, that model required modification. Nevertheless, the principal issue addressed in the west in the 1950s and in the east in the 1970s was the same for both detente policies: what the neighboring country had suffered at the hands of Berlin in the years after 1871. Like Adenauer before them, Brandt and Scheel never lost sight of that fact. The specific questions Bonn had to answer varied, but the legacy of twentieth-century German foreign policy—particularly that of the Third Reich—was constant. This legacy was one of mistrust of German intentions and capabilities in both eastern and western Europe and a determination never again to be vulnerable to German threats and demands.

In the early 1950s, the French had dealt with their own skepticism of the West German commitment to peace and democracy by "containing" the Federal Republic in a western European economic community and a military alliance dominated by the United States, even as they offered cooperation and equality to the new state.[34] Similarly, the Soviet Union had contained "its" German state in COMECON and the Warsaw Pact, and the other countries of eastern Europe, despite their antipathy to Moscow, relied on Soviet military strength to counter a resurgence of German aggression, against which Soviet propaganda constantly warned, from the Federal Republic.[35] Brandt's government, like those of his CDU predecessors, had no interest in the use of force to revise the postwar European status quo. Nevertheless, it had to deal with a collective historical memory that associated conquest and extermination with the name of Germany. This required the Federal Republic to treat the fears born of that memory seriously, no matter how little relationship existed between them and Bonn's foreign policy goals.[36]

The path to detente in the east led not to one capital, Paris, but to three: Moscow, Warsaw, and East Berlin. It also required the renunciation, vis-à-vis Prague, of Bonn's claim that the 1938 Munich Agreement remained valid. By integrating four million Sudeten Germans into its political and economic life in the 1950s, the Federal Republic had, de facto, accepted the 1945 borders of Czechoslovakia. Its tenacity in defending the Munich Agreement had had more to do with Bonn's juridical claim to be the sole successor state of the Third Reich than with any political intentions to dispute Prague's sovereignty over the Sudetenland.[37] The willingness to renounce this claim, finally abandoned in the 1973 Prague Treaty, opened the way for political and economic consultations between the Federal Republic and Czechoslovakia during the Prague Spring of 1968.[38]

The Warsaw Pact armies that destroyed Czechoslovakia's short-lived hopes for domestic liberalization also had a profound effect on West Germany's concept of detente in eastern Europe. Both CDU Foreign Minister Schröder and his SPD successor had misjudged the extent, in one vital area, to which the model offered by their country's rapprochement with France could be duplicated: the freedom to negotiate a new relationship with Bonn that existed in Prague and the other eastern European capitals in the 1960s was in no way comparable to Paris's independence in 1950. Robert Schuman had surprised and irritated his British and American colleagues with his proposal for the ECSC and, despite London's hostility to it, had prevailed. Four years later, Paris blocked establishment of the EDC, despite enthusiastic American support for it. Weakened psychologically and materially by war in Europe and in its colonies, France had, nevertheless, a degree of influence and room to maneuver within the western alliance that no Warsaw Pact state, twenty years later, possessed. After August 1968, the Federal Republic implicitly recognized that the paths to the capitals of eastern Europe could not be traveled simultaneously. The first road had to lead to Moscow, and it had to be traveled before the GDR set up political roadblocks more effective than those erected on the land corridors to Berlin twenty years before.

An attempt to draw a parallel between the role of Washington in the Federal Republic's policies of western detente and of Moscow in its eastern detente would be false, however. In many respects, Moscow was both Paris *and* Washington within the Warsaw Pact. The Wehrmacht had been within sight of the Kremlin in the winter of 1941–1942, Leningrad had lived under German siege for nearly three years, and millions of

Soviet civilians, as well as the soldiers of the Red Army, had died in the struggle to free their country from German occupation. Like its Warsaw Pact allies, Moscow had its own memories of the plans Berlin had had for all of them, and which it had partially implemented, in a Europe organized on the racist ideology of National Socialism.[39]

Although American and German armies had twice met in combat since 1917, Americans had no historical memory of occupation and extermination comparable to the one that linked, despite all their differences, the capitals of Europe, from Paris and the Hague to Moscow and Belgrade. Dealing with that memory in the east required that the Federal Republic develop east-west confidence-building measures comparable in intent and in psychological effect to those represented by the ECSC, the Paris Accords, and the Common Market within the west. It also required, as much as in the French case, the coupling of bilateral and multilateral initiatives, the renunciation of demands for an immediate and parallel quid pro quo, and a capillarization of detente to the grassroots. Finally, it required a differentiation between two tasks: dealing with those issues arising out of the Cold War and settling those that stemmed from Berlin's two attempts to establish German hegemony in east-central Europe. The Federal Republic shared with its NATO allies the first task, but the second was uniquely its own, as it had been twenty years before vis-à-vis France.

In both 1950 and 1969, West Germany found itself trying to break out of an inferior position in its political maneuvering room compared to Paris, in the first case, and to Moscow, in the second. In both periods, Bonn's ability to affect issues of vital importance to it was severely limited: in 1950, because of its status as a defeated and occupied power; in 1969, because of foreign policy doctrines based on the illusion that what had been lost on the battlefields of World War II could be won back, in conjunction with powerful western allies, without West German concessions.[40] All coercive options were, in both cases, foreclosed to Bonn by both external and internal factors. Chief among them in 1969 was the opposition of all mainstream political parties in the Federal Republic, and of its western allies, to the use of force—after two world wars—in a nuclear age. West Germany's political leadership and the overwhelming majority of its citizens were far more deeply committed to the prevention of a third European war than to modification of the status quo associated with Yalta and the Berlin Wall.[41] Like Adenauer's Frankreichpolitik and unlike Prussian-German foreign policy from 1864 to 1945, the Brandt-Scheel Ostpolitik sought to change the German status quo without threatening the peace of Europe.

Therefore, the option left to that foreign policy was compromise and reconciliation. Or, as France's president had described his own concept of east-west relations in the 1960s: the development of a process of detente-entente-cooperation, leading to a "Europe of the nations," from the Atlantic to the Urals.[42] The Federal Republic had twenty years' experience with this process in the west, where its relationship with France had evolved from hostility, before 1945, through detente in the 1950s, to entente in the 1960s and cooperation as that decade ended. Under the foreign policy leadership of Willy Brandt, Bonn began to encourage the same evolution in east-west relations that it had accomplished in western Europe with its Frankreichpolitik. The SPD foreign minister from 1966 to 1969 and chancellor from 1969 to 1974 had complicated problems to handle, but he had clear advantages over his CDU predecessor in the early 1950s: the economic and military dynamism of the Federal Republic—which France had once feared—and the relationship between Bonn and Paris that had developed since 1950.

Brandt's byword—that the Ostpolitik could take place only in conjunction with the broadening and deepening of the Westpolitik—was a shorthand reference to those advantages.[43] They were the chief weapons in the Federal Republic's diplomatic arsenal in the late 1960s, but their effectiveness would only be demonstrated over the long haul. At the outset, the difficulties arrayed against Bonn seemed formidable indeed. In his years as foreign minister, the SPD leader had to be content with positive results from the Grand Coalition's new eastern policies chiefly within the western alliance and in Bonn's relations with the neutral and nonaligned states of Europe and the Third World.[44]

The tacit abandonment of the Hallstein Doctrine in Bonn's resumption of diplomatic relations with Yugoslavia and its establishment of them with Romania in 1967, as well as its declared willingness to include its disagreements with the "second state on German territory" in a renunciation of force agreement with Moscow, brought the Federal Republic a new reputation overseas during the three years of the Grand Coalition.[45] Its support for the 1967 Harmel Report, in which the Atlantic Alliance indicated its willingness to pursue detente with the Warsaw Pact, was one signal of the change in Bonn's policies. West Germany relinquished its attempts to prevent its allies from negotiating with Moscow, out of fear that the western allies would make concessions in their positions on Germany, and began to participate in shaping multilateral negotiations between members of the two blocs.

At the same time, it began its own bilateral efforts in the capitals of the Warsaw Pact. As Brandt later wrote, his country began "to look after its own affairs, and not always to rely on someone else to speak for it."[46] Virtually overnight the Federal Republic ceased to be an obstacle to detente and became the innovator of proposals for east-west dialogue. However, major changes in the relationship between eastern and western

Europe and between the two German states were still over the horizon in 1968. On the scale of detente-entente-cooperation, whether real progress had been made was hard to see.

With his entry into the chancellery in October 1969, Brandt at last had the opportunity to apply the Federal Republic's strengths to the process of evolution along this scale. His three years as foreign minister of the Grand Coalition had enabled him to demonstrate Bonn's recognition of its assets as an economic leader of the European Community, a pivotal NATO ally, and France's closest diplomatic partner. Limited as these assets appeared to be in 1969, relative to Soviet hegemony in eastern Europe, the historical legacy of German conquest and extermination, and the mutual suspicions of the Cold War, the Brandt-Scheel foreign policy counted on the self-interest of Moscow and its allies, over the long term, to work in the Federal Republic's favor.

West Germany's economic strength was its clearest asset, given the failure of the Warsaw Pact governments to match the economic growth and prosperity of western Europe. Bonn could offer expertise, technology, and hard currency in negotiations with its eastern neighbors, things that could otherwise be obtained, at the time, only from the United States. Moreover, it needed foreign trade in a way that Washington did not in the late 1960s, giving West Germany an interest in economic relations for their own sake, as well as in their expected positive political fallout.[47] Moscow and its allies needed what the Federal Republic had to offer financially and technologically, but they were willing to see only so many political strings attached, as the dispute with the United States on most favored nation treatment and the 1975 Jackson Amendment later showed.[48] Bonn had a technological advantage over the other countries of western Europe and a political advantage over Washington.

A further aspect to the economic advantage enjoyed by the Federal Republic was the historic normality of Germany's leading economic role in east-central Europe. In the years before 1914, the expanding industries, scientific research institutes, and technical universities of Wilhelmine Germany had been leaders in the employment of Europe's industrial workers and the education of the twentieth-century's first generation of technocrats. In eastern Europe, this role added a new dimension to a centuries-old tradition of teaching in medicine, theology, and the humanities at the German-speaking universities of the region. It meant, at the turn of the century, that Germany not only ceased to be a country of emigration, chiefly to the United States, but began to import its first guest workers, principally from the Austro-Hungarian Empire.

The legacy of this tradition was central to the success of Brandt's foreign policies. Curiously enough, Germany's leading economic role historically was so self-evident that Bonn seemed to exploit it almost unconsciously as a factor in the detente equation. Brandt wrote later that his conversations with Yugoslavia's president were conducted in German.[49] Like many of his generation in the last years of Hapsburg rule, Tito had learned the language while working "as a wandering craftsman" in Wilhelmine Germany and as a soldier in the Imperial Austrian army.[50] Their association of the German language with technical training and technological development, as well as the historical orientation of the region toward German industrial centers, predisposed the elites of eastern Europe toward what Germans could contribute to their own economies. As East Berlin was nervously aware, the Federal Republic had a lot more to offer than did the GDR.[51]

Less self-evident than its economic assets was the advantage Bonn had because of its military strength within the western alliance. On the face of it, the existence, the size, and the reputation of the Bundeswehr would appear to be an obstacle to east-west reconciliation, as a West German army, had it existed, surely would have been to the detente process with France twenty years before. The impact of the Federal Republic's armed forces and its membership in NATO on the east-west equation was more complicated. Of crucial importance were two things: the pivotal role of the Bundeswehr in NATO's strategy on the central front, which gave Bonn a ticket to the top table within the alliance; and the integration of the Bundeswehr in the NATO command, which demonstrated to the countries of eastern Europe—as it once had to France—West Germany's renunciation of the unilateral use of its military potential.

Had the Federal Republic not had a critical mass of military security behind its overtures to the countries of the Warsaw Pact, its interest in negotiation would have run the risk of appearing to stem from fear and weakness. Had it possessed its actual level of military preparedness outside of the alliance, however, its diplomatic initiatives could have reminded both its eastern and its western neighbors of historical memories that Bonn sought strenuously to avoid resurrecting: the partitions of Poland, Rapallo, and the Molotov-Ribbentrop Pact. Moscow spent a good part of Brandt's years in the foreign ministry railing against West German militarism and revanchism, but its ultimate response to the overtures of the SPD-FDP government demonstrated that the Bundeswehr within the Alliance had brought an essential element to the detente process: the confidence that enabled all parties on both sides to make concessions.

The final, often overlooked, asset the Federal Republic brought to its first east-west overtures was perhaps the most important, precisely because it made the country's economic and military role in western

Europe possible: its relationship with France. Brandt's younger supporters, in the heyday of his Ostpolitik, tended to look back critically on Adenauer's policies and the priority the first chancellor had given to good relations with France and the United States.[52] Part of this criticism—that the magnet theory had proved untrue in the end—was justified and increasingly shared by the Federal Republic's political leadership. A good deal of it, however, rested on a blithe perception of economic and political cooperation between Bonn and Paris as the normal state of affairs—an astounding assumption, when measured against the history of the Franco-German relationship.

The efforts at detente in the 1950s had been so successful that many younger West Germans could not conceive of a Franco-German relationship that had once been at least as negative and destructive as that that existed during the Cold War between Bonn and Moscow or East Berlin. Their critique of Adenauer's Frankreichpolitik rested on the assumption that West Germany could have had a positive relationship with *both* eastern and western Europe in the early 1950s, but that the Cold War and Adenauer's historical and ideological biases had gotten in the way.[53] The fatal flaw in this argument was its failure to take into consideration that what *could* have gotten in the way of Bonn's detente with Paris were French fears that its neighbor would once again conduct a pendulum diplomacy toward eastern and western Europe in order to maneuver between them.

By 1960, the SPD as a party had overcome its internal resistance to accepting the premises of Adenauer's foreign policies.[54] Many individual Social Democrats who knew France best, however, had come to the conclusion long before that no alternative existed to an emphasis on building a relationship of trust between the two countries, the absence of which had long plagued Europe. The construction of that relationship in the first postwar years clearly implied the abandonment of any attempts at playing off Paris and Moscow against each other and denying skeptics in France any opportunity to claim, however wrongly, that Bonn harbored such ideas.[55] After two world wars—the second made possible, from France's perspective, by the 1939 Molotov-Ribbentrop Pact—Paris demanded of Bonn a willingness to make the choice that Adenauer had already favored and Stresemann had opposed in the 1920s: to give clear priority to Germany's relationship with France and to its role within western Europe.

The Brandt government knew what its youthful partisans had forgotten: the depth of French mistrust and the opposition Paris had mustered for five years (from 1945 to 1950) against the restoration of a major German political, economic, and military role in Europe. The rhetoric of western European cooperation had become increasingly reflective of genuine mutual trust, but in its early years—as a younger generation failed to see—it had often been the blanket under which France sought to contain, with Bonn's tacit acquiescence, West Germany's economic and political potential. Ironically, the once disastrous Franco-German relationship, transformed by Adenauer's Frankreichpolitik, had become, for the SPD-FDP coalition, Bonn's chief diplomatic asset.

This was true for three reasons. First, freed from the quarrels between the two countries that had twice devastated it since 1914, western Europe had reached a level of economic prosperity and political stability that made it, if not a magnet, certainly a positive example of social and Christian democratic government to the countries of eastern Europe. The "capitalist" states, and the working and property-owning classes within those states, had cooperated with each other to bring about postwar economic recovery. Combined with the absence of conflict between the "imperialist" colonial powers during two turbulent decades of decolonization, the development of western European cooperation was a formidable argument against the inevitability of Marxist economic and political expectations.

Second, the depth of the rapprochement with France meant that the Federal Republic, despite its squabbles with Paris over NATO and British membership in the EC, was virtually assured of western tolerance and understanding in its pursuit of Ostpolitik. As France went, so would West Germany's other western neighbors go, as Bonn was well aware. Had Paris acted on fears of another Rapallo, its reaction would have had repercussions throughout NATO and the EC, but the French supported Brandt's concept of bilateral West German initiatives, linked to NATO consultation and quadripartite negotiations on Berlin. If any doubt remained about the durability of the Schuman-Adenauer-DeGaulle legacy, Paris's encouragement of the Federal Republic's eastern policies was clear evidence of the historic change in French foreign policy.[56] The Frankreichpolitik had made an ally out of an enemy. For the first time in modern German history, the Federal Republic could dare to envision, in the long term, a positive and enduring relationship with both eastern and western Europe.

Finally, its relationship with Paris was an asset to Bonn's Ostpolitik because of the impact their rapprochement had on the Soviet Union and the countries of eastern Europe. This impact had several dimensions. First, it was a demonstration of Bonn's good faith, especially to Poland, where West German rhetoric was subject to doubt, but where there was no doubt of how bad Franco-German relations had once been. Second, the other countries of eastern Europe were reassured that the Federal Republic was linked in a western community with France, a country with which they had a historic relationship and which was politically and militarily able to balance West German economic strength. This mitigated the fear, historically explicable, that any future economic and political relationship would be with Bonn alone, or with a community dominated by the Federal Republic.[57]

The final and most important dimension of Franco–West German rapprochement was its deathblow to an era of Russian-Soviet foreign policy. Bonn and Paris had effectively foreclosed one of Moscow's options; the Rapallo card could be played to effect only in a climate of mistrust between the two western countries that no longer existed. It took Moscow some time to realize that the Frankreichpolitik that West Germany had pursued had not been tactical and that, restored to economic and military strength, Bonn would not be tempted to abandon its new Locarno for a new Rapallo. In the end, however, the Federal Republic's commitment to consultation with France on east-west issues and to expansion of the European Community left the Soviet Union with little doubt that such hopes were in vain. Moscow's realization that Franco–West German reconciliation was a reality was a critical factor in the Federal Republic's favor as it began to negotiate changes with its eastern neighbors in the Cold War status quo.

Brandt's Convictions

The Social Democrats came to the chancellery in 1969 convinced, as Adenauer had been twenty years before, that a historic mission of reconciliation and reorientation of their country's foreign policy lay before them.[58] The focal point of this mission, psychologically, was Poland. Brandt wrote later, "Reconciliation with Poland had the same historical significance as Franco-German rapprochement. . . . [It] was a moral and political duty."[59] Because "no land had suffered more from Hitler's war and the extermination policies of his state, party, and military machine," Poland was, in eastern Europe, what France had been in the west two decades earlier: the cornerstone on which West Germany would build a solid foundation of east-west relations—or would fail to do so.[60]

Brandt's government called on West Germans "to be courageous enough to take on [their] own history and its consequences."[61] This meant the recognition that "German unity was not on the world's agenda" and the acknowledgment of both the territory and the communist government of postwar Poland.[62] It also meant replacing the eastern policies of the Adenauer years with ones that did not deny the reality of the status quo that had developed since 1945. As Brandt noted, Soviet

Foreign Minister Andrei Gromyko had called Bonn's eastern policy, as long as it failed to deal with "the question of the existing borders," a "shell with no substance."[63]

A year before he became chancellor and a month after the Warsaw Pact invasion of Czechoslovakia in August 1968, Brandt spoke in Geneva to the Conference on Nuclear Non-Proliferation. He recalled his predecessor, Gustav Stresemann, who had spoken of the need for European reconciliation in his maiden speech to the League of Nations, and of "the horrible price paid by the people of Europe because they did not heed his and Briand's warnings." Despite Moscow's repression of the Prague Spring, said the West German foreign minister, the countries of western Europe "could not answer others' use of force in such a way that tensions were increased."[64] He later wrote of "a common interest—the will to survive in the nuclear age," which was also part of the postwar east-west status quo: "This nation at the heart of Europe cannot live permanently in fear, enmity, or hate with regard to its eastern neighbors."[65]

With the change of one adjective, Konrad Adenauer might have used the same words to explain his commitment to rapprochement with France. For his part, Brandt, unlike Kurt Schumacher, had supported the process of reconciliation with France in the 1950s, "emotionally desired and rationally required" by the new West German state.[66] As Bonn initiated its policy of east-west detente, "which would stand or fall with Franco-German agreement on it," Brandt had before him the example of Jean Monnet.[67] In the uncertain days of 1950, Monnet had been able "to bring reason into play through the power of conviction."[68] Twenty years later, Willy Brandt did the same.

Notes

1. One of the continuing debates among German historians concerns whether Adenauer actually believed that his "policy of strength" would have a magnet effect on eastern Europe. In all probability, his opinion changed over time, as American and Soviet policies both adjusted to the establishment of "their" blocs after 1955. In any case, Adenauer certainly saw the question as secondary in his lifetime to that of reconciliation with France and cooperation with Bonn's neighbors in *western* Europe and did not believe that West Germany could pursue those goals and reunification simultaneously. The charges made by Adenauer's critics that he saw West German foreign policy as a choice between Locarno and Rapallo, and that he chose Locarno, are probably true; whether, as his critics imply, he should be pilloried for the choice is another matter. For an attack on Adenauer's policy of "unconditional alliance with the West" (a phrase that recalls the Allies' wartime policy of "unconditional surrender"), see Rolf Steininger, *Eine vertane Chance: Die Stalin-Note vom 10. März 1952 und die Wiedervereinigung* (Bonn: J.H.W. Dietz, 1985). Steininger's premises were attacked by

Adenauer's diplomatic adviser, Wilhelm G. Grewe, in *Die Deutsche Frage in der Ost-West Spannung* (Herford: Busse-Seewald, 1986). For a less polemical summary than Steininger's of Bonn's policies toward eastern Europe and the USSR before 1969, see Richard Löwenthal, "Vom Kalten Krieg zur Ostpolitik," in Richard Löwenthal and Hans-Peter Schwarz, eds., *Die Zweite Republik* (Stuttgart: Seewald, 1974), pp. 604–699.

2. Peter Bender, *Die Ostpolitik Willy Brandts* (Reinbek bei Hamburg: Rowohlt, 1972), p. 16, puts the emphasis on the hopeful signs of differences with Moscow represented by these events in eastern Europe. Viewed from the euphoria of the first Brandt administration, this interpretation is understandable, but in the late 1950s, despite the twentieth CPSU party congress speech and the Austrian State Treaty, Khrushchev's Soviet Union, largely because of its policies at home and in eastern Europe, did not inspire much confidence abroad that it had changed greatly after Stalin. As Audrey Kurth Cronin commented in *Great Power Politics and the Struggle over Austria, 1945–1955* (Ithaca, NY: Cornell University Press, 1986), p. 163: "The crushing of the Hungarian revolt by Soviet troops in November 1956 made obvious the limits of the new Soviet approach to independence and neutrality."

3. As John Lewis Gaddis eloquently argued in *Strategies of Containment* (New York: Oxford University Press, 1982), both George Kennan's original containment doctrine and containment policy as it evolved after 1947 postulated that changes could be induced in Soviet foreign policy. The question was whether those changes could best be brought about by intimidating Moscow, through a policy of strength (predicated on the perception of virtually unlimited American resources) or by encouraging the USSR to develop a less paranoid view of its role in the world, through a policy of compromise and recognition of Soviet security interests (often predicated on the opposite perception of limited American means).

4. As in West Germany, whatever their differences of opinion on how to influence Moscow and despite their rhetoric, American foreign policy decision-makers of both political parties had tacitly ruled out a military confrontation with Moscow as too dangerous in a nuclear age. From Dulles to Kennedy, they held out the hope that "sooner or later, freedom would triumph, partly through the example of American vitality." Time may yet prove them right. See Stephen E. Ambrose, *Rise to Globalism* (New York: Penguin, 1983), pp. 247–248.

5. A development, described by Peter Bender, *Die Ostpolitik*, p. 18, as "a relaxation of east-west tensions and a hardening of the status quo," which could have had ominous implications for both German states; they faced the possibility of Germany again finding itself (as in 1945) the object of negotiations between the World War II allies on the future of Europe. For Willy Brandt, in 1961 the governing mayor of West Berlin, the building of the wall was the turning point in his determination to take the initiative, within the western alliance, in "the task of developing a new relationship with the great power to our east." The first chapter of Brandt's memoirs of the 1960s and 1970s, *Begegnungen und Einsichten* (Hamburg: Hoffmann und

Campe, 1976), p. 41, which contains the above quote, is not coincidentally entitled "The Wall."

6. Brandt, *Begegnungen*, p. 212: "We ran the danger of always begging for favors or of being blackmailed" because of Bonn's demand that third states wishing to have diplomatic relations with the Federal Republic not recognize the GDR. Combined with the 1961 Berlin crisis, the proliferation of new states after 1960, as the decolonization process picked up speed, only exacerbated Bonn's problems with implementation of the Hallstein Doctrine because potential economic and political relationships and membership in the United Nations were sacrificed on the altar of its claim to the *Alleinvertretungsanspruch*, "the sole right of [Germany's] representation."

7. "The Westpolitik," wrote Bender, *Die Ostpolitik*, pp. 10–12, "was successful because its goals lay within the realm of the possible" and because Bonn's politicians were conscious, in their dealings with their western European counterparts, of the moral legacy of the Third Reich, "which had political consequences. In the West, [the Federal Republic] was modest, willing to compromise, and prepared to make preliminary unilateral concessions."

8. Especially the United States, when seeking a West German contribution to western European defense with an intensity that almost torpedoed the ECSC. As Jean Monnet wrote in *Memoirs* (Garden City, NY: Doubleday, 1978), p. 349: he had "to prevent French policy vacillating between rigid opposition [to a West German army] and the temptation to compromise under pressure from the United States, backed by almost all her allies." The problem for Franco–West German relations in the early 1950s was twofold: the overly optimistic U.S. expectations of western European union and the United Kingdom's enthusiasm for the idea, as long as London was not required to participate in its realization. Neither Bonn nor Paris ever had to deal with opposition to their *detente* from neighbors and allies, although British and American concern over their *entente* developed in the early 1960s, when DeGaulle seemed to want to supplant western European and Atlantic cooperation with a "special relationship" between Bonn and Paris.

9. Adenauer's 1955 visit to Moscow was well described by Carlo Schmid, a member of the West German delegation, in his *Erinnerungen* (Bern: Scherz, 1979), pp. 564–582. In *Die Zeit* on the eve of the Kohl-Gorbachev summit, Theo Sommer, "Fäusteschütteln, Händedrücken," October 28, 1988, recalled the Adenauer visit.

10. Ernst Weisenfeld, *Welches Deutschland soll es sein?: Frankreich und die deutsche Einheit seit 1945* (München: C.H. Beck, 1986), pp. 72–73.

11. Bender, *Die Ostpolitik*, pp. 11–14.

12. Ibid., p. 13.

13. Ibid., p. 12.

14. As it was, Weisenfeld, *Welches Deutschland*, p. 72, described the Saar problem as "the last remaining impediment to close Franco-German cooperation," the settlement of which opened the way to "virtually linear progress" in the development of their working relationship.

15. In the mid-1960s, one-quarter of all West Germans were immigrants, from the GDR or from formerly German lands in eastern Europe. For a

discussion of the implications of this migration for the early Federal Republic, see Ralf Dahrendorf, *Society and Democracy in Germany* (Garden City, NY: Doubleday, 1967), pp. 106–112.

16. Alfred Grosser, *The Western Alliance* (New York: Vintage, 1982), pp. 212–216.
17. Ibid., p. 216.
18. Brandt, *Begegnungen*, pp. 141–142, deplored the debate between West German "Gaullists" and "Atlanticists," the former failing to see that DeGaulle's policy of independence for *France* was not one the General would have supported for the Federal Republic, the latter expecting too much from their "special relationship" with the United States; Brandt managed to treat DeGaulle's initiatives, not as a challenge to the existence of the western alliance, but as a challenge to reform NATO's (and Bonn's) relationship with Moscow: the NATO countries accepted this challenge in the 1967 Harmel Report on the Future Tasks of the Alliance.
19. Diether Raff, *Deutsche Geschichte vom Alten Reich zur Zweiten Republik* (München: Max Hüber Verlag, 1985), pp. 355–356.
20. Bender, *Die Ostpolitik*, p. 17.
21. Brandt, *Begegnungen*, p. 128.
22. Ibid., pp. 212–216.
23. Ibid., p. 216; Brandt noted that, in Africa, Bonn got too much credit for Germany's relinquishing its colonies in 1919, "as if this had been a farsighted and courageous act," but that it could not escape the charges of neocolonialism leveled against the west in the late 1960s.
24. Ibid., p. 220; Brandt wrote that Bonn was in danger of becoming "the last Cold Warrior."
25. Bender, *Die Ostpolitik*, p. 29, comments that the climate of Bonn's relations with eastern Europe actually grew worse in the 1960s because the Federal Republic, which "in reality could do nothing about [German] reunification, defended lost positions against all reason."
26. The numerous memoirs and other books about formerly German eastern Europe that have been published in West Germany since the late 1970s represent a radical change from the silence that characterized the approach to the topic in the 1960s (with the exception of a vocal minority that belonged to revanchist refugee organizations). The one exception at the time, and a notable one, was Marion Gräfin Dönhoff's *Namen die keiner mehr nennt* (München: DTV, 1986), first published in 1962. Its title *Names No Longer Spoken* reflects the reality of that year. Two of the best recent books on this topic are Christian Graf von Krockow, *Die Stunde der Frauen* (Stuttgart: DTV, 1987), and Karl Schlögel, *Die Mitte liegt ostwärts* (Berlin: Siedler, 1986). Schlögel (p. 8) calls the constriction of the Germans' own image of their place in that part of Europe "between France and the Soviet Union" (*Zwischeneuropa*) the "Wall in one's head," as a result of which the idea of central Europe has been replaced by the Cold War's terminology of an "eastern bloc."
27. Felix Gilbert, *A European Past* (New York: W.W. Norton and Company, 1988), p. 198.
28. The "bridge between east and west" image is commonly applied, not always

with approval, to Brandt's Ostpolitik, but he sounded an even more important note for Germans when he spoke at the Foreign Policy Association in New York in 1964 of "building bridges from the past to the future." As Brandt noted (*Begegnungen*, p. 141), his speech caused some sensation by not being more critical of the emerging policies of General DeGaulle.

29. By the 1980s, it had become possible to speak approvingly again of Prussian history and of the Prussian virtues, "a consciousness of duty, combined with mutual tolerance," as did Richard von Weizsäcker, then governing mayor of West Berlin, when he opened the 1981 Prussian history exhibit there. This speech, "Was Preussen heute bedeutet," is found in Richard von Weizsäcker, *Die deutsche Geschichte geht weiter* (Berlin: Siedler, 1983), pp. 261–267.

30. Hans-Peter Schwarz, *Adenauer* (Stuttgart: DVA, 1986), pp. 625–630.

31. Marion Gräfin Dönhoff, *Von Gestern nach Übermorgen* (München: DTV, 1984), pp. 144–147.

32. "A bold, constructive act," Monnet called the Schuman Plan in his *Memoirs*, p. 288, and quoted his 1950 proposal (p. 295): "World peace can be safeguarded only through creative efforts which match the dangers which threaten it."

33. And ironically, in part, for the same reason: Paris was in danger of being isolated in 1949–1950, as the German policies of its two allies in Washington and London underwent a fundamental change; two decades later, Bonn was in danger of being isolated, as its NATO allies began to negotiate, not only with Moscow, but also with Peking. Monnet knew that Paris would not be able to "brake" for long the rehabilitation of (West) Germany, and Brandt knew, as Bender wrote (*Die Ostpolitik*, p. 60) that, as east-west negotiations developed, "It was Bonn, not Moscow, that would feel the pressure. To avoid [diplomatic] isolation in the West, Bonn had to define a new position towards the East."

34. Schwarz, *Adenauer*, p. 719.

35. Bender, *Die Ostpolitik*, p. 13.

36. Brandt recalled (*Begegnungen*, p. 157) that DeGaulle had warned him that the pursuit of a new Ostpolitik was "fundamentally a psychological question, that "the psychology of [Poland and the USSR] with regard to Germany must be modified." This had also been true of France twenty years earlier.

37. Bender, *Die Ostpolitik*, p. 89.

38. Brandt, *Begegnungen*, pp. 543–549.

39. See Mikhail Gorbachev's comments on his own memories of the war in his *Die Spiegel* interview, no. 43 (October 24, 1988): 23.

40. Willy Brandt, ". . . *wir sind nicht zu Helden geboren*" (Zurich: Diogenes, 1986), p. 52.

41. As Bender noted (*Die Ostpolitik*, p. 50), Brandt's predecessors had not had any intention of using force as an instrument of Bonn's foreign policy; moreover, all of them had made that clear. However, the 1969 SPD-FDP coalition was the first West German government willing to link renunciation of force to the specific border and existential questions that existed between the Federal Republic and the states of the Warsaw Pact.

42. Weisenfeld, *Welches Deutschland*, pp. 109–110.

43. Brandt, *Begegnungen*, pp. 145, 189.
44. Bender, *Die Ostpolitik*, pp. 45–46.
45. And a new self-confidence in western Europe that was not always pleasing to Paris, which by the 1968 currency crisis had begun to fear that Bonn's evident economic strength and developing political role made desirable a rethinking of the French veto on British entry into the Common Market. See Grosser, *The Western Alliance*, pp. 250–252, and Weisenfeld, *Welches Deutschland*, pp. 111–112. Paris's perceptions were not false; Brandt, *Begegnungen*, p. 222, described his country at the end of the 1960s as "more grown up," with more weight in the councils of western European and Atlantic cooperation.
46. Brandt, *Begegnungen*, p. 222.
47. Jürgen Nötzold, "Der Beitrag der Wirtschaftsbeziehungen zur Stabilisierung der Entspannungspolitik," in Horst Ehmke, Karlheinz Koppe, and Herbert Wehner, eds., *Zwanzig Jahre Ostpolitik* (Bonn: Verlag Neue Gesellschaft, 1986), pp. 267–276.
48. Ibid., pp. 274–275.
49. Brandt, *Begegnungen*, p. 232.
50. Ibid.
51. Bender, *Die Ostpolitik*, p. 90.
52. Brandt himself never succumbed to the temptation. Unlike Schumacher, as a young politician in Berlin he had supported the Schuman Plan, and in his memoirs (*Begegnungen*, p. 641) he drew the explicit (and apt) comparison between his Ostpolitik and the Westpolitik of Konrad Adenauer, calling Franco-German cooperation the "model" for peaceful cooperation in Europe. See also Monnet, *Memoirs*, p. 319.
53. This continues to be the assumption of many West German works, such as Steininger's on the supposedly "lost opportunity" of the 1952 Stalin Note, but it is an analysis found neither in French histories of Bonn's foreign policy nor in assessments written by West Germans, such as Weisenfeld, with long years of experience in France. Weisenfeld's discussion of the Stalin Note and West German rearmament (*Welches Deutschland*, pp. 56–69) emphasizes precisely what many younger West German authors overlook: France's "fear of Rapallo" and the confidence Adenauer inspired in Paris by his clear commitment to western European integration *and* his lack of interest in neutralization plans for Germany.
54. At the Godesberg (1959) and Hannover (1960) party conferences and in Herbert Wehner's 1960 speech to the Bundestag, the bases for a new SPD foreign policy were laid, in which NATO and the new European Economic Community were accepted as the starting point for an attempt to "overcome" the Cold War status quo. See Willy Brandt's speech to the Hannover conference, November 25, 1960, "Politik für Deutschland," in *Auf der Zinne der Partei* (Bonn: J.H.W. Dietz, 1984), pp. 21–40. The Godesberg Program is found in Dieter Dowe and Kurt Klotzbach, eds., *Programmatische Dokumente der deutschen Sozialdemokratie* (Bonn: J.H.W. Dietz, 1984).
55. In part, as Schwarz pointed out (*Adenauer*, p. 833), because Adenauer feared Franco-Soviet cooperation as much as France feared a new Rapallo.

56. Weisenfeld, *Welches Deutschland*, pp. 113–116, points out that this support of Bonn did not always come easy for Paris, especially in the Pompidou years. DeGaulle's successor was not bothered by "the expression of German national sentiment, which he considered normal," but by the possibility of "a German-Soviet game in central Europe" that could lead to the "Finlandization" of the continent. The historic change was not that Paris never had doubts, but that it had the confidence not to base its foreign policy on those doubts.

57. Helmut Allardt, *Moskauer Tagebuch* (Frankfurt am Main: Ullstein, 1980), pp. 287–288 and 315–316.

58. Brandt, *Begegnungen*, p. 240.

59. Ibid., p. 242.

60. Ibid., p. 240.

61. Ibid.

62. Ibid., p. 246.

63. Ibid., p. 255.

64. Ibid., p. 252.

65. Ibid., p. 165.

66. Ibid., p. 133.

67. Ibid., p. 145.

68. Ibid., p. 135.

part three

BEYOND RAPALLO—THE LESSONS
OF LOCARNO IN THE EAST

6

CSCE AND A "COMMON EUROPEAN HOUSE"

A *Framework for East-West Dialogue*

Well into the 1970s, if not beyond, both practitioners and observers of Franco–West German relations could believe that nothing much had changed in the years since the signing of the Elysée Treaty in 1963. Willy Brandt and his SPD successor in the chancellery, Helmut Schmidt, sounded very much like their CDU predecessors when they spoke of Bonn's relationship with Paris. Two FDP foreign ministers, Walter Scheel and Hans-Dietrich Genscher, echoed their predecessors from the SPD and CDU in calling that relationship the cornerstone of their country's European and international role.[1] Private individuals and public officials involved in the daily implementation of the cultural, economic, and political agenda set by the two countries used a vocabulary already familiar in the late 1950s to describe their common interests and goals.[2]

Something fundamental had changed, however. Konrad Adenauer, Carlo Schmid, and the majority of those committed to rapprochement between France and the Federal Republic in the 1950s had seen that rapprochement as the first priority of the new West German state because they envisioned for it a *western* European future, in which good and cooperative relations with France would be essential. By the late 1960s, West Germany's political leadership and a younger generation of voters had begun to see good relations with Paris as essential for a somewhat different reason: because they enabled Bonn to initiate policies aimed at a revision of the postwar status quo, including the division of Germany and Moscow's hegemony in eastern Europe. By the early 1970s, the Federal Republic's relationship with France had become a means, not an end, of Bonn's foreign policy, because one end, the foreclosure of the possibility of a new Franco-German war, had already been achieved.

On the June day in 1974 when Günter Gaus opened the doors of the first permanent West German diplomatic mission to the German Democratic Republic, Bonn's relationship with Paris underwent a fundamental change. For twenty-four years, since Robert Schuman had invited the Federal Republic to join France in the establishment of the ECSC, approbation from the French capital had been the most sought-after pedigree of international respectability for the West German leadership.[3] Paris spoke for Bonn in places where it could not speak for itself: in much of eastern Europe and the Third World and in the principal organs of the United Nations. The entry of both German states into the UN in the fall of 1973 had heralded the era that dawned definitively nine months later, when Bonn and East Berlin began to speak officially and directly to each other. The decades in which West and East Germany had been important members of their respective alliances, but with ambiguous attitudes toward and roles in the broader international system, were over.

Fourteen months later, on August 1, 1975, the signing in Helsinki of the Final Act of the Conference on Security and Cooperation in Europe (CSCE) by the thirty-five participating states confirmed that a second phase of postwar European history had begun. The characteristics of that phase were bound to be somewhat uncomfortable for those used to dealing with the more clear-cut ties uniting the states of western Europe with each other and the United States and dividing them from the states of the Warsaw Pact that had developed in the first postwar period. For Americans, West Germans had been their least ambiguous Cold War ally for almost three decades, and the uneasiness of much of the American political leadership was reflected in the amount of time devoted by the SPD-FDP coalition to public relations in New York and Washington.[4] A West German state unhampered by its own Hallstein Doctrine or territorial claims in eastern Europe was a new factor in international politics.

Not only for Washington and Bonn's western European neighbors, however, but also for many of its own citizens, the need to define a role for the Federal Republic in the changed environment it had helped create was a painful process.[5] In many respects, rethinking the (western) European role they had assumed in the Adenauer years was far more difficult for the leadership and the voters of West Germany than its original articulation. Their options had been limited in the early 1950s. Twenty years later, tampering with the successful Westpolitik in order to define a new European role through the pursuit of an active Ostpolitik appeared to many of them both unnecessary and, to the extent that it made their western allies uneasy, dangerous—all the more reason for its supporters to elaborate an Ostpolitik that drew on the familiar institutions of the Westpolitik.

The treaties that created the climate in which these institutions could develop were the product of the diplomacy of the Federal Republic under the leadership of Willy Brandt and Walter Scheel. By 1974, Brandt had resigned as chancellor, unwilling to continue in that office after the revelation that one of his close associates had been an East German spy, and Scheel had left the foreign ministry to become West Germany's fourth president. In the years after 1974, two chancellors, Helmut Schmidt of the SPD and Helmut Kohl of the CDU, and one FDP foreign minister, Hans-Dietrich Genscher, set the tone and the tempo of Bonn's policies in and toward eastern Europe. The institutions their governments encouraged drew on the Franco–West German models of the 1950s—multilateral intergovernmental organizations, sister cities and other cultural and educational exchanges, and bilateral cooperation in specific areas of mutual interest—to develop an ongoing and expanding dialogue between the Federal Republic and its eastern neighbors.

The follow-up meetings of the Conference on Security and Cooperation in Europe have provided the principal venues of the first model since 1977, playing the role that NATO and the ECSC played in Bonn's Frankreichpolitik. At the same time, the initiatives of individual cities and private organizations have characterized the second area of dialogue, as they did between France and West Germany in the 1950s and continued to do in the years after the Elysée Treaty established the Franco-German Youth Office to support such exchanges. Finally, the West German government has actively sought environmental protection, transportation, and trade issues, among others, appropriate for the expansion of "functional" cooperation between the Federal Republic and the countries of eastern Europe.[6] Like the proponents of western integration in the 1950s, Bonn has acted on the belief that the practice of technical cooperation, where possible, changes political perceptions, opens further areas of dialogue, and has a positive spillover on the handling of other outstanding issues.[7] To its proponents, the benefits of pursuing simultaneously these three paths to detente were convincingly demonstrated by Bonn's success in undoing, within one generation, the legacy of decades of the mutual "hereditary enmity" between France and Germany.

The evolution of Ostpolitik's three-pronged approach bears study, both because of its similarity to Bonn's earlier Frankreichpolitik and because of the differences inherent in the nature of the governments and societies with which West German policy has had to deal in eastern Europe. The optimism generated by the comparison to the successful detente with France in the 1950s is tempered for many practitioners of the derivative policies toward the east, precisely because of the virtual impossibility of developing private, nongovernmental contacts with individuals and groups in the states of the Warsaw Pact.[8] Nevertheless, both the West German government and the states, municipalities, and individuals who have begun to implement the Frankreichpolitik triad toward eastern Europe, especially Poland and the German Democratic Republic, have concluded that a broadening and deepening of the government-to-government detente is possible. How have they proceeded, and why do they believe that an eastern Locarno, including a Locarno from below, is a realistic goal?

First, because the Brandt and Schmidt governments created a legal and political framework within which the three-pronged detente could be pursued. It consisted, first and foremost, of four treaties: the Federal Republic's own bilateral treaties with the Soviet Union, Poland (both 1970), and the German Democratic Republic (1972), and the 1971 Quadripartite Agreement among the United States, Britain, France, and the Soviet Union on the status of Berlin. The conclusion of the four treaties made possible east-west agreement on the calling of the Conference on Security and Cooperation in Europe in late 1972.[9] Not only did CSCE formalize the presence of two German states on the European stage and the Warsaw Pact's acceptance of an ongoing role for the United States and Canada in the political evolution of Europe, but also it brought together every state on the continent, except Albania, for unprecedented consultations on the social, economic, political, and security issues facing all of them. Since then, "for the Europeans, [CSCE has become] their forum for dealing with the division of Europe."[10]

The three bilateral treaties and the Quadripartite Agreement had other results. For the first time in a quarter-century, the status of Berlin was no longer an issue likely to provoke an east-west conflict. The treaty signed in Berlin in September 1971 by the four wartime allies, in the former headquarters of the Allied Control Council, effected a major change in their relationship. Unlike Bonn's bilateral treaties, it did so, not by acknowledging a changed status quo, but by reaffirming the rights in and the responsibilities for Berlin of the four occupying powers.[11] Like the participation of Canada and the United States in CSCE, the agreement of the three western allies and their Soviet protagonist to reaffirm their wartime decisions meant that Bonn's pursuit of detente would be carried on in a broader east-west framework. The Brandt government had made both West German ratification of the Moscow and Warsaw Treaties and its negotiation of the Basic Treaty with the GDR contingent on the successful conclusion of the Quadripartite Agreement.[12]

Those bilateral treaties, together with the 1973 treaty between West Germany and Czechoslovakia, were the final piece of the legal and political framework necessary for Bonn's pursuit of detente with its eastern neighbors. In them, the Federal Republic essentially did two things: it renounced the use of force as a means of its foreign policy, and it acknowledged the reality of the territorial changes in the borders of 1937 Germany that had come about since, and as a result of, World War II.[13] Bonn's acceptance of the Oder-Neisse line as the western border of Poland, its acknowledgment of Soviet and Polish jurisdiction in what had been German East Prussia, the abandonment of the claim that the 1938 Munich Agreement remained legally valid, and the decision to establish relations with the German Democratic Republic were all essential to the detente framework.[14] The Ostpolitik pursued since 1974 by West German governments led by both principal political parties, the Social and Christian Democrats, and carried out by their Free Democratic foreign minister consists of implementation of the commitment to "the necessity and possibility of east-west cooperation" that was contained in the Brandt-Scheel treaties.[15]

"Change Through Communication"

In addition to the flexible and prudent treaty framework negotiated by the first social-liberal coalition, the Federal Republic's practitioners of Ostpolitik, by the late 1980s, had other reasons to be cautiously optimistic that they would be able to broaden and deepen east-west cooperation by using Bonn's earlier detente with Paris as a prototype. The formula the SPD developed in the years after the building of the Berlin Wall to describe its concept of detente was that of *Wandel durch Annäherung* ("change through communication"), the utilization of an east-west dialogue to break down the barriers that had grown up between the states of eastern and western Europe during two decades of Cold War.[16] The toppling of the barriers between the Federal Republic and France and the other countries of western Europe had indeed been the result of the west-west dialogue of the 1950s.

The east-west concept differed from its west-west predecessor by postulating *two* kinds of change, however: the gradual destruction of the barriers between the states of eastern and western Europe, but also a gradual political liberalization within the countries of the Warsaw Pact.[17] This task had clearly not been part of the Frankreichpolitik, the success of which had depended on the recognition by Bonn and Paris that their two democracies shared an obligation to each other and to Europe to make war between them an impossibility. So, too, the success of the Ostpolitik required a determination to deter, not only each other, but war itself on the part of political leaders in both eastern and western Europe.[18] However, the closed societies of eastern Europe offered their western neighbors little reason to trust their good faith in pursuing this goal. The SPD concept contained an implicit challenge to the political hegemony of the Communist parties of eastern Europe because the implementation of the eastern treaties and the CSCE Final Act required their acquiescence in the long-term penetration of their societies not only by western Europe's technology and hard currencies but also by its ideas.[19]

Since the early 1970s, the need for that technology and currency has combined with the communications revolution to create a more congenial climate than was once expected for the development of the Federal Republic's policy of change through communication. The failure of the economies of eastern Europe to produce, in some cases, even the basic necessities of food and fuel has been exacerbated by their citizens' increasingly accurate information about their western European neighbors' standard of living. In addition to economic failure, moreover, the 1980s brought growing awareness of the serious environmental problems created by the combination of eastern Europe's aging industries and its leadership's insistence, for two decades, that air, land, and water pollution did not take place in Communist societies.

The April 1986 nuclear accident at Chernobyl brought into focus the factor impelling the countries of the Warsaw Pact down the path to detente and cooperation offered by the Federal Republic: their ability to protect the lives and welfare of their own citizens increasingly depended on technological and political cooperation with the countries of western Europe. At the same time, as former West German president and foreign minister Walter Scheel said in June 1986, "The accident at Chernobyl [made Bonn] wonder whether the technological underdevelopment of the East is really in our own interest."[20] Western Europe was clearly not immune from the effects of that underdevelopment.

The recognition of mutual dependence had also characterized the Franco–West German rapprochement of the 1950s. Initially, as with the first stage of Ostpolitik, the acknowledgment of that dependence was limited to two areas: security, a common interest in avoiding a third world war; and economic growth, at that time the reconstruction of postwar Europe. However, both Bonn and Paris, by cooperating in the areas they found unavoidable, also found themselves going down a road that led to new mutual ties and interests. The question that remained open for the Federal Republic in the early 1970s was whether the political leadership of the Soviet Union and its allies would allow a similar process to take place between their societies and West Germany's. In the 1980s, perhaps reluctantly, Warsaw, East Berlin, and Moscow seem to have answered that question in the affirmative—over a much longer time frame.[21]

The extent to which the Ostpolitik had become an integral part of the Federal Republic's foreign policy became clear by 1983, in the midst of Bonn's controversy with Washington over implementation of NATO's two-track decision. Soon after, the extent to which the countries of the Warsaw Pact had themselves become wedded to the process also began to be apparent. In West Germany, for the first time since the days of the Hallstein Doctrine, the Christian Democrats recaptured the chancellery in September 1982, and held onto it in the 1983 and 1987 elections. Contrary to the expectations of many observers within the Federal Republic and abroad, who expected a return to the good—or bad, depending on their point of view—old days before 1969, the CDU did not attempt a reversal of the eastern policies instituted by its SPD predecessor.[22] The new government remained committed to the deployment of NATO's intermediate-range nuclear forces (INF), but despite the CDU's rhetoric, no "turning point" occurred in the pursuit of detente with the Soviet Union and its allies.

East of the Elbe, neither the election of a CDU-led West German government nor the freeze in the Soviet-American relationship of the early 1980s dissuaded Moscow and its allies from the attempt to maintain and expand their economic and political relations with the Federal Republic. American and French concern that Bonn was overly ready to conciliate the Soviet Union reached its high point in the months from the 1983 West German election campaign to the cancellation of East German leader Erich Honecker's visit to the Federal Republic in 1984.[23] Despite overt Soviet threats to the West German government and electorate that detente was in danger, however, the voters gave the CDU-FDP coalition a mandate to continue its government; the West German parliament approved the stationing of Pershing II and cruise missiles in the Federal Republic, as called for by the 1979 NATO two-track decision; and Bonn maintained its attempt to reschedule the Honecker visit (which finally took place in 1987). All in all, the results of the Soviet intimidation campaign refuted Bonn's western allies' sometimes "unrealistically low opinion of the common sense of the German public and political leadership."[24] The thinly veiled nervousness emanating from Paris and Washington appeared to reflect the inherited concern that a new pendulum policy—Rapallo for Locarno—would emerge in Bonn in the early 1980s. It did not happen.

What did happen was twofold. First, what American ambassador Jonathan Dean called Bonn's "West-East policy" had begun to give West Germany "a distinctive foreign policy role and an identity that takes account of its history and geopolitical situation."[25] Because the policy "corresponds to Germans' sense of their national role," *whether* to pursue Ostpolitik has ceased to be a partisan political issue in the Federal Republic. Despite domestic political debate over *how* to carry out specific aspects of it, broad "nonpartisan support for the new German West-East role among the public and the major institutions of German society is evident."[26]

Second, although less easy to identify, given the nature of their societies, the extent to which the Soviet Union and its allies had recognized their own interest in maintaining and expanding a dialogue with the Federal Republic was becoming clear by the late 1980s. Their technological, environmental, and economic problems certainly played a major role in establishing their stake in the Ostpolitik process, but a decade of participation in it had also created its own momentum. In 1975, both Moscow and Washington had deprecated the importance of the human rights commitments made at Helsinki.[27] They were both wrong. Bonn's attitude toward the possibility of expanding "human contacts," through implementation of its own bilateral treaties as well as through the CSCE process, was far more positive than that of the two superpowers, as was the attitude of many of the neutral CSCE participants.[28] Compared to its American ally, West Germany was willing to settle for less spectacular human rights successes, a distrust of spectacular successes, given past German experience with them, being characteristic of its foreign policy as a whole.

Nevertheless, Bonn was well aware that its economic and technological strength gave it a certain amount of influence over the policies of the eastern European governments toward freedom of movement and expression, especially when combined with pressure from private human rights groups in both eastern and western Europe.[29] During the CSCE follow-up meeting in Vienna in November 1986, the Soviet Union was exposed to intensive, daily demonstrations and seminars protesting its human rights violations, including a fire set at the massive war memorial commemorating the Red Army's arrival in Vienna in 1945.[30] Part of the West German calculation was that Moscow could not forever ignore the negative effect of such incidents, provoked by its own policies of repression at home, on its attempts to influence West German and western European public opinion on other issues.[31]

The other calculation made by the Federal Republic in the 1970s was essentially a cost-benefit analysis. It postulated that the financial costs born by West Germany—economic benefits to eastern Europe—would eventually produce benefits—costs, to the Communist governments there—in the area of human contacts. However, this was no Jackson Amendment by another name. Bonn expected that results would be visible only indirectly and over the long term, as the self-imposed isolation of the Communist states began to be pierced by a variety of contacts with western Europe.[32] This cost-benefit analysis appears to have been correct.

By the late 1980s, West German business trips and tourism had brought the expected financial benefits to the Warsaw Pact states, but they also increased the interest of eastern Europeans in professional and personal contacts abroad, access to western television (now available by satellite), and a better standard of living.[33] In a unique position vis-à-vis the Federal Republic, the GDR especially found that pressure from its citizens to see West Germany, whether or not they had relatives there, made keeping human contacts a one-way street more difficult.[34] On both sides, "in view of the near total isolation of the two German states from one another in the 1950s," "remarkable" changes had taken place since the early 1970s.[35]

Given this evolution over nearly two decades of Ostpolitik, Bonn may be said to be following the model of its earlier Frankreichpolitik at a slower pace, a pace dictated by the nature of eastern Europe's closed societies. Any comparison to the Bonn-Paris relationship at its twenty-year mark, 1970, cannot fail to note how much more quickly two open societies established trust and confidence in each other, despite a history of war and occupation. The number of agreements reached by the Federal Republic with its eastern neighbors, on transportation, trade, environmental, and other issues, since the early 1970s is encouraging, but the fact that all these issues were dealt with in government-to-government agreements is not. Much of the Frankreichpolitik of the 1950s was initiated and implemented by private organizations and individuals, with little input from—and sometimes without the knowledge of—the two governments. Given the political systems with which West Germans have had to deal in eastern Europe, such initiatives have not been possible.

The German-German "Special Relationship"

The government and people of the Federal Republic are well aware of the limits this places on their efforts to effect an enduring east-west detente, especially their attempts to encourage an eastern Locarno from below. Nevertheless, their nation's history and its geostrategic position on the continent, the vast majority of West Germans believe, leave them no other option. As Ambassador Dean noted, the debates about the desirability of Ostpolitik that characterized the early 1970s in the Federal Republic no longer exist; the governing parties and the opposition Social Democrats all

> firmly adhere to the new, broader definition of the German international position that combines close ties to the United States and to the European Community with a sustained effort to achieve a modus vivendi on political issues and arms control with the Soviet Union, the GDR, and the other Warsaw Pact states.[36]

The implementation of this "new, broader definition of the German international position" requires of Bonn policies different from those it pursued in the twenty years during which West Germans "considered that they faced a stark, mutually exclusive choice" between their role in western Europe and the alternatives hinted at by the Soviet Union.[37]

The Federal Republic has focused its efforts on furnishing the "common European house." The concept enables it to link the existing structures of the Westpolitik, particularly the European Community (EC), with the developing structures of the Ostpolitik, particularly CSCE, by elaborating a mutually dependent role for both of them. Bonn has sought to make the general thrust of its Ostpolitik part of Franco–West German consultations.[38] At the same time, it has elaborated two strands of that eastern policy: its inner-German relationship (Deutschlandpolitik) with the GDR and its relationships (Ostpolitik) with the other countries of the Warsaw Pact. Juridically, and given the nature of the domestic debate on the Brandt-Scheel treaties at the time, the Federal Republic had reason to make a distinction between the two in the early 1970s. Today, the distinction is significant for other reasons.

Within the broader framework of the Federal Republic's pursuit of detente with all the Warsaw Pact states, including the GDR, Germany's national history and the importance of the human contacts issue contrive to give the inner-German relationship a special character. With or without the Basic Law's call for German reunification, the two states share a common language, a common geographic position at the heart of Europe, and a common past. They also share—although only for a few more years—a generation of leaders who survived exile or imprisonment in the 1930s and 1940s and who drew different conclusions from their experiences at the hands of the Third Reich. Many of the founding fathers of both states worked together in initial postwar attempts to reestablish a German political infrastructure. Well into the 1980s, the Federal Republic's second representative to the GDR, Klaus Bölling, was a former member of Erich Honecker's Young Communists (FDJ) in the late 1940s, and the East German leader himself was a "west" German from the Saarland who grew up there in the interwar years of its administration by the League of Nations. West German Foreign Minister Hans-Dietrich Genscher was an "east" German.[39]

This special relationship does not mean that an inner-German consensus on future political reunification ever developed. Legally and politically, the Federal Republic is bound by its own constitution to work toward that goal.[40] Over the past two decades, however, the nature of the other German state, not its existence, has become Bonn's principal concern.[41] West Germans have begun to emphasize, not reunification, but self-determination for the German people and the permeability of the inner-German border.[42] The political consensus that exists in the Federal Republic is twofold: that the two German states have a special responsibility for peace in Europe and that West Germans have a special responsibility for the political and economic well-being of the people of the GDR.[43] This consensus distinguishes the Deutschlandpolitik from Bonn's relationships with the other countries of eastern Europe.

For its part, officially, the German Democratic Republic does not recognize the concept of an "inner-German" relationship. East Berlin deals with Bonn, as with any other country, through its foreign ministry. It has, however, accepted the compromises necessary from Bonn's viewpoint: the exchange of permanent representatives, not ambassadors, and the management of the two states' relationship by the chancellery, not the foreign office, in the Federal Republic. It has also accepted other aspects of West Germany's concept of a special relationship, most notably—and advantageously—the special trading relationship with Bonn that brings the GDR many of the benefits of EC membership without the costs.[44]

Whether there is a consensus for or against German political reunification in the East German public is hard to tell, but a growing number of West German observers believe that there too the principal interest is in reform of the East German state, not in its abolition.[45] Still, in practice, if not in official policy, the GDR has enabled the Federal Republic to develop its concept of a special inner-German relationship. In the area of Europe's peace and security, East Berlin has gone further, explicitly accepting a special responsibility of the two German states to contribute to east-west detente and stability. The most forthright expression of this was contained in the communiqué issued by the Federal Republic and the GDR following the meeting of Helmut Schmidt and Erich Honecker at Werbellinsee (GDR) in December 1981.[46]

Measured against the two preceding decades of mutual hostility, the relationship that began to develop between West and East Germany in the early 1970s has already made a radical difference in the lives of millions of Germans. It has also made a radical difference in the political calculations of their respective allies in NATO and the Warsaw Pact. Bonn and East Berlin have altered the Cold War equation predicated on the two German states' mutual suspicion and, having changed that equation, have made necessary a reassessment of the German role in Europe. In this, too, the Deutschlandpolitik resembles the Frankreichpolitik, which altered a long-standing European security equation predicated on the constant of Franco-German hostility.

In its practice, the inner-German relationship is also beginning to resemble more closely Bonn's earlier detente with Paris. This resemblance is no accident. In many respects, the Federal Republic's goals are the same, and the nonpolitical obstacles, such as language, are fewer. The millions of West Germans with friends and relatives in the GDR have their own reasons to be interested in the development of better inner-German relations, but millions more have a natural curiosity about the historic German heartland of Brandenburg-Prussia. In the 1950s, the depth of interest in France and support for the policies of Franco–West German detente were strongest in the borderlands along the Rhine and Moselle.[47] In the 1980s, the Elbe borderlands are those most able to see the physical results of a better relationship between Bonn and East Berlin, in the type and extent of traffic across the border, but all West Germans share an interest, as did an earlier generation with regard to France, in turning confrontation with their neighbor into dialogue.

Weizsäcker, Genscher, and the Foreign Policy Consensus

The pursuit of that dialogue, the work of Gustav Stresemann and Aristide Briand, has found a second generation of individual political leaders committed to practice toward East Berlin, Moscow, and their allies what two generations of West Germans have practiced toward Paris. As Locarno had Stresemann and the Frankreichpolitik had Adenauer, the evolution of Bonn's eastern policies has also been shaped by key individuals, Willy Brandt and Helmut Schmidt in the 1970s, Foreign Minister Hans-Dietrich Genscher after 1974, and, since 1984, by West Germany's president, Richard von Weizsäcker. Without the direct political role given by the Basic Law to the chancellor, Weizsäcker has nevertheless been crucial to the further development of Bonn's policies of east-west detente in the 1980s. Like Brandt, he has become the voice of a Federal Republic willing to confront the consequences of Nazi Germany's policies for Germans and their neighbors. He also plays a role, however, that neither Adenauer nor Brandt was able to fill: Weizsäcker symbolizes both faces, east and west, of West Germany's foreign policy, and the nonpartisan domestic consensus in support of it.

Both within the Federal Republic and abroad, the president has come to embody a new West German political maturity four decades after the end of World War II. He does so through a combination of his personal background, his political convictions, and his understanding of the nature of the West German presidency. Unlike Brandt, who, like other socialists, was forced into foreign exile in the 1930s, Weizsäcker came from an aristocratic, Protestant family with a tradition of diplomatic service. He served as a Wehrmacht officer on the Russian front and, as a young lawyer, participated in the defense of his father at the trial of the foreign office leadership in Nuremberg. He was active in the early efforts of the Lutheran church (EKD) to promote inner-German detente in the 1960s and was the first Christian Democratic mayor of West Berlin in the early 1980s. His older brother, a highly respected physicist, is a leader of the anti-nuclear weapons movement in the Federal Republic.

In a way that has surprised many West Germans, this president has found a way to speak for the vast majority of them. Unlike the SPD leadership in general, Weizsäcker makes no secret of the importance to him and his politics of his religious convictions. Unlike the CDU leadership in general, however, he is not Roman Catholic, but Protestant, with close ties to the Lutheran church in East Germany. He personifies what both the postwar SPD and the CDU sought: the infusion of individual ethics into politics and the end of the divisive confrontation between German Catholics and Protestants. At the same time, like most Germans, he was neither in a concentration camp nor in exile during World War II. Weizsäcker fought for his country, while his father, like many older Germans, found himself in the service of a government for which no Prussian concept of apolitical public administration had adequately prepared him. In many respects, the wartime and postwar experiences of their family, despite its aristocratic background, were more typical of the average German's than were the experiences of politicians in the resistance or in exile abroad.[48]

Today, in many respects, the president is also typical of the majority of West Germans who favor detente with East Germany and its Warsaw Pact allies but not at the expense of their country's friendship with France and role within western Europe. The chord struck by Weizsäcker is a new phenomenon in West German politics and, for that matter, in modern German politics. Neither Stresemann nor Adenauer spoke for a nonpartisan majority of their countrymen. Stresemann pleased some of his constituents with Locarno and others with his implementation of Rapallo, but neither his foreign policies nor Weimar's democracy could rely on broad-based, nonpartisan support. Adenauer's Frankreichpolitik survived early SPD opposition only to become entangled in the West German debate over the Franco-American squabbles of the 1960s, just as it was achieving its goal of rapprochement between Paris and Bonn.

In the early 1970s, Brandt's Ostpolitik unleashed a domestic political war with the opposition Christian Democrats and with some members of the FDP, despite their party's participation in the governing coalition. As a result, the CDU brought the eastern treaties to the West German Supreme Court for a judgment on their compatibility with the Basic Law and, by using the constitution's provision for a constructive vote of no confidence for the first time, attempted to bring down the government.[49] The attempt failed but forced an early federal election in 1972. In the late 1970s, disagreements within the SPD-FDP coalition on how to continue to combine the pursuit of east-west detente with Bonn's obligations in the western alliance contributed to schisms within both the SPD and the government and to the establishment of the Greens.[50] Until the mid-1980s and Weizsäcker's eloquent speech commemorating the fortieth anniversary of the end of World War II in Europe, a West German leader seemed unlikely to be able to articulate both an Ostpolitik and a Westpolitik that met the approval of his countrymen and their neighbors in eastern and western Europe.

In addition to the West German president, however, other individual political leaders have also been instrumental in advancing Bonn's policies of east-west detente. The practice of West German foreign policy since 1974 has depended on FDP Foreign Minister Hans-Dietrich Genscher, his tenure encompassing the entire CSCE follow-up process and all but a few months of West Germany's membership in the United Nations. Moreover, Genscher has served under chancellors from both parties, Helmut Schmidt and Helmut Kohl, and like Weizsäcker, has given expression to the nonpartisan West German consensus in favor of pursuing both the Ostpolitik and the Westpolitik, which the CDU and the SPD, respectively, once so vigorously opposed. To an entire generation of Germans and other Europeans, Genscher has come to embody the foreign policy of the Federal Republic.[51]

Individuals from other friendly nations were important to the success of West Germany's Ostpolitik from the beginning. In its initial stages, the ties that existed among the Socialist and Social Democratic leaders of Europe, especially through the Socialist International, played a major role in establishing contacts with the leaders of eastern Europe. Willy Brandt's relationships, dating from his war years abroad, with Austrian chancellor Bruno Kreisky and Swedish prime minister Olof Palme were of special importance.[52] Their two neutral states were able to provide Bonn—and the SPD before and after its years in the chancellery—with informal mechanisms of dialogue that were not always possible in diplomatic negotiations with the states of eastern Europe.[53]

One of the principal differences between the Federal Republic and the countries of the Warsaw Pact, however, is the extent to which Bonn's pursuit of east-west detente is not tied to the policies or tenure of specific leaders. The lesson of Locarno, that friendship between three great statesmen was not an adequate basis for a foreign policy of understanding and cooperation, was well learned in western Europe. Certainly in the beginning, Adenauer's Frankreichpolitik and Brandt's Ostpolitik had both depended on specific individuals for their momentum. However, the fear that Bonn's Frankreichpolitik depended on Adenauer or that its Ostpolitik was dependent on the presence of the SPD in the chancellery turned out to be groundless.[54] By the end of the 1980s, both the western and eastern policies articulated by the Federal Republic's FDP foreign minister and its Christian Democratic president had a broad, overlapping constituency throughout West Germany.

East of the Elbe, the situation has been different. Indeed, one of the paradoxes of the Ostpolitik and a major difference with the Frankreich-politik is its dependence on a degree of centralization of decision-making in eastern Europe that in the long run it hopes to break down. The relationship between East Berlin and Moscow is a particular example of the irony of Bonn's position. Walter Ulbricht's GDR in the 1960s was reluctant to have Moscow undertake negotiations with the three western allies on the rights and responsibilities of the four powers in Berlin and with the Federal Republic on the nonuse of force.[55] It was especially unwilling to enter into discussions with West Germany on the basis of "two states, one nation," as desired by Bonn. In the end, only because Moscow was in a position to force Ulbricht from office and to see that he was replaced by a man willing to support the development of an inner-German detente, Erich Honecker, was it possible for the Brandt-Scheel government to negotiate the treaties that formed the basis of its Ost- and Deutschlandpolitik.[56]

In the 1980s, the situation is much the same. The control exercised by Moscow in eastern Europe, which worked to the disadvantage of Bonn's foreign policy toward Czechoslovakia in 1968 but to its advantage toward the GDR three years later, is a major element in West German expectations of the reform policies of Soviet president Mikhail Gor-bachev. In Prague and East Berlin, leaders reluctant to undertake economic and political reforms may be forced to do so by a combination of pressures emanating from Moscow and from their own countrymen. In June 1987 in East Berlin, demonstrators called on their government to take down the Berlin Wall—in the name of the Soviet leader.[57] As the decade ended, the Federal Republic again found itself in the somewhat uncomfortable position of hoping that Moscow could impose its will—this time for domestic reform and east-west cooperation— on its Warsaw Pact allies, as it once did on the GDR.[58] One of the long-term goals of Ostpolitik, to encourage the political independence of the countries of eastern Europe from the Soviet Union, is paradoxically dependent in the short term on the effectiveness of Moscow's control.

The Institutionalization of East-West Detente: CSCE

Encouraging movement in eastern Europe beyond this stage of dependence on the commitment of specific leaders to the detente process requires the application, as it did in Adenauer's West- and Frankreichpolitik, of the other three lessons of Locarno. The Federal Republic has sought to instigate, in the east-west dialogue, a self-perpetuating process rooted in institutions. Like the ECSC and its successor organizations of the European Community within western Europe, the Conference on Security and Cooperation in Europe in the 1980s has provided the mechanism for the establishment of working relationships between the foreign offices of eastern and western Europe. It is the only forum where diplomats of the two blocs and of all the neutral states of Europe meet on a regular basis (because Switzerland is not a member of the United Nations).

The European Coal and Steel Community that established the basis for the new postwar relationship between France and the Federal Republic was based on two principles accepted by its six founding states: the recognition of their sovereign equality and the delegation of certain areas of national decision-making authority to a supranational authority.[59] The Conference on Security and Cooperation in Europe is based on ten principles accepted by the thirty-five signatories of the 1975 Helsinki Final Act. These principles are:

1. Mutual recognition of their sovereign equality
2. Nonuse of force
3. Inviolability of frontiers
4. Territorial integrity of states
5. Peaceful settlement of disputes
6. Nonintervention in internal affairs
7. Respect for human rights and fundamental freedoms
8. Self-determination
9. Cooperation between states
10. Good faith fulfillment of international obligations[60]

The first six principles had already been accepted by the Federal Republic as the basis for its relations with the countries of the Warsaw Pact in its bilateral treaties with the Soviet Union, Poland, and Czechoslovakia.[61] The acceptance by those countries, including the GDR, of the last four principles at Helsinki is the basis of Bonn's institutionalization of the detente process through CSCE and, especially with East Germany, bilaterally.[62]

This institutionalization has taken two forms since 1975. Multilaterally, Bonn has supported the expansion of the east-west dialogue through the CSCE follow-up meetings held in Belgrade from 1977 to 1978, Madrid from 1980 to 1983, and Vienna from 1986 to 1989. Further CSCE meetings on specific east-west issues have also been held in Budapest, on cultural contacts; Stockholm, on confidence-building measures and disarmament in Europe (CDE); Ottawa, on freedom of movement; and Bern, on human rights.[63] The Federal Republic has been an active participant in all of these meetings, which, from its perspective, offered advantages to the Ostpolitik similar to those provided to the Frankreich-politik by the framework of the ECSC and, especially in its early years, the European Community.

Chief among these advantages was the multilateralization of issues that would be more intractable on a bilateral basis. As the ECSC once provided the mechanism by which the appearance of excessive unilateral concessions on the part of either France or the Federal Republic could be avoided, CSCE provides a mechanism by which the compromises of all enable the compromises made by a single state to take place. As the European Community, in its first years especially, gave West Germany a voice in the economic and political development of western Europe that might otherwise have been unacceptable to many of its neighbors so soon after World War II, the CSCE process gives the countries of the Warsaw Pact and the European neutrals a voice in shaping the east-west dialogue that they would not otherwise have. It permits the "German Question" to be discussed in a wider forum. As the American ambassador John Maresca noted, "Although it was never mentioned publicly, and rarely discussed even in private," the CSCE was "about Germany, and . . . the status of that divided nation in the future."[64] So was the ECSC.

In its working groups, the Conference on Security and Cooperation in Europe reflects the de facto tripartite division of the continent into three groups of states: the NATO allies, members of the Warsaw Pact, and the neutrals. In its plenary sessions, however, the conference meets as a gathering of individual states seated in alphabetical order, not within their respective groups. Moreover, in the corridors of Stockholm's Kulturhuset and Vienna's Hofburg, national representatives from Poland, Portugal, the United States, Bulgaria, Finland, and the other thirty participating states have had an opportunity for discussion and debate provided them nowhere else. The CSCE has been compared to the Congress of Vienna, but in many respects its atmosphere more closely resembles that of the League of Nations, and its Locarno tea parties, of the late 1920s.[65]

West German foreign policy as practiced at the CSCE, although primarily an aspect of Bonn's Ostpolitik, is also aimed at another goal: to enhance political cohesion among the countries of western Europe. To that end, at Stockholm in January 1986, Foreign Minister Genscher and his French counterpart, Roland Dumas, arrived together and made a joint proposal to the opening session of the final round of the CSCE meeting on confidence-building measures and disarmament in Europe (CDE).[66] Paris and Bonn share a fundamentally Gaullist conception of the role of the CSCE—based on the cooperation of states, not of blocs, from the Atlantic to the Urals.[67] However, Bonn takes this concept a step further by envisaging the eventual dissolution of the blocs and their replacement by an all-European "peace order," possibly with a formal organizational structure of its own, responsible for the continent's security and development.[68]

As was the case when Willy Brandt and Walter Scheel were negotiating Bonn's eastern treaties, the Federal Republic's interest lies in pursuing policies in the CSCE and toward the Warsaw Pact in general that have been agreed on with France. However, the very development of the CSCE process, the inner-German relationship, and other forms of bilateral and multilateral cooperation between West Germany and its eastern neighbors makes this increasingly difficult. Bonn and Paris inevitably part company at a certain point: their attitudes toward the postwar status quo in Europe.

Jonathan Dean categorized the position of the Federal Republic on the GDR as one that "must be objectively described as revisionist, though not with the usual negative connotations of this term."[69] In fact, Bonn's position on postwar Europe is revisionist, no longer in the negative sense of upholding the Munich Agreement or the Oder-Neisse line, but in the sense that West Germany accepts the logic that dismantling the Warsaw Pact, a goal with which France would not argue, also means dismantling NATO.[70] This change, in turn, would mean an entirely new context for relations between the two western allies. Paris has never had to face the question of the strength of the Franco–West German relationship in a world without an east-west confrontation and without British and American troops in the Federal Republic.

Because of West Germany's success in applying the second lesson of Locarno to its Ostpolitik, however, the day may not be far off when France confronts that possibility. The institutions of dialogue established at Helsinki and Stockholm; the increasing use of existing multilateral organizations, such as the U.N. International Atomic Energy Agency (IAEA), for the east-west dialogue; and the growth of bilateral coopera-tion between the Federal Republic and its eastern neighbors all indicate that the detente that Bonn has been pursuing with eastern Europe since the late 1960s is moving slowly toward entente. It has already taken longer than the thirteen years that elapsed between Paris's proposal of the Schuman Plan and the signing of the Elysée Treaty, but the process to which the Federal Republic is committed has acquired a momentum that "it is doubtful that any Western ally can" stop.[71] Indeed, probably only a Soviet military move against western Europe could discourage it now.

Bonn has been in a curious position for over a decade. As Ambassador Dean wrote, in its inner-German relationship, West Germany

> has the tremendously difficult task of convincing its own allies and the Warsaw Pact states that it is doing nothing that is on balance injurious to their interests, while at the same time convincing its own electorate that it is doing something significant for German interests. Its diplomacy has done a brilliant job in this effort.[72]

West German diplomacy has been brilliant in concealing the extent to which the entire Ostpolitik, not just its Deutschlandpolitik, is revisionist. However, this very brilliance is potentially the source of new and apparently unexpected woes for the Franco-West German relationship. Gustav Stresemann once alienated his French colleagues by describing the need for Berlin to practice Metternich's art of "finesse" in its foreign policy.[73] Bonn's attempts to reassure Paris that the ultimate goal of the Ostpolitik, if reached, will not fundamentally alter the postwar structures of the Westpolitik—when, in fact, it will—have already resulted in ominous rumblings out of Paris that there is too much finesse in West German foreign policy today.[74]

Capillarizing Detente in a Common European House

Despite its brilliance, Bonn's diplomacy has not done a better job than any of its allies' in distinguishing a commitment to western European and Atlantic cooperation from a commitment to the structures set up to support that cooperation in the first quarter-century after the end of World War II. Without such a distinction, however, Bonn's Ostpolitik inevitably and increasingly appears at best naive and at worst duplicitous to Paris, as well as to Washington and London. As long as its policies toward eastern Europe were essentially aimed at promoting east-west *detente* between the blocs, Bonn could agree on a common strategy with Paris.[75] At the moment that detente becomes a reality, however, whether formally proclaimed or not, the evolution of *entente* between the Federal Republic and its eastern neighbors, and between western and eastern Europe, raises other questions. What role do the two states of divided Germany have then? What commitment does a Federal Republic endowed with a new central European role have to western European integration?

In a speech to Vienna's Danube-European Institute in August 1986, the West German foreign minister attempted to define how the Federal Republic saw its role in the CSCE process and in the furnishing of a "common European house" from the Atlantic to the Urals. For Bonn, CSCE was "an instrument for shaping Europe" in ways that will "give political effect to the general desire for more humanity, more security, and more community" among its peoples, a "dramatic, comprehensive forum which does not take the east-west confrontation for granted, but seeks to break it down."[76] The CSCE process had had "far-reaching effects on the relationship between the Federal Republic and the GDR and its other eastern neighbors," and especially on the lives of millions of individuals.[77] To describe it, Genscher used words like change, movement, and dynamic new beginnings.[78]

Calling on his audience to begin work on "the rebirth of our continent," the foreign minister declared that in a "common European house, people, ideas, and information must be able to move freely." Europe's identity rested on "its common history, its common culture, to which all the nations have made great contributions, and its common responsibility for the future of our continent."[79] Genscher's language could easily have been used—and was—to describe the concepts that underlay the process of detente between the Federal Republic and France in the 1950s. Then, too, the proponents of rapprochement between the two countries based their work on the common historical and cultural heritage of Carolingian Europe and on a common Franco-German responsibility for the future of Europe.[80]

At Vienna, Genscher declared that a "continuous bilateral and multilateral political dialogue between east and west is indispensable to the construction of a European peace order," both between the super-powers and between the states of eastern and western Europe. Cultural exchange was also indispensable, because without "knowledge and respect for the great cultural achievements of others, it is difficult to imagine a durable relationship without mistrust, disputes, and fear."[81] Again, his words could have been taken from any number of speeches made in favor of the cultural and political dialogue between France and the Federal Republic at its beginnings in the 1950s.[82] The skepticism that existed toward that dialogue at the time—whether it was either desirable or possible—was certainly a match for any faced by the CSCE process since 1975.

The legacy of the Frankreichpolitik's successful application of the lessons of Locarno is visible in all aspects of Bonn's attempt to broaden, deepen, and institutionalize participation in the east-west dialogue. This began in the early 1970s with the CSCE's initial meetings in Geneva and Helsinki. The inclusion of all the states of Europe (except Albania, at its own choosing), not only members of NATO and the Warsaw Pact, recognized their common interest in defusing the east-west military confrontation and expanding cooperation on the continent.[83] As well as including the neutral and nonaligned states in the developing framework of the east-west dialogue, Bonn favored a broadening of that dialogue beyond political and security issues into economic, educational, and other areas of concern to individual Europeans and a deepening of it, *within* states, to include private groups and citizens.

For the Federal Republic, this involvement of individuals was important not only because of the western commitment to human rights and of the specific issues it faced with the GDR and ethnic Germans in the other Warsaw Pact states but also because of the role individuals played in the establishment of detente with France in the 1950s and 1960s. West German foreign policy places far greater emphasis than that of its allies on the importance of creating a Locarno from below as part of the east-west detente process. For this reason, Bonn has been one of the principal supporters of all forms of educational, cultural, and artistic exchange with the countries of eastern Europe. Manifestations of this support include the Federal Republic's cultural agreements with Bulgaria and Albania in 1988 and with the GDR in 1986, the German cultural week held in Poland in October 1988, and the active role played by West Germany in the CSCE cultural forum in Budapest in 1985.[84]

Compared to the establishment of student exchange programs and sister cities between France and the Federal Republic a quarter-century ago, their development with the countries of eastern Europe has been a much more centralized process. Individual West German cities have had to work through the diplomatic representatives of the states concerned, not through private organizations.[85] Moreover, cities, schools, and other organizations have not always been free to choose their partners in the exchange; their preferences have sometimes been ignored, and a relationship with a different city or group offered. The exchanges, until very recently, were much more of a one-way street than they had ever been between France and the Federal Republic.[86] The emphasis on exchanging works of art, performances of theater groups, and organized sport clubs also reflected both the centrally controlled cultural policies of the states of the Warsaw Pact and their reluctance to permit the free movement of persons.[87] Breaking down these barriers to the kinds of exchanges West Germany would prefer is a task that did not confront the architects of the Frankreichpolitik.

Compared to the early 1970s, however, when exchange programs between the Federal Republic and its eastern neighbors were virtually nonexistent, the barriers to the exchange of persons and ideas, as well as cultural goods, have been eroded. With the success of the capillarization of detente with France as their model and with the CSCE Final Act as their point of reference, West German municipal and state governments in the mid-1970s began to explore ways to encourage the countries of eastern Europe to fulfill the pledge made at Helsinki to enhance the volume and the quality of human contacts. Once of the first initiatives was that of the Hanseatic city-state of Bremen to reestablish its cultural ties to the Polish, formerly German, Hansa city of Gdansk (Danzig).[88] A decade later, Erich Honecker's home state of the Saarland took the lead in finding sister cities in the GDR. The first East-West German city partnership, between Saarlouis and Eisenhüttenstadt, has led to nearly fifty others, including one between the historic Roman city of Trier, Karl Marx's birthplace, and Weimar, birthplace of the first German republic.[89]

The sister city relationship between Bremen and Gdansk, which celebrated its tenth anniversary in 1986, and the developing partnerships between cities on West Germany's border with France and East Germany's border with Poland represented the new interest in looking eastward among the people of the Federal Republic. Since the late 1960s, Saarlouis had had an active sister city relationship with the French port of Saint-Nazaire, but by 1986, at the local level as well as in Bonn, the Westpolitik and the Ostpolitik were no longer perceived as mutually exclusive alternatives.[90] Whether Paris and the French counterparts of West Germany's local and state officials shared this perception, however, was not yet clear.

Certainly, the immediacy of the problem of furnishing the "common European house," called for by Mikhail Gorbachev and François Mitterrand—and at Helsinki in May 1988 by Ronald Reagan—as well as by the West German foreign minister, was felt most acutely between the Rhine and the Elbe. Practitioners of an eastern Locarno from below in the late 1980s used the same language with which their predecessors had described the urgency of rapprochement and reconciliation with France in the 1950s: the responsibility of the past because of Germany's wars of conquest and extermination; the present for a better quality of life for the peoples of Europe; and the future to eliminate armed conflict. The success with which Bonn defined those responsibilities and implemented policies to meet them in western Europe allowed West Germans to turn their attention to the same responsibilities and to the need for comparable policies on their eastern borders.

In a speech to the Atlantic Treaty Association in September 1986, Chancellor Kohl struck this note when he described "the path which German policy has followed since the war" as one of "reconciliation with our neighbors."[91] This path, which "we have traveled with France and with many of our former enemies," is the one "we wish to follow with regard to our neighbors in central Europe, the peoples of the Soviet Union, and especially the Polish nation," he said. West German foreign policy, "from necessity and the most sincere conviction, pursues the goal of a system of peace in Europe" that will allow all the people of the continent "to live together without fear and in mutual trust."[92]

The Christian Democratic chancellor called attention to "the results of the work of the great men on whose shoulders we stand today," those who created the western detente of the 1950s and 1960s. Cooperation between the countries of western Europe "was made possible by the reconciliation of France and Germany and the uniqueness of their relationship."[93] As a result of that relationship, "at the end of this century of fratricidal wars in Europe, armed conflict between the nations of the European Community has become completely unthinkable." Whatever the disagreements within the EC, it was "a model of cooperation and coexistence which should be an example for Europe as a whole."[94]

The chancellor went on to reprimand himself and others for the tendency to refer to the countries of the European Community as "Europe." There were, he said, "important European countries which cannot now join the Community. But the Danube flows through Europe. And Prague and Krakow and Warsaw—and naturally Leipzig, Dresden, and Weimar—are also Europe." The foreign policy of the Federal Republic was predicated on the belief that "only understanding, cooperation, and the will to successful negotiations can overcome the division of Europe and the antagonisms of its different political systems." This policy was rooted in the CSCE Final Act, whose "signing in Helsinki marked the beginning of a process which has intensified the dialogue between the two halves of Europe, and set in motion expanded political, economic, and cultural cooperation" between the larger and smaller and the allied and neutral states of the continent.[95]

Quoting with approval Mikhail Gorbachev's use of the metaphor of the "common European house," Kohl touched on the principal difference between the conditions in which the Frankreichpolitik developed in the 1950s and those with which West German Ostpolitik had to deal in the 1980s: the nature of eastern Europe's closed societies. Although western Europe's "system for the protection of human rights is an example for the rest of the world," this was not true of the states of the Warsaw Pact. In the common European house, however, as Bonn conceived of it: "There can be no locked doors, no boarded-up windows. The gates must be open wide, in every direction, and openness and trust must characterize the relationships among its inhabitants." As it had been the basis of the Franco–West German detente of the 1950s, the development of mutual confidence was "an essential element in the evolution of a peaceful Europe from the Atlantic to the Urals."[96]

Since its first bilateral and multilateral initiatives toward eastern Europe two decades before, the Federal Republic had never under-estimated the amount of patience and time needed to encourage the conditions in which that confidence could grow. The nature of the centralized, closed societies east of the Elbe was one aspect of the Ostpolitik with which its western precursor never had to deal. The practitioners of that Ostpolitik, at the federal level and below, had daily evidence of their lack of the Frankreichpolitik's greatest asset, taken for granted at the time: the constitution of the Fourth Republic and the West German Basic Law. Their constitutions created the conditions in which detente, not only between the two states but also between their citizens, could flourish.

Despite the absence of those conditions at the outset of their Ostpolitik, neither the West German government nor those individuals engaged in the creation of an eastern Locarno from below believed that their task was hopeless. It was certainly more difficult than it had been in the west, but the responsibilities of the past, present, and future remained. For West Germans, those responsibilities were symbolized by Auschwitz, Chernobyl, and Hiroshima. The need to come to terms with the first, create the conditions in which economic and social progress was possible without the second, and establish a political climate in which the destruction of the third became unthinkable would not go away. As a result, no matter how difficult or frustrating, both Bonn's Ostpolitik and the need to define with France an acceptable blueprint of the common European house would remain.

Notes

1. Henri Menudier's "Deutsch-französische Beziehungen und europäische Integration," in Robert Picht, ed., *Das Bündnis im Bündnis* (Berlin: Severin und Siedler, 1982), pp. 140–168, is one of the best brief discussions of the continuity of Franco–West German cooperation through three generations of West German foreign ministers from the CDU, SPD, and FDP.
2. See the chancellor's farewell speech to the West German parliament, September 10, 1986, in Helmut Schmidt, *Die nüchterne Leidenschaft zur praktischen Vernunft* (Berlin: Verlag Rainer Röll, 1987), pp. 42–43.
3. A point made explicitly by Schmidt; ibid., p. 42.
4. Willy Brandt, *Begegnungen und Einsichten* (Hamburg: Hoffmann und Campe, 1976), pp. 90–96 and 378–389.
5. Peter Bender, *Die Ostpolitik Willy Brandts* (Reinbek bei Hamburg: Rowohlt, 1972), pp. 45–48.
6. The relevant documents are contained in two publications of the Bundes-

presseamt, Bonn, 1986: *Dokumentation zur Ostpolitik der Bundesregierung* and *Dokumentation zur Deutschlandpolitik der Bundesregierung.* The status of cooperation with the GDR was analyzed by Ernst Martin, *Zwischenbilanz: Deutschlandpolitik der 80er Jahre* (Stuttgart: Verlag Bonn Aktuell, 1986).

7. Heinrich Vogel, "Sicherheit als Problem aussenwirtschaftlicher Entscheidungen der Sowjetunion," in Horst Ehmke, Karlheinz Koppe, and Herbert Wehner, eds., *Zwanzig Jahre Ostpolitik* (Bonn: Verlag Neue Gesellschaft, 1986), pp. 265–266. The benefits of functional cooperation were first discussed by Ernst B. Haas, *Beyond the Nation-State* (Stanford: Stanford University Press, 1964).

8. Discussions with members of the Saarlouis-Eisenhüttenstadt sister cities committee, Saarlouis, Federal Republic of Germany, December 1986.

9. Jonathan Dean, *Watershed in Europe* (Lexington, MA: Lexington Books, 1987), p. 104.

10. Ibid., p. 115.

11. The Quadripartite Agreement is contained in *Dokumentation zur Ostpolitik*, pp. 70–72. Section I, paragraph 3 reaffirms the rights and responsibilities of the four powers.

12. Bender, *Die Ostpolitik*, pp. 102–107, and Brandt, *Begegnungen*, pp. 512–523.

13. Bonn's three treaties with Moscow, Warsaw, and Prague are contained in *Dokumentation zur Ostpolitik*, pp. 13–15, 21–23, and 50–52. Renunciation of force is provided for in Article 2 of the Moscow Treaty, Article II of the Warsaw Treaty, and Article III of the Prague Treaty. The inviolability of borders is recognized in Article 3 of the Moscow Treaty, Article I of the Warsaw Treaty, and Article IV of the Prague Treaty. Article I of the Prague Treaty declares the 1938 Munich Agreement null and void.

14. The Basic Treaty with the GDR is contained in *Dokumentation zur Deutschlandpolitik*, pp. 46–48. It provides for renunciation of force in Article 3.

15. Editorial on the significance of the CSCE/CDE Final Document, Stockholm, *General Anzeiger* (Bonn), September 26, 1986.

16. One of the sources of misunderstanding of Egon Bahr's 1963 concept, developed when he was press spokesman for the governing mayor of West Berlin, Willy Brandt, is the lack of a definitive English equivalent for the German word *Annäherung.* It has been translated as "coming closer together," "contact," and in other ways that, unfortunately, often imply a compromise of western democratic principles in order to reach a modus vivendi with the Warsaw Pact states. Another possible translation of the German word (a communications trench is an *Annäherungsgraben*) seems the best way to avoid this difficulty, while suggesting the necessity to link entities that require mutual contact; hence, "change through communication." See Helga Haftendorn, "Wurzeln der Ost-und Entspannungspolitik der Sozial-Liberalen Koalition," in *Zwanzig Jahre*, pp. 17–28.

17. Richard Löwenthal, "Vom Kalten Krieg zur Ostpolitik," in Richard Löwenthal and Hans-Peter Schwarz, eds., *Die Zweite Republik* (Stuttgart: Seewald, 1974), p. 667.

18. See Georgi A. Arbatov, "Internationale und europäische Sicherheit im Atomzeitalter, Entspannung und Abrüstung" and Egon Bahr, "Von der

Strategie der Abschreckung zur gemeinsamen Sicherheit," in *Zwanzig Jahre*, pp. 37–67 and 95–101.

19. Robert Legvold wrote, "with the fruits of economic involvement came the perils of political penetration. The Western powers now deliberately sought to use improved relations to force their ideas, tastes, and practices on the Socialist societies." Quoted in Vojtech Mastny, ed., *Helsinki, Human Rights, and European Security* (Durham, NC: Duke University Press, 1986), p. 52.

20. Scheel devoted much of his June 17, 1986, speech to the Bundestag, commemorating the thirty-third anniversary of the June 17, 1953, uprising in East Berlin, to the implications for Germany and Europe of the Chernobyl explosion. The speech is contained in Bundespresseamt, *Bulletin* no. 73 (June 19, 1986): 613–619.

21. See Mikhail Gorbachev's *Die Spiegel* interview, no. 43 (October 24, 1988): 28–29, and Max Schmidt, "Die politische Entspannung: Konsequenzen für ein neues Denken und Handeln," in *Zwanzig Jahre*, pp. 150–151.

22. Walther Leisler Kiep, "The New Deutschlandpolitik," *Foreign Affairs* 63, no. 2 (Winter 1984/5): 316–329.

23. Paris's concern was so strong that, six weeks before the March 1983 West German federal election, President Mitterrand gave his immediately (in)-famous speech to the Bundestag, calling on Bonn to implement the NATO two-track decision. Because the SPD, four months out of the chancellery, had repudiated the Schmidt government's support for Pershing and cruise missile deployment, the French Socialist president was effectively calling on West Germans to vote for a Christian Democratic chancellor. See Ernst Weisenfeld, *Welches Deutschland soll es sein?* (München: C.H. Beck, 1986), pp. 154–156.

24. Dean, *Watershed*, p. 249.

25. Ibid., p. 242.

26. Ibid.

27. John J. Maresca, *To Helsinki: The Conference on Security and Cooperation in Europe, 1973–1975* (Durham, NC: Duke University Press, 1987), pp. 217–218, 225–226.

28. Ibid., p. 229. Maresca's assertion that the continuation of the CSCE process depends on "the acquiescence of the two superpowers" is no doubt literally true, but it fails to convey the leverage of the eastern and western European states within their respective alliances, and of the neutrals, on the USSR and the United States. The negative repercussions of a withdrawal from the CSCE process are something neither Moscow nor Washington has been willing to face, given the other intra-alliance issues with which each has to deal. See also Dean, *Watershed*, pp. 110–115.

29. Jürgen Nötzold, "Der Beitrag der Wirtschaftsbeziehungen zur Stabilisierung der Entspannungspolitik," in *Zwanzig Jahre*, p. 271.

30. *Die Presse* (Vienna), November 6, 1986.

31. The West German attitude toward the east European dissidents has often been contradictory, especially within the SPD. There is, after all, an inherent contradiction between contributing economically to the stability of the governments of eastern Europe and encouraging political dissent there.

Willy Brandt's refusal to meet Lech Walesa during his 1984 visit to Poland set off a specific debate within the SPD on the party's commitment to human rights, but across the board, the practitioners of Ost- and Deutschlandpolitik have walked a thin line between encouraging dissent and cautioning eastern Europeans to go slow. See Horst Ehmke, "Frieden und Freiheit als Ziele der Entspannungspolitik," in *Zwanzig Jahre*, pp. 279–291.

32. Helmut Kohl, "Leitlinien und Grundüberzeugungen deutscher Aussenpolitik" (a speech to the Deutsche Gesellschaft für Auswärtige Politik, June 25, 1986), *Bulletin* no. 78 (Bonn: Bundespresseamt, July 1, 1986): 657–663.

33. Angela Stent, "Intra-German Relations: The View from Bonn," in Robert Gerald Livingston, ed., *The Federal Republic of Germany in the 1980s* (New York: German Information Center, 1983), pp. 19–30.

34. Martin, *Zwischenbilanz*, p. 58.

35. Dean, *Watershed*, p. 244.

36. Ibid., p. 254.

37. Ibid., pp. 239–240.

38. Weisenfeld, *Welches Deutschland*, pp. 162–164. Beginning in 1986, the Quai d'Orsay and the West German Foreign Office began a regular exchange of personnel. In 1988, one of the French diplomats detailed to Bonn was assigned to the desk dealing with Deutschlandpolitik. See *Der Spiegel* no. 16 (April 18, 1988): 45. In *Le monde diplomatique*, February 1989, Marcel Drach's "Une nouvelle donne dans les relations entre les deux Europes," p. 16, and Paul-Marie de la Gorce's "La diplomatie ouest-allemande à l'avant-garde de la détente," pp. 20–21, are both excellent summaries of West German and EC policies.

39. Klaus Bölling, *Die fernen Nachbarn* (Hamburg: Stern, 1984), pp. 12–24, and Theo Sommer, "Jenseits von Potsdam," *Die Zeit*, June 24, 1988.

40. Preamble and Article 146, *Grundgesetz für die Bundesrepublik Deutschland* (Bonn: Bundeszentrale für politische Bildung, 1984).

41. Marion Gräfin Dönhoff, "Mauer und Einheit: Zeit zum Umdenken," *Die Zeit*, May 1, 1987.

42. Ibid. See also Marion Gräfin Dönhoff, "Von der Geschichte längst überholt," *Die Zeit*, January 27, 1989.

43. Dorothee Wilms, *The German Question and Inner-German Relations* (Washington, D.C.: Konrad Adenauer Stiftung, 1987).

44. Stent, "Intra-German Relations," pp. 24–25.

45. Jürgen Schmude, "Deutsche in zwei Staaten—was treibt sie zusammen, was treiben sie miteinander?" in *Zwanzig Jahre*, p. 193.

46. Contained in *Dokumentation zur Deutschlandpolitik*, pp. 255–260.

47. Which shared a common history from Roman settlement of the Rhine through Charlemagne, the Hapsburgs, and Napoleon, and where extensive personal and professional ties already existed before 1945. See Edwina S. Campbell, "The Ideals and Origins of the Franco-German Sister Cities Movement, 1945–70," *Journal of the History of European Ideas* 8, no. 1 (1987): 83–84.

48. The federal president discussed the influence of these events on him in a 1964 speech at the Evangelical Academy, East Berlin, as one of the West

German participants ("then far from common") at an east-west conference on tragic historical anniversaries: among them, the outbreak of war in 1914 and 1939 and the July 20, 1944, attempt to assassinate Hitler, on which Weizsäcker spoke. The speech, "Der 20. Juli 1944—Attentat aus Gewissen," is collected with other speeches in Richard von Weizsäcker, *Die deutsche Geschichte geht weiter* (Berlin: Siedler, 1983), pp. 21–42. The resonance that the president has found in West German public opinion was reflected in early 1989 when Martin Wein's biography *Die Weizsäckers* (Stuttgart: DVA, 1988) hit the West German best-seller list. The book's subtitle is "the story of a German family." The president's nonpartisan approach came under attack within the CDU when he hosted a reception in honor of Willy Brandt's seventy-fifth birthday in January 1989. See Jürgen Leinemann, "Eine der grossen Leitfiguren der Welt," *Der Spiegel* no. 4 (January 23, 1989): 31–32.

49. Brandt, *Begegnungen*, pp. 567–571.
50. Hans-Dietrich Genscher, October 13, 1982, speech to the Bundestag, excerpted in Robert Leicht, ed., *Im Lauf des Jahres—Deutsche Texte und Dokumente 1982* (München: DTV, 1983), pp. 186–192.
51. A fact typified by a two-page ad in *Der Spiegel* (January 19, 1987): 94–95, urging support for the FDP in the upcoming Bundestag elections. The ad, signed by Marion Gräfin Dönhoff and Wolf Graf Baudissin, among others, urged West German voters to "save Detente! . . . German foreign policy should remain in the hands of Foreign Minister Genscher, to assure continuity, expertise, judiciousness, and reliability." Genscher as the personification of Bonn's foreign policy was also discussed by SPD leader Gerhard Schröder at a luncheon meeting of the Friedrich Ebert Stiftung, Washington, DC, June 29, 1988. Christoph Bertram's "Akrobat auf dem Schwebebalken," *Die Zeit*, February 17, 1989, discussed the problems Genscher's east-west balancing act had begun to encounter among Bonn's western allies.
52. Brandt, *Begegnungen*, pp. 207–209. See also Bruno Kreisky, *Zwischen den Zeiten* (Berlin: Siedler, 1986), pp. 351–354.
53. Brandt, *Begegnungen*, pp. 108–110.
54. Richard Löwenthal, "The German Question Transformed," *Foreign Affairs* 63, no. 2 (Winter 1984–85): 303–315.
55. Bender, *Die Ostpolitik*, pp. 89–92.
56. Karen Dawisha, *Eastern Europe: Gorbachev and Reform, the Great Challenge* (Cambridge: Cambridge University Press, 1988), p. 114.
57. Robert Leicht, "Wut an der Mauer," *Die Zeit*, June 19, 1987.
58. Marion Gräfin Dönhoff, "Die Weltpolitik vor der Wende?" *Die Zeit*, February 5, 1988.
59. Jean Monnet, in *Memoirs* (Garden City, NY: Doubleday, 1978), described Paris's insistence (p. 312) on "negotiations on the basis of the principles and essential undertakings contained in the French proposals of 9th May," which meant (p. 311) that "the method for negotiating the Schuman Plan was itself" not negotiable.
60. The text of the Final Act in German, one of the six official CSCE languages, is in *Dokumentation zur Ostpolitik*, pp. 122–189, as are the final documents of

the Belgrade and Madrid CSCE follow-up meetings. The Final Act in English, keyed to the discussion in his text, is found in Maresca, pp. 249–306, which also contains the final recommendations of the 1973 Helsinki consultations. The text of the Final Act, as well as President Ford's address to the August 1, 1975, summit and the list of signatories (not found in Maresca), is also contained in Richard P. Stebbins and Elaine P. Adam, eds., *American Foreign Relations 1975: A Documentary Record* (New York: New York University Press, 1977), pp. 283–360. Section 1, immediately following the preamble, contains the "Declaration on Principles Guiding Relations between Participating States."

61. And as the basis for membership of the Federal Republic (and the GDR) in the United Nations in 1973. See Brandt, *Begegnungen*, pp. 554–555.

62. Which the Federal Republic sees as a form of regional cooperation "in conformity with the purposes and principles of the Charter of the United Nations" (CSCE Final Act, Section 1). See Richard von Weizsäcker, "Die Bedeutung der Friedensfunktion der Vereinten Nationen" (speech on the occasion of the visit of the U.N. Secretary General to Bonn, July 11, 1986), *Bulletin* 86 (Bundespresseamt, July 16, 1986).

63. Mastny, *Helsinki*, pp. 16–33, and also pp. 304–311, for Bonn's assessment of the Ottawa experts meeting on human rights by the West German representative, Ekkehard Eickhoff.

64. Maresca, *To Helsinki*, p. 81.

65. In Vienna in 1986, said *Die Presse* (November 5, 1986), "The Congress had not yet danced." All of the "unique qualities" of the Locarno tea parties described by Jon Jacobson, *Locarno Diplomacy* (Princeton: Princeton University Press, 1972), p. 70, also apply to the CSCE process, which, like the Briand-Stresemann-Chamberlain meetings built around the League of Nations Assembly, has both a public and a private face.

66. Hans-Dietrich Genscher, speech to the forty-first General Assembly of the United Nations, New York, September 25, 1986, in *Bulletin* 113 (Bundespresseamt, September 30, 1986): 953–958.

67. As Weisenfeld pointed out (*Welches Deutschland*, p. 154), the difference between the Gaullist concept of the 1980s and its predecessor, both in France and in the Federal Republic, is that the late 1980s version postulates neither "tension with the United States" nor a "third force between the superpowers, but a Europe conscious of its own history, contributions, and interests." The ongoing involvement of the United States and Canada in the CSCE process, as much as if not more than their NATO membership, makes this concept possible; Moscow and its allies have acknowledged the interest of the North Americans in "security and cooperation in Europe" since 1972, most recently in Gorbachev's *Der Spiegel* interview, p. 30. See Brandt, *Begegnungen*, p. 558, on the USSR's original proposal for a CSCE excluding Washington and Ottawa.

68. Genscher, *Bulletin* 113, pp. 954–955.

69. Dean, *Watershed*, p. 242.

70. Raymond Aron, *Mémoires* (Paris: Julliard, 1983), p. 261, recalled that he wrote in 1949: "Like the Marshall Plan, the Atlantic Pact has no other final

goal than to make itself superfluous." Bonn's foreign policy is implicitly based on the same idea.

71. Dean, *Watershed*, p. 249.
72. Ibid., pp. 248–249.
73. Wolfgang Stresemann, *Mein Vater Gustav Stresemann* (Frankfurt am Main: Ullstein, 1985), pp. 373–379.
74. Among the more rabid, Brigitte Sauzay's *Le vertige allemand* (Paris: Olivier Orban, 1985), which caused a stir because its author was (and remained, after its publication) one of the French interpreters at Franco–West German summits; and among the more thoughtful, with a broad historical perspective, Stephane Roussel's *Les collines de Berlin* (Paris: Mazarine, 1985), by the longtime correspondent of *Matin* in Berlin and *France-Soir* in Bonn. As Roussel wrote (p. 287): "When Germany moves, the world pays attention."
75. As Weisenfeld (*Welches Deutschland*, pp. 175–182), pointed out, the West German formula of self-determination for the German people, if implemented, *could* lead to reunification; perhaps more than the Germans themselves, the French, given their own nationalism, are likely to assume that it *would* lead to one German state. That "the future shape of central Europe, in fifty or one hundred years," will be the result of "a common solution, which does not lead Germans and French, Poles and Czechs, back to their old discords," is the assumption of French policy, given two things: German patience and a prudent western assessment of the east-west balance of forces. Any sign that one or both are lacking in West Germany makes Paris nervous, as it did in 1983. See also Gesine Schwan, "Mitten im ganzen Europa," *Die Zeit*, January 27, 1989.
76. Hans-Dietrich Genscher, "Perspektiven einer europäischen Friedensordnung," Vienna, August 27, 1986, *Bulletin* 96 (Bundespresseamt, August 29, 1986): 807–813.
77. Ibid.
78. Ibid., p. 813.
79. Ibid.
80. Monnet, *Memoirs*, p. 287.
81. Genscher, *Bulletin*, 96, p. 812.
82. The proclamation of the sister city relationship between Lyon and Frankfurt am Main, October 15, 1960, included the following paragraph, typical of its day and a paraphrase of Genscher's words in Vienna twenty-five years later: "This union between the two cities is concluded in the hope of arriving at a true comprehension of the problems of each, at mutual tolerance and respect, thus preparing complete *entente* between the peoples of the two countries, in order to contribute to the establishment and maintenance of peace in the world." The full text is in *Partnerschaftsurkunden* (Stuttgart: Internationale Bürgermeister-Union, 1969), p. 12.
83. Maresca, *To Helsinki*, p. 13: "the voice of San Marino or Liechtenstein was theoretically equal to that of the United States or the USSR. While these ministates are perhaps poor examples because their personnel and resources were not sufficient for them to play a role equal to that of the larger countries, it is a fact that middle-sized states, such as Romania, Switzerland,

or the Netherlands, were able to deal with the great powers as equals in this negotiation, and did so."

84. Discussion with members of the West German delegation to the Budapest Cultural Forum, Bonn, February 1986. See also Genscher, *Bulletin* 96, p. 811, on "the reestablishment of a once self-evident common [European] discussion" and *Deutschland-Nachrichten*, November 23, 1988, October 19, 1988, and September 14, 1988.

85. Discussions with the mayor of Saarlouis and the former mayor of Bremen, on their cities' partnerships with Eisenhüttenstadt (GDR) and Gdansk (Poland), Saarlouis and Bonn, December 1986.

86. Saarlouis discussion, December 1986, and Martin, *Zwischenbilanz*, pp. 95–97: One of the key measures is the number of school children, students, and young people who participate in organized travel between West and East Germany, as compared to the numbers who participate in Franco–West German exchange programs. In 1982, 196 West German school classes with approximately 5,000 participants visited the GDR. The next year, about 13,000 children in 500 groups made the trip, and by 1985, there had been a tenfold increase, with 68,000 participants, over 1982. However, the East German youth organization (FDJ) permitted only 1,250 young people in thirty-eight groups to visit West Germany in 1982, and in 1983 unilaterally broke off east-west visits after only ten groups had participated. They were reinstituted in August 1985, with 1,020 young people in thirty-four groups visiting the Federal Republic that year.

The number of exchanges between French and West German schools, youth clubs, sport groups, and other institutions is so extensive and so decentralized that it is virtually impossible to give a definitive figure on the number of participants. Holger Mirek's *Gemeindepartnerschaften: Ein Leitfaden für Praktiker* (Kehl am Rhein: N.P. Engel, 1984) lists forty-two umbrella organizations for Franco–West German exchanges, and the West German Foreign Office's 1985 publication *Wege zur Freundschaft: Partner für deutsch-französische Zusammenarbeit* lists ninety-eight organizations active in Franco–West German nongovernmental cooperation. The Franco-German Youth Office (DFJW) established by the 1963 Elysée Treaty gave financial support to 109,847 activities from 1963 through 1984 in which 3,485,551 young people from both countries took part. In 1984, 127,579 participants in Franco–West German exchange programs received financial aid from the DFJW.

Neither activities that last less than five days nor the number of young people acting as hosts are included in the DFJW's figures, since short-term programs (mainly in the border areas) are not financed by the DFJW, and only "traveling" participants are counted, as they are the recipients of financial support. Moreover, many more young people, compared to the 1950s and 1960s, have the opportunity to make private visits to France or the Federal Republic, without having taken part in an organized exchange or as a follow-up to one. See Gert Hammer, *Das deutsch-französische Jugendwerk* (typescript, 1985), p. 10. Interview with Mr. Hammer, Deputy General Secretary of the DFJW, Bad Honnef, September 1985.

87. Martin, *Zwischenbilanz*, pp. 111–118.
88. Discussion with the former mayor of Bremen, Hans Koschnick, Bonn, December 1986.
89. Discussion with the mayor of Saarlouis and members of its sister city committee, Saarlouis, December 1986.
90. Ibid.
91. Helmut Kohl, "Ecksteine deutscher Politik," Mainz, September 17, 1986, *Bulletin* no. 106 (Bundespresseamt, September 23, 1986): 897–900.
92. Ibid., p. 898.
93. Ibid., p. 899.
94. Ibid., p. 900.
95. Ibid.
96. Ibid.

7

BONN'S FRANKREICHPOLITIK AT A CROSSROADS

National Neutralism: Impotence as Foreign Policy

The fundamental problem Bonn faces in elaborating its concept of a common European house is the wariness of the Federal Republic's own allies toward any German plan for the political organization of central Europe. Paradoxically, despite their greater suffering at the hands of Berlin in the twentieth century, the countries of eastern Europe have a longer historical memory of a positive German role east of the Elbe than do Bonn's western neighbors. A major German voice in their part of the world seems historically "normal." In the west, however, the negative images of Wilhelmine Germany's search for its place in the sun and Nazi Germany's racist expansionism color the attitudes of Bonn's allies toward an activist West German foreign policy aimed at reshaping the Yalta status quo, probably more than they realize and certainly more than they care to admit.[1]

Despite the polite rhetoric of NATO solidarity, the practitioners of West German foreign policy, of whatever party, have been acutely aware of this problem since 1949.[2] Public opinion in the Federal Republic and the parties of the left in opposition have not always seemed to share the government's concern for the way in which West German initiatives, whatever their intentions, will be interpreted west of the Rhine and across the Atlantic.[3] Then again, the practice of treading on eggshells in the elaboration of Bonn's foreign policy interests has become a vicious circle for the Federal Republic. Certain interests are too important for Bonn not to lead its allies, but the attempt to appear to be always following—what one writer called "the after-you-Valéry method"—takes its toll.[4]

West Germany is unlike any other state of the western alliance when viewed from within that alliance, but its global role since the early 1970s has made Bonn recognize other perspectives. The countries of Asia, Africa, and Latin America, themselves spared a close encounter with the recent German past, are free to see the Federal Republic without blinders: as a prosperous, democratic state concerned with the welfare and security of its citizens. Ironically, Bonn's allies are perhaps its most skeptical diplomatic partners, because they know simultaneously too much—more than the countries of the southern hemisphere—and too little—less than the nations of eastern Europe—about Germany. The chief foreign policy challenge for the Federal Republic is to convince its own allies that the changes it seeks in Europe will be positive for all of them, not just for Germans. Whether Bonn will succeed is still an open question.

Over the past decade, skepticism toward the policies pursued by the Federal Republic and, even more so, toward the policies advocated by large numbers of its citizens, has grown abroad. In France, this skepticism reached its peak in the mid-1980s, when a spate of books asking "whither Germany?" captured the concern of French government and, to a lesser extent, public opinion.[5] Looking at the Federal Republic from outside, French writers, as well as American and British observers, were struck by its apparently groundless pessimism, its fear of the future, and its self-image as a passenger in a vehicle over which it had no control—a mood describable only by that untranslatable German word, *Angst*.[6] Why were West Germans, citizens of one of the few states in the world where social and political justice were both paid more than lip service, so dissatisfied with themselves? What dangerous foreign policies would grow, as they had in the past, out of German dissatisfaction?

Bonn's allies in Paris and Washington were especially concerned with the phenomenon that by the mid-1980s had become known as "national neutralism."[7] It was identified chiefly with the amorphous West German peace movement, galvanized into action by NATO's determination to begin installation of Pershing II and cruise missiles in the Federal Republic in the fall of 1983. However, national neutralism was less a policy espoused by that movement as a whole than a distillation of the principal elements of its critique of Bonn's foreign policy since 1949. This made it no less dangerous in the eyes of the French. The foreign policy Paris had come to expect of Bonn was one of *western* orientation, rooted in the *western* military alliance and the *western* European community. If the peace movement's critique gained majority support in the Federal Republic, the unexplored paths it might lead to could not be predicted.

The two components of national neutralism were especially shocking to observers west of the Rhine because, for thirty years, neither had seemed to play a major role in the policies of the Federal Republic. Nationalism, as the French knew it among themselves and as the Germans had known it for nearly a century and a half before 1945, was rhetorically invoked on West German public occasions, but Paris had come to regard the speeches of Bonn's politicians as a decorative part of the political landscape, without practical significance.[8] Bonn's support for the political and economic integration of western Europe, as well as its military integration in the Atlantic Alliance, had made the Federal Republic France's partner and ally. Despite their own nationalism, the French had grown used to the West Germans' repudiation of their recent nationalist past. Bonn's tenacity in pursuing its Ostpolitik, combined with the peace movement's charges that German reunification had been unnecessarily sacrificed to Adenauer's dreams of a Carolingian western Europe in the 1950s, gave Paris an unexpected shock.[9] French withdrawal from the NATO military command was one thing; the serious possibility that West Germans fifteen years later would elect a government with a mandate to refuse implementation of an Alliance decision was another.

At the same time, this manifestation of German nationalism was clearly different from its predecessors. Unlike them, it was not characterized by a self-image of power and prestige, but by one of impotence and inferiority.[10] The operative metaphor in the West German political debate became, ironically, Poland after 1790, in the years of partition.[11] However, the fate of German nationalism at the Congress of Vienna was also invoked. The peace movement's critique paradoxically read German history in much the same way that Wilhelmine expansionists had read it: as a conspiracy among the great powers to maintain a balance of power in Europe and peace among themselves by keeping Germany weak and divided.[12]

The remedy prescribed for the perceived frustration of legitimate German nationalism in the years after 1945 was different, however. Unlike the last German emperor, Wilhelm II, national neutralists did not overestimate the ability of their country to impose political solutions on Europe militarily. Unlike Bismarck, the first German chancellor, they did not even see limited possibilities to do so. On the contrary, their analysis postulated the possibility of political change in Europe only through a demonstration of German abnegation and led them to link German nationalism with neutralism for the first time since the early 1950s.[13]

Their concept of a neutralized Germany was based on a curious combination of historical and contemporary self-images. On the one hand, it implicitly—sometimes explicitly—regarded eastern European and Soviet fears of West German militarism and revanchism as legitimate, implying that the Federal Republic was hardly without means, including the use of force, to advance its interests.[14] On the other hand, it pictured West Germany within the western alliance as barely able to articulate its own interests, an impotent victim of the policies of is allies.[15] Faced with the technological possibility of nuclear annihilation, it postulated a supreme German interest in opting out of the east-west struggle.[16]

The neutralist prescription, which was nothing if not solicitous of the security concerns of the Warsaw Pact states (except, perhaps, those of the GDR for its own political existence), assumed the acceptability to those states of German reunification, provided that national unity and neutralization went hand in hand.[17] In that sense, to advocate neutralization was to be a German nationalist and to reject it, as had Konrad Adenauer and two generations of West German political leaders, was to betray the national cause. The critique turned the priorities of the Federal Republic's founding fathers upside down, assuming—as they had not—that unity would not require the sacrifice of justice and freedom by the people of the Federal Republic, or worse still, not caring if it did. This was a major difference between the national neutralists and such early postwar leaders as Kurt Schumacher. Although the SPD believed then that more could have been done to prevent the division of Germany, it was always more interested in what kind of Germany emerged from the war than in a reunified nation at any price.[18]

Among the neutralist remedy's many internal contradictions was its lack of interest in the security concerns of Bonn's allies and its characterization of their relationship with the Federal Republic. Supposedly the pawn of its three principal western allies in the Cold War and unable to defend its own economic and political interests within the western alliance, West Germany was nevertheless urged to execute a maneuver most unlikely for a pawn: to pursue unilaterally national reunification and military and political self-neutralization. A West German foreign policy more alarming to Paris and Washington is hard to conceive, but this was of little importance in the national neutralist critique. French and American concerns for the future security of western Europe were not accorded the legitimacy granted the revanchist nightmares of the states of the Warsaw Pact. Instead, those concerns were invariably taken as evidence of an occupation mentality toward the Federal Republic and an ideologically determined "enemy image" of the Soviet Union. Any delineation of their own security interests by the United States and France inevitably fueled the national neutralist self-portrait of West Germany as the pawn of the principal western players.[19]

The practitioners of West German foreign policy, the politicians and diplomats with whom Paris and Washington dealt in the early 1980s, clearly did not see their country in the same light as did their national neutralist critics.[20] On the contrary, they recognized that the Federal Republic was itself a principal player in the east-west game. Unfortunately, they were not above avoiding unpleasant political confrontations at home by implying their own lack of influence over unpopular decisions of Bonn's allies, such as France's refusal to include its nuclear forces in east-west arms talks or the American strategic defense initiative (SDI).[21] This tendency was doubly irritating to a French government concerned with the national neutralist drift in West German public opinion and dependent for its economic and military security on Bonn's commitment to NATO and the EC.[22]

However, what was new and most alarming to Bonn's allies in the 1980s was the growing tendency among West Germans to make a distinction between *German* interests and *western* interests and apparently to regard the two as incompatible.[23] They had a disquieting sense of having witnessed such a development in Germany before and the failure of Weimar's democratic forces to rise to the situation. If the Federal Republic were to pursue the policies implicit in the national neutralist critique, France feared that the perception of German impotence would soon become a self-fulfilling and contagious prophecy; the future of Europe would be shaped, not by Franco–West German leadership, but by German acquiescence in Soviet hegemony.[24]

Unspoken Disagreements with Paris

France's concern to stem the national neutralist tide manifested itself in the recklessness with which a Socialist president from Paris endorsed the foreign policies of a Christian Democratic chancellor in Bonn in an election year.[25] By the 1980s, however, despite François Mitterrand's plea for NATO's implementation of the two-track decision, French diplomacy was astute enough to recognize the impossibility of demanding of its ally a choice between east and west: West German Ostpolitik had become a permanent part of the European political landscape. What was needed was a strategy designed to ensure that the Federal Republic would, in the future as it had in the past, regard its eastern policies as the companion of, not a substitute for, the West- and Frankreichpolitik.[26]

Not surprisingly, this was also the strategy adopted by the CDU-led West German government elected in March 1983. The Christian Democrats' election victory was itself reassuring to Bonn's allies abroad, although there was a tendency to misinterpret it in the United States.[27] West Germans had been asked to choose between the SPD, which had repudiated its own support for the NATO two-track decision but which was clearly in favor of continuing an active Ostpolitik in pursuit of east-west detente, and the CDU, which had once vigorously opposed the abandonment of the Hallstein Doctrine and the eastern treaties. In other words, voters ran the risk of electing a party that might abandon the Westpolitik for the Ostpolitik or its opponent, thought willing to do the opposite. In fact, the reelection of the Free Democrats to the governing coalition was clear evidence that West Germans favored the continuation of both policies. As CDU support for those policies soon showed, somewhat to Washington's (and many West Germans') surprise, so did their new government.[28]

Under the continuing direction of FDP Foreign Minister Hans-Dietrich Genscher after 1983, West German strategy was not to change Bonn's support for the Westpolitik but to change the role of its western policies in the overall foreign policy of the Federal Republic.[29] To the West German public, the CDU-FDP government attempted to show, as its SPD-FDP predecessor once did, that the Westpolitik enabled the Ostpolitik to take place and that without it the goals of the Federal Republic in eastern Europe, both for itself and for the people of the Warsaw Pact states, could not be reached. This was a tricky business. To succeed, it required the cooperation of Bonn's principal partner in Europe and the western alliance, Paris.

Whatever else had happened since the summer of 1914, one thing had not changed for German foreign policy in seventy-five years. The relationship with France remained the determining factor of good or bad German relations with the other principal western power, first Great Britain and then the United States. Politicians and diplomats of both Weimar and Bonn, from Gustav Stresemann to Helmut Schmidt, had learned that this was true and focused their foreign policy on their country's relationship with France. Other leaders of both countries, chief among them Adenauer, Schuman, and Monnet, knew instinctively that a modus vivendi between them would eventually carry the English-speaking powers along, despite their momentary irritation with the ECSC or the Elysée Treaty. As long as France understood and accepted what West Germany was trying to accomplish in Europe, the two countries' other western allies would raise no serious objections.[30]

In his 1985 Stimson lectures at Yale University, Helmut Schmidt described his own evolution over thirty years from an Anglophile to an Atlanticist to a Francophile West German politician.[31] Schmidt was almost startlingly frank in his declaration that "Germans will remain on the Western side only if the French help them and bind them to the West" and that this could not be done "by an American president coming from Georgia, California, or any other state."[32] The former chancellor was convinced that "German interests within Europe can be pursued only to the extent that the French are involved and support them."[33]

Schmidt was undoubtedly correct, but what are "German interests within Europe"? Can Paris support them? Clearly not, if those interests are defined according to the national neutralist critique. Just as clearly, however, the West German government itself has never defined German interests in that way. Bonn's attempt since 1983 to elaborate compatible eastern and western policies reflects a continuation but also a redirection of the efforts of earlier West German governments to do the same. Critical to the attempt is the Federal Republic's ability to convey to its western European neighbors, particularly France, its own sense of a German role in eastern Europe and a desire to participate—if only to a limited extent—in it. If Bonn fails to do so, French understanding of and tolerance for West German foreign policy is likely to falter. The result would not be Bonn's abandonment of its eastern policies but a rift between the two western neighbors that would be disruptive and destructive to the fabric of Europe.

Both of them understand the pivotal nature of their relationship, and this knowledge is the positive aspect of their attempt to define foreign policies that meet their respective national interests.[34] The negative aspect, on the West German side, is an unwillingness to confront the possibility of clashing interests and a tendency to assume that they must be compatible because the alternative would be too dreadful to contemplate; on the French side, the expectation is that Bonn will ultimately defer to Paris if the latter demands it.[35] The Franco–West German relationship has functioned on the basis of these two assumptions because both countries have studiously avoided confronting issues that might disrupt it. One of the principal questions facing Bonn is whether the evolution of its eastern policies will allow this to continue. Chances are, it will not; Paris had no difficulty understanding and supporting Bonn's *concept* of a common European house, but agreeing on a blueprint for it is another matter.

As issues on which their opinions are far apart become part of an east-west dialogue in the 1990s, agreement between Paris and Bonn on how to deal with them will become more important but not easier. In the months after the nuclear accident at Chernobyl in April 1986, the divergence in view between Paris and Bonn on both energy and environmental issues became apparent.[36] For years, Bonn had had to deal with bilateral problems arising out of French pollution of the Rhine, acid rain, and the construction of the French nuclear power plant at Cattenom, on the West German border. The Federal Republic also had a nuclear industry, however, and, despite its vocal environmental and antinuclear movements, it was determined not to let such issues stand in the way of good relations with France.[37]

Outside Europe, Bonn also turned a blind eye to events and issues with which it had little desire to associate, but that it knew were important to France's definition of its global interests. Despite widespread private condemnation of French actions in 1985 against the Greenpeace ship *Rainbow Warrior* in New Zealand waters, both government and opposition politicians in the Federal Republic were publicly circumspect.[38] Similarly, France's involvement with highly dubious governments in central Africa, Paris's arms sales policies in the Third World, and its atmospheric testing of nuclear weapons were treated with kid gloves by West German politicians and journalists.[39] The condemnation such policies would have received if pursued by the United States, for example, was spared the French government.

Effectively, Bonn sought to establish a division of labor: its acceptance, if not support, of French policies outside of Europe in exchange for French acceptance of West German policies there. Or, as Helmut Schmidt rather disingenuously characterized it, acquiescence in the French belief

> that after centuries of continuous spiritual and political development it is natural and legitimate for France to play a world role. But a nation of 55 million people cannot play such a role effectively if it does not have friends and allies who follow French leadership.[40]

Signs of Bonn's following French leadership around the world were few and far between, but West German rhetoric, at least, accorded France its global role.

The tacit division of labor was possible because, until the 1980s, neither Bonn nor Paris had to pay a very high price for the policies of its ally. West Germany's economy was strong enough to bear the financial burdens of both membership in the EC and the Ostpolitik. France's global role was generally supported by its other NATO allies, and countries like New Zealand had no interest in attempting to pressure Bonn to take their side against Paris. The Federal Republic was safely able to assume that France's overseas policies, even when distasteful, would extract no cost from West Germans.[41] Until concern for the Ostpolitik seemed capable of pulling Bonn away from its NATO commitments and French environmental and energy policies appeared potentially lethal as well as expensive and annoying, the two countries managed to agree where they could and otherwise remain silent. Bonn's attempt to put flesh and blood on the Ostpolitik skeleton may change their ability to do so.

The Burden of Auschwitz

In the 1970s, any comparison of the extent of relations between the Federal Republic and the countries of eastern Europe with that between France and West Germany would have seemed ludicrous. A decade later, the comparison is less farfetched. Certainly, the developing pattern is clear. Exchanges of university students and professors, sister cities relationships, joint economic ventures, and environmental-energy cooperation are proliferating between the Federal Republic and its eastern neighbors. For West Germans, the ties being reestablished east of the Elbe are an especially poignant reminder of their historical contribution to the development of modern Europe.

Helmut Schmidt said at Yale that Bonn's western neighbors "do not fully grasp . . . that the Germans carry a heavy burden from the great injury . . . inflicted upon them with respect to their national identity."[42] The former chancellor was referring to the division of his country, but the greatest injury to Germany's national identity is not political division or even the separation of its people. The spirit Bonn wishes to exorcise is the image of Germany in the eyes of its neighbors, especially in the west, as the one nation in Europe that has not, on balance, made a positive contribution to the history of the continent. The name of Germany brings to mind the name of Auschwitz.

West Germans themselves, in their current debates over historians' interpretations of their recent past, are clearly torn between believing the negative image and wanting to believe a more positive one.[43] A new era of peace, disarmament, economic prosperity, and political freedom throughout Europe, as a result of German initiatives, would clearly tip the scales toward a more positive self-image. Other western Europeans do not, indeed, "fully grasp" what that would mean to their German neighbors.

Ironically, then, to be more like the French, Bonn is intent on pursuing policies that have the potential to bring it into conflict with Paris. Amid their own "emotional confusion stirred by feelings of guilt, postwar achievement, atonement, pride and moral uncertainty," West Germans envy their French neighbor one thing:

> It is its respectability. That is what Bonn would like to have a share in. Diplomatic and political initiatives undertaken by France, even the most adventurous, are somehow acceptable to the world community. With a few exceptions, they seldom arouse deep resentment.[44]

In sharp contrast, West German policies "dare not be too assertive, lest Frenchmen and other Europeans remember [the German] role in two world wars."[45] With its support for a common European house and the

European peace order with which to furnish it, Bonn believes it has found policies that will restore a positive identity to the German nation and enable it to regain not only the respect of its neighbors but also its own self-respect. The same hope fueled the Frankreichpolitik in its early years.[46]

In that sense, Bonn's concern with the wounds inflicted on Germany's national identity reflects the historical legacy symbolized by Auschwitz. The other nations of Europe all have pages in their history books they would rather forget, but only Germans supported a government that made no secret of its intent to destroy the legacy of the eighteenth-century Enlightenment, to use the teachings of Christianity to justify expulsion and genocide, and to subjugate the rest of Europe in the service of a Germanic master race.[47] Nothing like it had been seen in the history of modern Europe, and in the early 1930s many Germans and early admirers of the Third Reich abroad could scarcely imagine that National Socialism would actually practice what it preached. Unfortunately, it did.

Their failure to look more closely at where their country was going and why has haunted the people of West Germany ever since. By the 1980s, political leadership was almost completely in the hands of those too young to have held responsible positions before 1945, and the question of individual guilt for the crimes of Nazi Germany was no longer, if it ever was, the Federal Republic's principal dilemma. The central issue was West Germans' ability to see in the actions of their elected political leaders and in the foreign policy of their country motives other than the accumulation of power for power's sake at work.

As a result, West German diplomats and politicians have an exceedingly difficult role. Their constituents demand a moral content to their foreign policy far beyond that demanded of their French, or even American, colleagues.[48] Over the past ten years, the higher purpose— beyond the survival and prosperity of the Federal Republic—that Bonn has made its own is the evolution of east-west detente into an entente between the states of eastern and western Europe. Instead of regarding Franco–West German entente and the European Community that accompanied it as an end in itself, West Germany has come to see them as a model for cooperation throughout the continent.[49] This evolution in attitude toward the Frankreichpolitik and the EC does not mean that West German support for them has declined. It does mean, however, that what Bonn expects of them today is quite different from its early expectations.

Whether France and the other members of the EC fully understand the implications of the Federal Republic's shifting attitudes toward its role in western Europe is not yet clear. For that matter, Bonn itself sometimes seems to be wavering between the 1960s and the 1990s, in part, no doubt, because of the bureaucratic division of labor within the foreign office, which makes the daily coordination of policies toward western and eastern Europe difficult. For West German diplomats, contacts and cooperation with France have become routine, but initiatives toward eastern Europe and the Soviet Union still receive political attention at the highest level. Such a pattern of priority to adversaries, not allies, is characteristic of not only the Federal Republic's foreign policy but also that of most countries, including the United States.[50] Inevitably, France was the focus of West German foreign policy at a time when turning a "uniformly awful" relationship into a productive one was the task at hand.[51] The same task confronts the Federal Republic in eastern Europe today.

The Challenge of Chernobyl

One of the areas in which Bonn has chosen to pursue this task is scientific and technological cooperation. The Federal Republic has, in the area of civil technology, clear advantages over all the countries of the Warsaw Pact, and its political leadership is well aware of the eastern European need for the expertise and equipment West Germans can provide. For their part, the state governments of Bavaria and Baden-Württemberg, where West Germany's high technology boom is centered, are as interested for economic reasons in encouraging technological export as Bonn is for political reasons.[52] Profit and politics are not the only reasons behind the Federal Republic's commitment to technological cooperation with eastern Europe, however.

At the International Atomic Energy Agency (IAEA) in 1986, the Federal Republic made its clearest statement of the importance of scientific and technological cooperation to West German foreign policy.[53] The issue of immediate concern to the IAEA members meeting in Vienna was the aftermath of the April 1986 accident at the Soviet nuclear plant at Chernobyl. The Federal Republic, with its proposal for IAEA action on the safety of nuclear facilities, had been one of the chief movers behind the three 1986 Vienna meetings designed to focus attention on the general issue of nuclear safety, as well as on Chernobyl.[54] Bonn had several issues with which to deal, not the least of which was, again, its geographic position and its many neighbors.

The Federal Republic, like France, is officially committed to the maintenance and expansion of nonmilitary nuclear power. In the aftermath of the 1973 OPEC oil embargo, the SPD-FDP coalition undertook a nuclear development program designed to reduce West German dependence on foreign oil. In the 1970s, the utilization of nuclear energy was also regarded as more environmentally sound than the continued use of high-polluting coal. Nevertheless, the growing environmental and antinuclear movements in the Federal Republic were already questioning the government's policy by the late 1970s. With the accident at Chernobyl, doubts about nuclear power moved into the political mainstream, with the SPD repudiating the support it had given nuclear energy while in the chancellery.[55]

For West German foreign policy, however, the domestic development of nuclear power was the least of its concerns. Whatever Bonn did at home, it was surrounded by states committed to nuclear energy—and by states committed to its abandonment. At the 1986 meetings of the IAEA, the Federal Republic's neighbor to the east, Austria, spoke out unequivocally against nuclear power.[56] Its neighbor and ally to the west, France, spoke just as eloquently in its defense, using, moreover, many of the same arguments: Third World development, environmental protection, and the rights of future generations.[57] Denmark, West Germany's neighbor to the north, affirmed its nonnuclear policy; Belgium confirmed its commitment to expand its nuclear program.[58] Further afield, Bonn's EC partners from Dublin and Athens joined Copenhagen in rejecting nuclear energy, and the Soviet Union agreed with France on the need to continue its development.[59]

No one reading the records of the IAEA debate could fail to be struck by the effect of such disparate views on the West German commitment to international cooperation. On the one hand, its geographic position alone gave the Federal Republic an undeniable interest in its neighbors' development of their nuclear programs. The level of French technology and training in the management of nuclear energy was acknowledged to be one of the best, if not the best, in the world, but the results of human error or a failure of quality control would very likely be felt throughout Europe, not only within the borders of France. Bonn had even more reason to support international technological cooperation when it looked eastward. Not only did its geographic position and population density expose the Federal Republic to the same risks it faced from the west (and from its own nuclear plants) but the level of political and technological management in the countries of the Warsaw Pact posed additional risks.[60]

The American foreign policy debate over the desirability of maintaining technological supremacy over the Soviet Union had little resonance in West Germany.[61] Bonn was increasingly unlikely to take any comfort from the technological backwardness of its eastern neighbors. Unlike its French ally, West Germany was also disinclined to treat technology as a matter of national pride and status. Instead, Bonn's foreign minister described new technologies as a means to "influence behavior and societal structures in both the West and the East." They "promote[d] individual initiative, responsibility, and decentralization" and "enhance[d] the consciousness of European identity."[62] Whether the issue was the chemical pollution of the Rhine by industrial sources in France and Switzerland, the winter smogs produced by the GDR's high-sulfur coal, or the contamination of Europe's harvest by radiation from Chernobyl, the lesson for the Federal Republic was the same: the health and well-being of West Germans and all their neighbors demanded the development of reliable technology and the education and training to use it throughout Europe.[63]

As a result, the Federal Republic was a prime mover behind two 1986 IAEA conventions dealing with nuclear safety. Both of them, the Convention on Early Notification of a Nuclear Accident and the Convention on Assistance in the Case of a Nuclear Accident or Radiological Emergency, adopted on September 26, 1986, entered into force that year.[64] West Germany's first minister of the environment—a cabinet position created as a result of the accident at Chernobyl—spoke at Vienna of his country's support for the two agreements and of the responsibility of governments to "control and thus justify the risks that are undoubtedly associated with nuclear energy."[65] This could not be done "on the national scale, by one country alone," but only by international agreement. Only through international cooperation could states "technologically and thus morally justify the use of nuclear energy." The leitmotiv of West German foreign policy reappeared in the minister's statement: "We only fulfill our national obligations if we are aware of our responsibility towards the international community, that is to say, our responsibility towards all human beings."[66]

In 1986, before the IAEA meetings, Bonn signed an agreement with Moscow on scientific and technical cooperation, including basic research in nuclear physics and the planning, operation, and safety of nuclear power plants; additional agreements on the construction of a high-temperature reactor and nuclear safety were signed in October 1988 at the Kohl-Gorbachev summit.[67] West Germany's 1987 environmental and scientific agreements with the GDR and Czechoslovakia also dealt with the management of transboundary pollution problems and the transfer of control technology.[68] The cultural exchange agreement signed in 1986 with the GDR and similar agreements with Poland and the USSR provided for the exchange of university students and professors working in the basic and applied sciences, as well as in the humanities.[69]

From the West German perspective, the contacts established by these agreements were being *re*established. Scientific, technological, economic, and cultural interaction between Germans and their eastern neighbors was the norm, not the exception, until the middle of the twentieth century. Helmut Schmidt recalled this history in his description of his home, Hamburg, the Elbe River port that is still the destination of much of the trade carried on the inland waterways of east-central Europe. The origins of Hamburg's modern trading relationships with the Baltic ports of Poland, Scandinavia, and the USSR extend back to the Middle Ages. Ironically, this central location and the Elbe's role as part of the inner-German border have also given Hamburg and the neighboring West German state of Lower Saxony some of the more serious transborder pollution problems in Europe, thanks to the Warsaw Pact states' lack of environmental controls.[70]

In the months after Chernobyl, the readiness to discuss common environmental problems and to acknowledge their need for western control technology and expertise was a major change in the foreign policies of the Soviet Union and its allies. The countries of the Warsaw Pact had refused to participate in the United Nations Conference on the Environment in Stockholm in 1972; officially, socialist states did not have environmental problems.[71] Unfortunately, as many scientists from the Soviet Union and the countries of eastern Europe were well aware, socialist states had even worse environmental problems in the making. The combination of political blindness and the level of technology in their countries meant that the pollution of streams, lakes, and groundwater, acid rain damage to forests, air pollution, and the effects of strip mining and other land-(mis)management techniques went unchecked for nearly two decades after the environmental movement began to change concepts of growth in the west.[72]

The accident at Chernobyl was a turning point not only in the nuclear power debate but also with regard to the broader environmental health and security issues finally being faced in eastern Europe. In the final analysis, those issues led back to the central concern of Bonn's east-west strategy: freedom of movement and access to information. The Federal Republic rightly saw that, like it or not, their environmental problems at home and with each other would encourage the countries of eastern Europe to look for cooperation with western Europe and to provide the accurate technical information required by such cooperation.[73]

In this sense, Chernobyl, like Auschwitz, was important not only as a single event but also as a constant factor influencing Bonn's foreign policy. The Federal Republic could not alter the history that left it with the legacy of Auschwitz; neither could it change the industrial and scientific revolution that made such incidents as Chernobyl possible, although not inevitable. In his speech at the Danube-European Institute in the summer of 1986, Foreign Minister Genscher reiterated West

Germany's conviction that the technological and ecological interdependence of Europe was a fact. Its political divisions, whether among the members of the European Community or along the Elbe, had no bearing on this reality, except to make more or less difficult the cooperation necessary to deal with that interdependence.[74]

In its assessment of the Chernobyl factor, Bonn found itself at odds with Paris. A cartoon that appeared in the Federal Republic in early May 1986 captured the West Germans' mixture of incredulity and admiration when confronted by the French faith in the relevance of political borders to such problems as Chernobyl. Imposed on a map of France, a gendarme facing eastward extended his right arm and blew his whistle at a westward-drifting cloud of nuclear pollution, saying to it: "Stop! This is France!"[75] Although they could not help but admire the extent to which France's devotion to national autarchy had survived the twentieth century, West Germans were more than a little exasperated by the cast of mind that made this possible. It seemed to them to lie behind an entire range of French policies that made cooperation difficult, from Cattenom to the atmospheric testing of nuclear weapons.[76]

The Trauma of Hiroshima

From Paris's perspective, what made cooperation with Bonn difficult was an apparently naive West German approach to the concept of *raison d'état.*[77] One of the great strengths of French foreign policy remained the sincerity with which its constituency equated French leadership in the world with the general interest of the international system, a quality that was also—usually—an asset to American foreign policy as well.[78] East of the Rhine, the lack of self-doubt that plagued French leaders continued to be a cause of astonishment and some envy in the 1980s. West German diplomats and politicians did not live in so simple a world.[79] Instead, they lived in a world in which political decisions, at different times and at different places, had made possible Auschwitz, Chernobyl, and Hiroshima. At its core, West German foreign policy was far more pessimistic than its French or American counterparts.[80] Arguably, it was also far more pessimistic than its Soviet counterpart.

The pessimism of the West German worldview was somewhat mitigated, however, by the pragmatism of its foreign policy practitioners. The clearheadedness with which Bonn's diplomats had identified areas for east-west cooperation, on the model of the Frankreichpolitik, was more than matched at the state and local level. The east-west Locarno from below that began to develop in the 1980s reflected the West German experience with France in its pace, its nonpartisanship, its participants, and its modest expectations. In other words, West Germans adapted to the tempo of their foreign counterparts, looked to sports, music, and other areas of specific common interests to develop initial exchange programs, and recognized the political purposes to which "nonpolitical" relations between universities, schools, and cities could be put.

In the pursuit of West German foreign policy at this level, the connection between Hiroshima and Auschwitz was especially clear. If the establishment of a dialogue between the peoples of Europe was possible, then avoiding the armed conflict that would almost surely lead to more Hiroshimas might also be possible. In Paris and Washington, this West German concern with nuclear holocaust was usually analyzed in connection with Dresden and Berlin: the fear of again being the victims of war.[81] This analysis missed the point. The physical destruction of a war in central Europe, especially in a nuclear age, certainly had an impact on West German attitudes, but the psychological factor was even more important. West Germans did not fear being the victims of another Hiroshima as much as they feared being its perpetrator, even in self-defense. In addition to Auschwitz, the burden would be too much for the national identity to bear. Without an equivalent experience in their past, Bonn's allies had difficulty understanding fully the West German concerns for the future.

Exorcising the legacy of Auschwitz is an aspect of east-west detente unknown to the Federal Republic's western allies and one especially difficult for them to handle. Neither West Germany's geographic position nor its economic interests are unique; other western European countries share Bonn's concern for the security of their trade and borders. However, the issues of Germany's own making, whether tangible or psychological, are of a different order. West Germans are required to define a foreign policy role for themselves in a European and world order still based ultimately on the use of force, but they, of all nations, are perhaps most genuinely convinced of the ultimate futility of force as a means to an end.[82] Their history provides ample evidence that the short-term solutions force seems to offer are no answer in the long run.

Arguably, they are wrong to generalize. The histories of other countries give equally ample evidence of decisions reached because of the use or threat of force that have proved both durable and desirable, from the national independence of most states to the abolition of slavery. West Germany's two principal allies, France and the United States, are among the countries whose existence and form of government clearly result from the initially illegal use of force against existing authority. Paris and Washington are much closer to each other than either of them is to Bonn in their attitude toward the marshalling of power and the use of force in their foreign policies.[83] This alone hinders them from arriving at an understanding of the aims and expectations of West German diplomacy, and equally blocks the Federal Republic from comprehending its two allies' "certain idea" of global responsibility.

The observation and analysis of the twenty-fifth anniversary of the Elysée Treaty in January 1988 brought indications of a new West German willingness to face the differences in outlook and policy between Bonn and Paris. The events of the past decade, from the INF deployment debate to Greenpeace and Chernobyl, had made ignoring them increasingly difficult. The events of the next decade would indicate whether those differences were such that the expectations of the early postwar years had remained unfulfilled. If the rhetoric of the early Frankreichpolitik—and of Schuman's and DeGaulle's "Deutschlandpolitik"—had genuinely become reality, then the future of Europe would be one of leadership by the two western neighbors. If the mistrust of the 1920s could be rekindled in the 1990s, however, both France and the Federal Republic might be condemned, not again to war and chaos, but to impotence and irrelevance in shaping the future of the continent.

Notes

1. Zbigniew Brzezinski, "The Future of Yalta," *Foreign Affairs* 63, no. 2, Winter 1984/5): 296: "while the Europeans resent their historic partition, they fear almost as much a reunited Germany." Common wisdom though this is in the United States, it is at least debatable whether Europeans fear a reunited Germany because of what policies that state would pursue or because of the price that would have to be paid to Moscow to obtain reunification. See also Christoph Bertram, "Akrobat auf dem Schwebebalken," *Die Zeit*, February 17, 1989.

2. "The French," wrote Carlo Schmid, "will only be able to forget when they are certain that the Germans will never forget"; the leader of his own party made all the western allies wonder if the Germans had learned anything at all. Quoted in Willi Emrich, *Französisch-deutsche Freundschaftswoche vom 8. bis 16. Oktober 1960 in Frankfurt-am-Main* (Frankfurt: Verlag Waldemar Kramer, 1961), p. 89.

3. Beginning with Kurt Schumacher and again, after the golden days of western relations with the SPD from 1960 to 1975, opposition from the Social Democrats to nearly all the elements of western economic and security cooperation supported by Washington and Paris has been the rule more often than the exception. Needless to say, for the past decade the Greens have been even more of an anathema to Paris than the left wing of the SPD, given their opposition to NATO, nuclear power, and economic growth. See Ernst Weisenfeld, *Welches Deutschland soll es sein?* (München: C.H. Beck, 1986), pp. 152–153.

4. David Lawday, "France and Germany—The Odd Couple," *Economist* 271, no. 7082 (May 26, 1979): 28.

5. Brigitte Sauzay's *Le vertige allemand* (Paris: Olivier Orban, 1985) and Stephane Roussel's *Les collines de Berlin* (Paris: Mazarine, 1985) came at the end of a flood of articles and books asking, as did Jean François-Poncet in *Le monde* in 1981, "What's Germany up to now?" The West German Embassy in Paris was concerned enough in 1985 to sponsor a conference on the image of Germans in France forty years after the war. Conversation with Alfred Grosser, Paris, December 1985. A new wave seemed to be beginning in 1989; see, for example, Alain Minc, "Où va l'Allemagne?" *L'Express* no. 1963 (February 24, 1989): 20.

6. The French were not the only ones. In 1982, *Der Spiegel* put out a special report by Jürgen Leinemann, *Die Angst der Deutschen,* which was subtitled "observations on the nation's frame of mind." One of Leinemann's observations (pp. 81–82): "Without a consensus on the past and a common hope for the future, there is no hope for a more or less agreed-upon interpretation of the present."

7. David Gress, *Peace and Survival* (Stanford: Hoover Institution Press, 1985), pp. 68–76.

8. Fritz Stern, "Germany in a Semi-Gaullist Europe," *Foreign Affairs* 58, no. 4 (Spring 1980): 878, wrote that "In that extraordinary interlude in European history . . . from 1948 to 1973, one had assumed . . . that European peace was built on a permanently provisional solution of the German problem."

9. Sauzay, *Le vertige allemand,* pp. 253–255.

10. Hans-Peter Schwarz, *Die gezähmten Deutschen* (Stuttgart: DVA, 1985), p. 107, reprimands West Germans for their "fascination with the apparent impotence of the Federal Republic."

11. Used by, among others, Helmut Schmidt, in *A Grand Strategy for the West* (New Haven: Yale University Press, 1985), p. 54.

12. One of the more hysterical books, which accuses all of the *western* powers of seeing Germany as "booty or battlefield" is Oswald Feiler, *Moskau und die Deutsche Frage* (Krefeld: SINUS-Verlag, 1984). See especially the last chapter, designed to warm French hearts, on the desirability of reestablishing the "Reich" to the Memel border, in collaboration with the Soviet Union. The chapter is entitled: "In spite of everything, Germany has a future—but not in the West."

13. Schwarz, *Die gezähmten Deutschen,* pp. 170–171, compares the danger of West Germany's "unconditional pacifists" misleading the Soviet Union today with the false impression created by French and British pacifists in the 1930s; he is also scathing in his condemnation of Bonn's "official characterization" of its foreign policy as "peace policy," which only encourages public opinion to think more highly than it should of the "defeatist pacifists."

14. See, for example, the Greens' 1987 electoral program, section 5, "Einseitig abrüsten—Wir machen den ersten Schritt"; also *Friedensmanifest der Grünen,* Offenbach, October 2–4, 1981; and Matthias Küntzel, "Bonn will die europäische Atomstreitmacht," in the program for the Greens' seminar on Franco–West German military cooperation, Bonn, December 6-7, 1985.

15. See the Greens' *Militärgrossmacht Westeuropa,* attacking Paris's and Bonn's efforts to reactivate Western European Union (WEU).

16. See, especially, *Friedensmanifest der Grünen*, pp. 11–14.

17. Gress's chapter, "Eleven Neutralist Propositions," pp. 173–188, is the best summary in English of West German national neutralism and its illusions.

18. As Lewis J. Edinger, *Kurt Schumacher* (Stanford: Stanford University Press, 1965), pp. 155–159, points out, Schumacher remembered what the Communists had done in the 1920s to undermine the SPD and the Weimar Republic; as suspicious as he was of the motives of the western allies, he was even more so of Germans who took their orders from Moscow.

19. The west's *Feindbilder* (enemy images) and occupation mentality supposedly are shared by the West German government, which—to paraphrase Schumacher—acts as a "government of the Allies." Gress, *Peace and Survival*, pp. 181–184, discusses the growing tendency of the neonationalists on the left to argue "that West and East Germans and, in particular, the West and East German governments had common interests different from those of the United States and the Soviet Union." Schwarz, *Die gezähmten Deutschen*, pp. 134–135, is scathingly accurate in his critique of those "peace researchers" who have forgotten the lessons of the European balance of power and who believe Germans can opt out of power politics.

20. See Helmut Schmidt's *A Grand Strategy for the West*, his *Die Zeit* discussion with Richard Nixon, "Europa ist nich dekadent," July 11, 1986; and his *Die Zeit* articles, "Null-lösung im deutschen Interesse," May 15, 1987, "Der General und seine Erben," May 8, 1987, and "Europa muss sich selbst behaupten," November 28, 1986.

21. See Edwina S. Campbell, "Dilemmas of an Atlantic Dialogue," in Gale Mattox and John Vaughan, eds., *Germany Through American Eyes* (Boulder, CO: Westview, 1989).

22. Weisenfeld, *Welches Deutschland*, p. 175.

23. Feiler's book does this with more hysteria than most, but as Gress points out, the tendency to characterize German interests as different from those of either both superpowers or the west alone is common, and the identification of German interests with the west, the hallmark of the 1950s, is virtually nonexistent in the current political climate of the Federal Republic. The usual critique, as Gress notes (*Peace and Survival*, p. 184), begins with the concept of unique German interests, but then drifts eastward with the assumption that the USSR, as a European power, "shares a commitment to peace with western Europe" lacking in the United States. Even Helmut Schmidt (*A Grand Strategy*, p. 56), with his remark that "Germany [must] be politically oriented toward the West and bound closely to it," implies that "Germany" is not inherently a part of "the West," a rather remarkable assumption and a thought unlikely to occur to the leaders of any other NATO or EC country.

24. See Weisenfeld, *Welches Deutschland*, p. 116, on Pompidou's concern that West Germans could be tempted to acquiesce in a "pax Sovietica."

25. Ibid., p. 154.

26. Bonn's consultations with Paris on CSCE, using the EC's European Political Cooperation (EPC) process, have helped ensure this. See: Michel Tatu, "Aussenpolitik zwischen Ost und West," in Robert Picht, ed., *Das Bündnis*

im Bündnis (Berlin: Severin and Siedler, 1982), p. 84; Tatu's October 28, 1988, *Die Zeit* article, "Gute Reise, Kanzler!"; and Weisenfeld, *Welches Deutschland*, p. 122.

27. As a victory for the "Atlanticists"; if there are any 1950s-style Atlanticists left in West Germany, they are well hidden. In his 1985 Yale lectures, Helmut Schmidt (*A Grand Strategy*, p. 53), skirts the issue, noting that he changed from an Atlanticist to a Francophile "as a consequence of my own insight into the geopolitical situation of my country," not because he had been disillusioned by the United States. This is typical Schmidt—polite, but with the definite implication that he *was* disappointed with the U.S. lack of "insight into the geopolitical situation" of Germany. Also typically, Schmidt was more forthcoming when he discussed the same issue in German, in his final speech to the Bundestag, calling it a mistake to have insisted, as he and his colleagues did, on an "Atlanticist" preamble to the 1963 Elysée Treaty. See Helmut Schmidt, *Die nüchterne Leidenschaft zur praktischen Vernunft* (Berlin: Verlag Rainer Röll, 1987), pp. 42–43. See also Minc, "Où va l'Allemagne?," p. 20.

28. The CDU-CSU-FDP government declared in its program, presented to the Bundestag on May 4, 1983, that it would further develop the Ost- and Deutschlandpolitik initiated by the first SPD-FDP coalition and contained in the CSCE Final Act and the series of bilateral treaties signed from 1970 to 1973. The government program is contained in *Freiheit, Mitmenschlichkeit, Verantwortung* (Bonn: Bundespresseamt, 1983).

29. In Vienna in 1986, Genscher interpreted western European cooperation in a way that would no doubt have surprised Konrad Adenauer:

The process of unification of the twelve democracies linked in the European Community, with the goal of European Union, has a pan-European and global perspective. The future-oriented development of the EC would lose much of its force if it did not have the goal of simultaneously contributing to east-west cooperation in Europe. It falls to the Federal Republic of Germany inside the EC and to Austria outside it to call attention continuously to the needs of Europe as a whole—from the Atlantic to the Urals. The Federal Republic does this in conjunction with France, with which it has a unique relationship.

Hans-Dietrich Genscher, "Perspektiven einer europäischen Friedensordnung," Vienna, August 27, 1986, *Bulletin* 96 (August 29, 1986): 810. See also Gesine Schwan, "Mitten im ganzen Europa," *Die Zeit*, January 27, 1989.

30. Commenting on the 1920s, Jon Jacobson, *Locarno Diplomacy* (Princeton: Princeton University Press, 1972), p. 378, wrote:

Preoccupied with China, Russia, and the naval rivalry with the United States, [British Foreign Secretary] Chamberlain was content to entrust Briand, and to a lesser extent Stresemann, with the determination of how differences between them would be resolved. With regard to Europe, Britain occupied what Chamberlain called "a semi-detached position."

Although the anti-EC consequences of British detachment have usually been stressed (Schmidt, *A Grand Strategy*, p. 52: "Almost no woman or man in office in Whitehall thinks that the Atlantic Ocean . . . is broader than the channel"), one of the other consequences is that both London and Washington have almost always been more than willing to leave to the French and the Germans "the determination of how differences between them would be resolved." The major exception was American pressure to rearm Germany, and even then, two U.S. administrations of both parties waited three years for Bonn and Paris to play out the EDC negotiations. See Robert McGeehan, *The German Rearmament Question* (Urbana: University of Illinois Press, 1971), pp. 228–238.

31. Schmidt, *A Grand Strategy*, p. 53.
32. Ibid., p. 56.
33. Ibid., p. 55.
34. Stern, "Germany in a Semi-Gaullist Europe," p. 874, noted that their bilateral relationship in the late 1970s helped disguise West Germany's increasingly important global role.
35. Lawday, "France and Germany," p. 28:

[The Germans] are willing to forgive the French almost anything, including their nationalist ways and their obstinacy at the negotiating table, for the sake of maintaining the new friendship. Conduct which, from Britain or Italy, would be considered unacceptable tends to be regarded by the Germans as all part of the fun of courtship when it comes from France.

36. The differences between the vigorous French defense of nuclear power and the more circumspect West German vote of confidence in it at the Fall 1986 IAEA meeting in Vienna appeared minor, judging from the official speeches. Behind those speeches, however, are vastly different public attitudes toward nuclear energy in the two countries. By early 1988, according to a *Der Spiegel* poll, a majority within all West German political parties (CDU-CSU, 53 percent; FDP, 58 percent; SPD, 82 percent; Greens, 92 percent) favored the gradual phasing out of nuclear energy, while both civilian and military nuclear power enjoy broad public support in France. See statements by France and the Federal Republic of Germany, Thirtieth Regular Session, IAEA, Vienna, September–October 1986 *Der*; *Spiegel*, no. 9 (February 29, 1988): 47.
37. Roger de Weck, *Die Zeit* articles: "Misstöne und Verstimmungen," October 31, 1986; "Als wäre nichts geschehen," September 26, 1986; and "Eine Freundschaft ohne Wärme," January 29, 1988. For a rare French plea to listen to what West Germans are saying, see Luc Ferry, "Comprendre la RFA," *L'Express* no. 1963 (February 24, 1989): 21.
38. In Bonn in 1985, shortly after the French attack on the *Rainbow Warrior*, I discussed West Germany's circumspect, to say the least, reaction to the attack with a leading member of the Bundestag. I commented that, had it been the United States and not France, there would have been far more (and far more critical) press coverage, public demonstrations, and political criticism, from all

parties. He not only agreed but also remarked that he personally had pulled his punches when discussing the Greenpeace affair, precisely because it was France that was involved. Later, I had similar discussions with members of the West German Foreign Office, all of whom agreed that Germans, whether government officials, journalists, or private citizens, were far less likely to criticize France in public than they were the United States. Throughout this period, from the interception of the *Achille Lauro* hijackers to the bombing of Tripoli, their readiness to do the latter was evident.

39. Conversations in Bonn and Paris, 1985 and 1986. The Greens pointed out in a televised election debate in November 1986 that Bonn and Paris have failed to address fundamental differences on many security and economic issues, especially outside Europe; they got a rather hysterical reaction from the FDP foreign minister, who accused them of endangering West Germany's postwar rapprochement with France.

40. Schmidt, *A Grand Strategy*, p. 55.

41. Lawday, "France and Germany," p. 31, asserted that "long-term French and German international interests converge. It would still be difficult for Germany to send troops anywhere, except on some minor antiterrorist mission." Perhaps, but in my 1986 discussions with West German Foreign Office members, I found their reactions to the opposite scenario far more interesting: the possibility that Bonn might one day be asked to pay a price for Paris's independent foreign policies outside Europe, a terrorist attack on a French nuclear facility, for example. The West German diplomats were genuinely surprised, I think, by a scenario they had not considered but admitted was not improbable.

42. Schmidt, *A Grand Strategy*, p. 53.

43. The "historians' debate" that began in 1986 is only the current round in the ongoing West German preoccupation with the German past and its implications for the future. See Gordon Craig, "The War of the German Historians," *New York Review of Books*, January 15, 1987. For a good summary of the nation-state dilemma and its impact on Franco-German relations, see Wolfgang Mommsen, "Auf der Suche nach nationaler Identität: zur Diskontinuität deutscher Staatlichkeit," in *Das Bündnis*, pp. 40–66. See also, among numerous *Die Zeit* articles: Wilhelm Ribhegge, "Stellenweise Glatteis," February 13, 1987; Robert Leicht, "Nur das Hinsehen macht uns frei," January 2, 1987; Ernst Nolte, "Die Sache auf den Kopf gestellt," October 31, 1986; Thomas Nipperdey, "Unter der Herrschaft des Verdachts," October 17, 1986; and Hagen Schulze, "Fragen die wir stellen müssen," October 3, 1986. The entire spring/summer 1988 issue of *New German Critique*, no. 44, was devoted to the historians' debate. It includes translations of several of the key West German contributions and commentary on them.

44. Lawday, "France and Germany," p. 31.

45. Ibid., p. 28.

46. Werner Weidenfeld, *Konrad Adenauer und Europa* (Bonn: Europa Union Verlag, 1976), p. 191.

47. Primo Levi, *The Drowned and the Saved* (New York: Summit Books, 1988), p. 21:

The Nazi concentration camp system still remains a *unicum*, both in its extent and its quality. At no other place or time has one seen such a phenomenon so unexpected and so complex; never have so many human lives been extinguished in so short a time, and with so lucid a combination of technological ingenuity, fanaticism, and cruelty.

48. Schwarz, *Die gezähmten Deutschen*, pp. 54–56.
49. In his fall 1986 speech to the Atlantic Treaty Association, Chancellor Kohl declared that the European Community was "a model, which should be an example of how nations throughout Europe can live together and cooperate with each other." Helmut Kohl, "Ecksteine deutscher Politik," Mainz, September 17, 1986, *Bulletin* 106 (Bundespresseamt, September 23, 1986): 900. In his memoirs, *Begegnungen und Einsichten* (Hamburg: Hoffmann und Campe, 1976), p. 641, Willy Brandt wrote:

The model case of Franco-German cooperation has made clear what positive energies can be awakened for the durable anchoring of peace on our continent. I remain convinced that we should understand the policy of European unification and the policy of detente as two great parallel actions which depend on each other.

50. The Auswärtiges Amt is certainly not unique in this regard. As Stanley Hoffmann, "Choices," *Foreign Policy* no. 12 (Fall 1973): 32, wrote: "Modern government—not just in the United States—seems to be able to deal best only with the urgent." I worked on the French Desk of the West German Foreign Office for three months in 1986, and there are advantages to the routine that characterizes Franco–West German relations in the 1980s, among them, the expertise, commitment, and breadth of experience of diplomats on both sides who have worked with each other for years, sometimes decades. The disadvantage, in a world of crisis management, is the lack of high-level attention devoted to issues unlikely to produce spectacular successes or failures. I have elsewhere (*Consultation and Consensus in NATO* [Lanham, MD: University Press of America, 1985], pp. 157–163) characterized these issues, usually with allies, as "cooperative/non-time-sensitive" issues; relations with adversaries usually involve "confrontation/close of business" issues that require high-level political decisions and make diplomatic careers. Perhaps in the nature of things, this means that Franco–West German relations have become, as Richard Neff ("NATO Political Consultation–Fact or Myth?", *NATO Review* 23 [January 1975]: 9) said of NATO consultation, "workaday and blue collar, nether a noisemaker nor a newsmaker." Chancellor Kohl described his November 1988 summit with François Mitterrand in much the same way, but with a more upbeat tone, when he said, "The sensation is that there is no sensation." Quoted in *The Week in Germany* (New York: German Information Center), November 10, 1988.
51. Lawday, "France and Germany," p. 36.
52. Conversations at the Baden-Württemberg Ministry of Economic Affairs, Stuttgart, December 1986.

53. Statement by the Federal Minister for the Environment, Nature Conservation and Nuclear Safety, First IAEA Special Session, Vienna, September 24, 1986.

54. "Explanatory Memorandum Submitted by the Federal Republic of Germany," IAEA Board of Governors/2257, May 14, 1986, and "Measures to Strengthen International Cooperation on the Safety of Nuclear Installations" (Draft resolution submitted by the Federal Republic of Germany), IAEA board of Governors/2258, Vienna, May 20, 1986.

55. "Election Program of the Social Democratic Party," Nuremberg, August 1986. For an analysis of the SPD's security platform, see Edwina S. Campbell, "Nuremberg and Beyond: Defining a New SPD Security Policy" in *Security Perspectives of the West German Left: The SPD and the Greens in Opposition* (Cambridge, MA, and McLean, VA: Institute for Foreign Policy Analysis and Pergamon-Brassey's, 1989), pp. 40–65.

56. Statement by the Federal Minister for Foreign Affairs of the Republic of Austria, First IAEA Special Session, Vienna, September 24, 1986.

57. Discours de l'Administrateur Général du Commissariat à l'Energie Atomique (France), Vienna, September 29, 1986.

58. Allocution du Secrétaire d'Etat à l'Energie (Belgium) and Statement by the Danish Minister for the Environment, Vienna, September 26, 1988.

59. Statement by the Head of the USSR Delegation to the Special Session of the IAEA General Conference, Vienna, September 24, 1986, and "Programme for Establishing an International Regime for the Safe Development of Nuclear Energy" (Proposals by the USSR), IAEA General Conference GC(SPL.I)/8, September 8, 1986; Statement by the Delegation of Greece and Statement by the Irish Minister of State for Foreign Affairs, Vienna, September 25, 1988.

60. Discussion of transborder nuclear safety issues with members of the IAEA Secretariat and the West German IAEA Delegation, Vienna, November 1986.

61. Genscher, "Perspektiven," p. 811: "I have often warned against a technological division of Europe. Cooperation in Europe must adapt to the state of technology, not yesterday's technology, but the technology of today and of tomorrow."

62. Ibid.

63. Ibid.: "Out of date, dangerous, and environmentally unsound methods of production and power plants pose chronic and acute ecological problems for all of us."

64. Conversations with IAEA and West German officials, Vienna, November 1986. See also "Draft of a Final Document—Special Session of the General Conference" (Note by the Director General) GC (SPL.l)/4, Vienna, September 24, 1986, and IAEA Press Release PR 86/8, Vienna, May 22, 1986.

65. Statement by the Federal Minister for the Environment, Nature Conservation and Nuclear Safety, First IAEA Special Session, Vienna, September 24, 1986.

66. Ibid.

67. *The Week in Germany*, October 28, 1988, and July 25, 1986.

68. *The Week in Germany*, June 12, 1987, and October 9, 1987.
69. *Dokumentation zur Deutschlandpolitik* (Bonn: Bundespresseamt, 1986), pp. 261–266, and *Deutschland-Nachrichten* (New York: German Information Office), November 18, 1987.
70. Schmidt, *Grand Strategy*, p. 26. See also Karl Schlögel, *Die Mitte liegt ostwärts* (Berlin: Siedler, 1986), pp. 39–55. In November 1988, Bonn was finally able to announce that talks with the GDR on cleaning up the Elbe would begin in early 1989, despite the two countries' continuing disagreement on the exact location of the inner-German border where it follows the river. *The Week in Germany*, November 18, 1988.
71. Statement by the Secretary of State on the Stockholm Environment Conference, Department of State Press Release 133, June 5, 1972.
72. David A. Kay and Eugene Skolnikoff, eds., *World Eco-Crisis: International Organizations in Response* (Madison: University of Wisconsin Press, 1972).
73. IAEA and West German officials both confirmed that more than rhetoric was behind the USSR's proposals for international cooperation (GC (SPL.I)/8):

    Events [like Chernobyl] show how small, in fact, is the world we live in, how great is the interdependence of States. The realities of the nuclear and space ages make it imperative for the peoples to see themselves as members of one family on planet Earth. The conclusion that the Soviet Union has come to, following the Chernobyl accident, is clear and unambiguous: wide-ranging international cooperation and joint efforts are necessary to guarantee nuclear safety in the broad sense of the word.

74. Genscher, "Perspektiven," p. 810: Protecting the lives and well-being of our peoples requires that we be able to judge the environmental hazards originating in the territory of other states. These hazards know no political or ideological border. Seveso and Chernobyl are warnings. They were not only recognized in the West."
75. In the *Badische Zeitung* (Freiburg im Breisgau), May 1986.
76. See *L'Express*'s dossier on the twenty-fifth anniversary of the Elysée Treaty, "France-Allemagne: le drôle de couple," January 22, 1988, pp. 41–51.
77. Schwarz, *Die gezähmten Deutschen*, pp. 143–151.
78. In his introduction to the collection of his speeches published before the March 1986 National Assembly elections, *Refléxions sur la politique extérieure de la France* (Paris: Fayard, 1986), p. 10, François Mitterrand asked if his country "should cease to be what the centuries have made of France." His answer (p. 13): "No, patriotism is not dead!" While working in the Auswärtiges Amt, I wrote a commentary on Mitterrand's book; its ideas and much of its phraseology were virtually identical to that in Ronald Reagan's 1986 State of the Union message, delivered shortly before. The French president (pp. 18–19) spoke of the importance of French independence of action, which he called "a way of seeing things, a belief in oneself, a will to endure."
79. Conversations in Bonn, 1985 and 1986.
80. The much discussed "Europessimism," and its accompanying symptoms in

the early 1980s, was more a West German disease than a western European one. Roussel, *Les collines,* pp. 287–288, remarked that "History seems to have condemned the German people to a perpetual search for its own identity." Already "cut off from the world of yesterday," the German past, by the Third Reich, they had also lost "their unconditional faith in America" and the dream of a united western Europe that they had embraced in the 1950s. Like Faust, says Roussel, Germans once sold their soul to the devil in return for the promise of "a new youth, a Reich that would dominate the world," and, since being liberated from the bargain, have not regained their balance. See also Leinemann, *Die Angst,* p. 112: "The German past all too easily provides examples and vocabulary which distort the current situation." Minc ("Où va l'Allemagne?," p. 20) remarks that "relations with the East are reborn, the American tie is weakening, the European dream remains."

81. Schwarz, *Die gezähmten Deutschen,* p. 166.
82. Ibid., pp. 49, 57–59.
83. Compare the opening lines of the 1985 West German Defense White Book with the opening line of the Minister of Defense's introduction to *The 1984–1988 French Defence Programme.* From the latter: "In an international environment characterized by a multiplicity of threats and with a world-wide economic crisis adding to the tension, France must have the means to ensure her security, preserve her independence and fulfill her international obligations." From *Zur Lage und Entwicklung der Bundeswehr:* "The security policy of the Federal Government serves the maintenance of peace in freedom. It is a policy of peace."

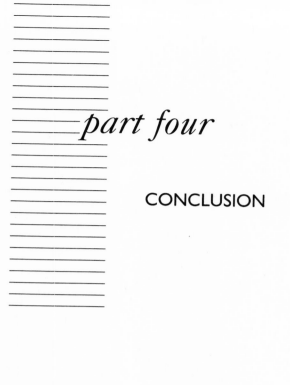

part four

CONCLUSION

8

IDENTITY AND RESPONSIBILITY: GERMANY'S PAST AND EUROPE'S FUTURE

There Is No Pendulum

The first thirty years in the history of the Federal Republic were marked by an effort on the part of West Germans to reiterate and reinforce their ties to western Europe. They seemed conscious of the fragility of their country's claim to membership in the western community.[1] The hopes placed in the first expansion of the European Community, the praises sung of the warm relationship between the French president and the West German chancellor during the Giscard-Schmidt years, and the intensity with which mainstream politicians sought to ignore growing domestic disenchantment with postwar West German society all testified to Bonn's self-conscious pursuit of a role within the west that would reaffirm the political rehabilitation of a defeated nation. One of the characteristics of the 1980s was a decline in the manifestations of this search for acceptance by its western European and Atlantic partners in the foreign policy of the Federal Republic.[2] Is the search over?

In many respects, it is. The rumblings of discontent with the Federal Republic that emanated from Paris and Washington throughout the 1980s reflected, in large part, their lack of preparedness for the change in tone and emphasis in Bonn's diplomacy. For the first time in their relationship, West Germany's political leaders seemed not to care very much what their American or French counterparts thought of a particular course of action; worse than that, they let their disinterest show.[3] Worried observers on the Seine and the Potomac naturally began asking if the changed tone meant major substantive changes as well; if so, then whither Germany, again?

The response to the new West German diplomacy has come most clearly from Paris. With the fall of the Schmidt government in 1982,

French foreign policy faced the prospect of a new situation in Bonn: a nonpartisan West German foreign policy simultaneously *less* Atlanticist than France's and *more* determined to do something about the division of Europe into east-west blocs than General DeGaulle had ever been. The combination was a new factor in the Franco-German equation, and it led to an ironic role reversal: twenty years after France's withdrawal from the unified NATO command, Bonn's pleas to Paris for fidelity to the Atlantic Alliance began to echo back across the Rhine. Since the early 1980s, the French government has been the most vocally Atlanticist of any on the continent.[4]

In response to the prominent and growing role of West German diplomacy in the search for a new system of peace between the states of eastern and western Europe, the French emphasis on the American connection was neither unwise nor unwelcome; it was certainly not unexpected. However, did the French recognize what was happening in Bonn? A French foreign minister in the 1920s sought to "organize" the peace of Europe at Locarno and with the Pact of Paris.[5] By the late 1980s, one of his most energetic successors at organizing post-Yalta, post-Helsinki Europe was clearly West Germany's foreign minister. Like all of his predecessors, Hans-Dietrich Genscher represented a Federal Republic conscious of the question lurking behind the policies of every French government: what hold has the Rapallo temptation on West Germany today? In the 1960s, when the answer seemed quite clearly none at all, Paris was able to pursue its independent course within the Alliance; the French attack on Atlanticism was made possible by the West German commitment to it. When Paris thought of Rapallo then, it was as an option Bonn had rejected in favor of being "inflexibly anchored in the western alliance, a voluntary captive of it."[6] Rapallo was not much discussed in public.

In the 1980s, however, the word appeared frequently in French discussions of the foreign policy of the Federal Republic.[7] Perceptions of a West German "drift to the east," the rebirth of "Mitteleuropa," and a new "Rapallo," already widespread with the two-track decision debate, were given further impetus by Mikhail Gorbachev's arrival in the Kremlin and the clear preference of West German public opinion for a "denuclearized" Europe in the wake of the 1987 INF treaty.[8] How many French voters could actually identify Rapallo was another question, but, like "entangling alliances" for Americans, the invocation of its specter had become a ritual of the Franco-German relationship. Was it only a ritual or did the French still see (West) German policy as a pendulum swinging between east and west? Did they still seriously wonder if Rapallo could promise Bonn more than Locarno?

If so, they were asking themselves the wrong question, but possibly to dangerous effect. Historical inertia, embodied in foreign policy prescriptions and applied to the radically changed realities with which a country has to deal (witness "no entangling alliances" in 1930s America), is a factor to be reckoned with. If, despite a different global context, such prescriptions are maintained as the basis of policies, they can create a reality of their own. If Paris thinks it sees a pendulum in the foreign policy of the Federal Republic, it may one day find one. However, West German diplomacy has no pendulum, for a simple reason: Bonn, as many have observed, is not Weimar, and its foreign policy is not that of Berlin in the 1920s.

The constant Paris correctly sees in the foreign policy of its West German ally is a deep and continuing historical interest in the economic, cultural, political, and human development of eastern Europe.[9] This interest was temporarily discredited by the policies of the Third Reich, symbolized by Auschwitz, and disavowed by the first generation of political leaders in the Federal Republic, who saw, correctly, that they had no other choice. Many of that generation, Konrad Adenauer chief among them, wanted no other choice; in his lifetime, Germany's role in eastern Europe had led to very little but disaster, from Lenin at the Finland Station to the Warsaw Ghetto. The attraction of a democratic Federal Republic closely tied economically and politically to France was self-evident.

In its early years, the Federal Republic made a choice between Rapallo and Locarno that was both real and symbolic. It abandoned a foreign policy goal—German reunification—that could have been pursued only through unacceptable compromises with the Soviet Union, and it linked the fate of the new West German democracy to that of France and its other western European neighbors. In the course of elaborating the core of this foreign policy, the Frankreichpolitik of the 1950s and early 1960s, Bonn developed a new understanding of Locarno. No longer seen by the foreign policy practitioners of the Federal Republic as solely a choice for western Europe—which it was, in its two historical contexts of the 1920s and 1950s—Locarno became a *process* of establishing cooperative relationships between countries mutually dependent on each other for their survival, whether they liked it or not. This concept of Locarno is the dominant characteristic of the foreign policy of the Federal Republic today.

The Third Option

Consequently, from Bonn's point of view, the question behind French skepticism is fundamentally flawed. It presupposes that only two options, the historic choice between Rapallo and Locarno, are available to the foreign policy of the Federal Republic. The third option of an east-west detente taking the triad of the Frankreichpolitik as its model has not yet found a firm place in the psychology of the Franco–West German relationship. However, it is the option Bonn has been pursuing since the early 1970s. Both West German public opinion and all mainstream political parties in the Federal Republic are committed to the continued application of the Frankreichpolitik process, derived from Locarno, to their country's Ostpolitik. The successful utilization of this process in the establishment of better relations with the GDR and the other countries of eastern Europe, including the USSR, has become the principal goal of West German foreign policy.

The extent of the nonpartisan consensus on the pursuit of the eastern policies reflects, not the failure, but the success of the earlier Frankreichpolitik. Bonn's search for approbation within western Europe is over because the Federal Republic found the equal voice in its councils it was seeking in the 1950s, and it did so chiefly because of the process adapted from the failure of Locarno to the Frankreichpolitik. The mutual trust and confidence built by successive French and West German governments in the multilateral institutions of western Europe—and the reinforcement of that confidence by private citizens creating a Locarno from below—is the success story Bonn hopes to replicate in its eastern policies.

As the West German understanding of Locarno changed, so too did the definition of German interests in Europe. French speculation on the existence of the historical Locarno-Rapallo pendulum compares Bonn and Berlin in complete disregard of the fundamentally different foreign policy agenda of the Federal Republic. Given the nature of the post-Versailles international system and of the Weimar Republic, Berlin's diplomacy was predicated on the existence of essentially antagonistic and potentially conflictual relations between the states of Europe. In a sort of funhouse-mirror image of the nineteenth-century balance of power, Berlin attempted to skew the balance in post-1919 Europe in such a way that revisions to the Versailles Treaty could one day be made—against the will of its defenders, if necessary, whether France in the west or Poland in the east. This policy did not rule out the eventual use of force, once Germany was in a strong enough position diplomatically and militarily to reestablish a central German political role in eastern Europe.[10]

This description of Berlin's foreign policy is not in the least applicable to Bonn. The Federal Republic has no interest in direct German political control of eastern Europe. If it were possible—and West Germans have no illusions that it is—the overwhelming majority of them would find it undesirable.[11] The continuing psychological costs of the last two German drives for European hegemony are burdensome enough. Furthermore, Bonn has no delusions of even a reunited Germany becoming a rival there to the Soviet Union; the European and global balance is not that of the 1920s, when Berlin and Moscow (and Rome, Paris, and London, by omission or commission) still determined the political fate of their neighbors. The political role, sui generis, of the two global powers, Moscow in the east and Washington in the west, is not disputed by Bonn.

Not only does West German foreign policy have no interest in the political goals that mesmerized Berlin in the 1920s, but it also categorically repudiates two of the basic tenets of Berlin's diplomacy: the essentially competitive and antagonistic nature of economic and political relations between the states of Europe and the willingness to use force as a means to achieve foreign policy goals.[12] (Weimar diplomacy was not unique in this regard; all the states of post–World War I Europe took a disastrously autarchical approach to their economic and political interests.) In the sharpest possible contrast to Berlin, Bonn sees the survival and prosperity of Europe and of all its nations as dependent on the elimination of the use of force, the peaceful management of political competition, and the expansion of cultural, technological, and economic cooperation. What can the supposed choice between Rapallo and Locarno mean to a country that sees its interests so differently from the first German republic?

Not a great deal, which is precisely the problem with the Rapallo specter that sometimes seems to be haunting France. Although the French perspective on Germany continues to postulate the two options of Rapallo or Locarno, east or west, Bonn's foreign policy is predicated on the existence of a third option: a European-wide Locarno, especially a Locarno from below. One of the principal questions confronting the Federal Republic is whether France can understand this third option and, if so, if it will participate in its elaboration. The answer depends on the degree to which both allies can agree on two things: that their own relationship is an appropriate model for the development of east-west relations in Europe, and that the Gaullist goal of an interdependent Europe of independent states from the Atlantic to the Urals can be achieved only if the Federal Republic rather than France plays the principal role in its accomplishment.

For some time now, Bonn has forcefully proclaimed that the Franco–West German relationship is a model for the rest of Europe, and, rhetorically, Paris seems to agree.[13] However, the rhetoric is not without internal contradictions because, at the same time, their relationship is described as a unique one.[14] The dilemma was present at the creation: the postwar relationship between the Federal Republic and France and the institutions of postwar western Europe came into the world together, with the Schuman Plan for the European Coal and Steel Community. In the early 1960s, the Fouchet Plan for interstate consultation of the (then) EC Six and the Elysée Treaty itself rekindled the argument between those partisans of western Europe who saw the Bonn-Paris axis as an attempt to sabotage political and economic integration and those who argued that broader and deeper European cooperation could be built only on that axis.[15] Within the European Community, the relationship between the two countries has always led a double life, seen by some as a detour, by others as the high road to EC development.[16]

Since the mid-1960s, however, leaving the philosophical debate behind, the countries of western Europe have in practice looked to the Franco–West German relationship as the key to the success of their economic and political cooperation. The development of European Political Cooperation (EPC) since the mid-1970s and, in the 1980s, attempts to breathe life into military cooperation in the Western European Union (WEU) have both been predicated on the centrality of Bonn's and Paris's willingness to cooperate with each other.[17] Whatever the theoretical debates, forty years of western European cooperation have confirmed the primacy of the relationship between France and West Germany. At the same time, the other EC countries have not necessarily regarded that relationship as a model to be emulated in its details; given the uniqueness of the mutual hostility between France and Germany historically, their reconciliation was also unique within western Europe. It had "an historic resonance" and would "not be easily supplanted by any other arrangement."[18]

Neither the nations of western Europe nor the United States had an interest in preventing the establishment of a good relationship between Bonn and Paris. Indeed, given both the history of Franco-German conflict and the need during the early years of the Cold War for the rapid development of western European economic and political cooperation, all of them had a great deal to gain from the success of Bonn's Frankreichpolitik. Reconciliation between the two neighbors meant peace and prosperity for the smaller nations of western Europe and the elimination of one of British foreign policy's perpetual problems, the need to deal with French anxieties about Germany. As Monnet recognized, no real opposition could be raised, despite London's misgivings about the ECSC, to any plan that promised to free the continent from the curse of recurring Franco-German wars.[19] As a result, the priority given by Adenauer's Federal Republic and Schuman's France to finishing the work begun by Stresemann and Briand received general acclaim.

In the broader context of Europe as a whole, however, the Franco–West German entente appeared somewhat different. Their rapprochement tilted the scales of economic and political strength in Europe decisively in favor of the western half of the continent. When it joined NATO in 1955, West Germany contributed critical territory and man-power to the Atlantic Alliance, but more importantly, throughout the 1950s and 1960s, its policy of reconciliation with France brought psychological reassurance to Paris and to western Europe as a whole that German economic and political potential, for the first time in this century, would be used *for* their mutual benefit. Given the nature of the Cold War, however, this potential would also be used, if necessary, in the defense of western Europe *against* the Soviet Union and the eastern European members of the Warsaw Pact. The other side of the Federal Republic's policy of detente with France was its role in the east-west conflict.

Since the early 1970s and with increasing candor since 1982, Bonn has attempted to enlist its relationship with Paris in the pursuit of policies based on the assumption that the east-west conflict is counterproductive and designed to make it obsolete.[20] In effect, West German detente policies over the past decade have analogized the postwar east-west rivalry to the historical Franco-German enmity and have sought to apply the remedy successfully used to defuse that conflict in the 1950s and 1960s. This poses a dilemma for France by forcing Paris to rethink both its relationship with Bonn and its attitudes toward the Soviet Union and the Warsaw Pact. Can France agree with West Germany that the nature of the Soviet threat has changed since the 1950s and that the techniques of reconciliation developed by their own detente can be usefully applied to eastern Europe and the USSR? Can Paris share Bonn's perception of a third option, supplanting Rapallo and Locarno in the historic sense? Or will a foreign policy dispute result between them because France will conclude that West Germany's pursuit of Ostpolitik is rooted in wishful thinking about the nature of Moscow's foreign policy and will lead to the *pax Sovietica* Pompidou feared?

Mitteleuropa and a Carolingian Past

Pessimistically, two reasons for a potential foreign policy dispute be-tween the two allies cannot be ruled out. First, the strength of the hold the Rapallo complex has on the French mind is no accident, and it is not solely related to distrust of Germany based on past experience. Instead, that distrust is itself an aspect of a broader issue facing the two allies: their fundamentally different conception of international relations as a whole. Both French foreign policy and the public opinion that supports it are rooted in the classical European concept of a competitive state system that, since the Peace of Westphalia in 1648, has spread around the world. Characteristic of that system is the ultimate possibility of the use of force—in other words, the reliance of states, in the final analysis, only on themselves for the maintenance and advancement of their own interests.[21]

Also characteristic of it is the assumption that states are held in check—deterred—from advancing their own self-defined interests by the readiness, psychological and material, of other states to counter moves toward regional or global hegemony. In other words, French foreign policy (like that of most states, including the United States, Great Britain, and the Soviet Union) assumes the existence of antagonism in the international system. In this respect, the French concept of international relations is much closer philosophically to the Weimar Republic's than it is to Bonn's, which is predicated on the belief that states' own long-range interests, properly defined, exclude the use of force and include the development of cooperative relationships with each other.[22]

Undoubtedly a good deal of truth lies in Bonn's foreign policy assumptions, especially in a nuclear age. However, a lot can be said for Paris's skepticism; states, after all, may not properly define their own long-range interests. The fact that France and West Germany are both right about the current state of the international system will not relieve them of the practical problem of arriving at a common interpretation of their western detente and its applicability to east-west detente today. They need to define what mixture of cooperation, competition, and hostility toward the countries of western Europe characterizes Soviet foreign policy forty years after Stalin's policies provoked the Cold War. The arrival of Mikhail Gorbachev in the Kremlin in 1985 did not make this task any easier.

The second problem facing the relationship between Bonn and Paris is related to the strength of the Rapallo complex and the French attitude toward international politics. The substance of Bonn's current foreign policy goals in Europe is almost purely Gaullist.[23] The Federal Republic aims at making the eastern European states more independent of Moscow politically, while simultaneously working to create conditions in which all the Warsaw Pact states, including the Soviet Union, will become more responsive to internal pressures for freedom of movement and information and more economically and culturally interdependent with the nations of western Europe. Despite their common Gaullist approach to the continent's future, Paris and Bonn face a dilemma: the historical and cultural reality is such that the Federal Republic alone, of all the countries of western Europe, is in a position to carry out General DeGaulle's concept. French support for West German policies presupposes a willingness on the part of Paris to see Bonn take a political lead in central Europe that runs contrary to all past French suspicions of a German Mitteleuropa.

Considerable debate has ensued recently in Europe over the historical existence of this Mitteleuropa. What was it? Did it ever exist as its partisans imagine it or has it assumed mythical proportions in the imagination of generations too young to remember the reality of the early twentieth century? Wasn't the actual state of affairs—the atrophied Hapsburg bureaucracy, the stifling Hohenzollern bourgeoisie, the petty squabbles of the Balkan nationalities—less to be lamented than fin-de-siècle romanticism would have it? No doubt. However, the way Europe *was* during the era in question is less important than the way Europe is *imagined* to have been by the partisans of east-west detente today.

The role Mitteleuropa plays in the elaboration of West Germany's Ostpolitik was played in its Frankreichpolitik by the western Christian empire of Charlemagne.[24] To the people and governments of western Europe in the first two postwar decades, Carolingian Europe symbolized their aspirations for diversity in unity. Under the umbrella of the Latin Christian heritage that united them, the nations of the continent were to find their way back from the divisive nationalism of the nineteenth century. In the modern border town of Aachen, Charlemagne's imperial capital, France, West Germany, and the Low Countries found the appropriate symbol for their postwar cooperation. Once the center of an empire, Aachen had become in the twentieth century a provincial city on a fortified frontier; the goal of statesmen like Schuman, Adenauer, and Belgium's Paul-Henri Spaak was to make it literally and figuratively the heart of western Europe again. They succeeded, and the Charlemagne Prize given by the city of Aachen to François Mitterrand and Helmut Kohl in November 1988 recognized the historic significance of the Elysée Treaty and the pivotal role of France and West Germany in the construction of Europe.[25]

By the 1980s, the *idea* of Mitteleuropa had come to represent the same unwillingness to tolerate indefinitely the hostile borders of the contemporary east-west conflict. Like Carolingian Europe, the historical Mitteleuropa of the Hohenzollerns and Hapsburgs had certainly been romanticized into an ideal it never reached in practice. What it represented for Europe nearly a half-century after the end of World War II, however, was the freedom from political control with which ideas and people had once moved within a vast area from the Low Countries to western Russia. German was, in fact, the lingua franca of this central Europe, the language of the arts and sciences at universities from Czernowitz in Austrian Poland to Bonn in the Prussian Rhineland.[26] As a symbol for the goals of the Federal Republic's Ostpolitik, this Mitteleuropa was as apt as the image of Charlemagne's empire for its Frankreichpolitik.

Carolingian Europe had one major advantage, however: it was sufficiently remote in time to be untainted by association with the darker side of either modern German or modern French nationalism. Since 1933, that could not be said of Mitteleuropa. The use that National Socialist Germany made of the major cultural and economic role of Germans in east-central Europe cast a dark shadow over it that only began to fade in the 1980s and again reveal the older, historical German role in a more positive light.

In the French consciousness, however, and in that of many of Bonn's western allies, few aspects of the role of Germany in the European heartland seemed positive. The consolidation of Berlin's political control there after 1871, from Russia to the western borders of Alsace and Lorraine, gave Germany the agricultural and industrial base from which it mounted its twentieth-century invasions of the Low Countries and France.[27] To find its way to a policy of consistent support for the Federal Republic's Ostpolitik, Paris must overcome its understandable historical reluctance to see a potential new German power base take shape in the center of the continent. It has, in other words, to convince itself that the aims of West German foreign policy today are different from those of Berlin historically and that renewed German political influence in Mitteleuropa, like equality for Bonn in the Carolingian Europe of the 1950s, would be to the advantage of France and of Europe. That is the task confronting the two western allies in the 1990s.

Complicating it is the level of public enthusiasm for the Ostpolitik within the Federal Republic, especially for that aspect of it involving the GDR, Bonn's Deutschlandpolitik. This response is in no way surprising, but it is nevertheless somewhat painful for the partisans of the older Frankreichpolitik.[28] The French and their language, not just in West Germany, have a reputation that precedes them for being difficult to know. Despite their best efforts, those who love France face an uphill battle, certainly in the Anglo-Saxon countries, to communicate their affection to those around them; in West Germany, however, the difficulties of getting along with the French have unique historical and political overtones. Even in the early 1960s, in the heyday of their efforts to establish a new relationship between the Federal Republic and its neighbor, West Germans complained that the French were simply not as easy to fathom as the more engaging and sympathetic Austrians.[29]

What was true of Austria then seems true of the GDR today and, to a certain extent, of the other countries of eastern Europe. Language is a major part of the problem; those West Germans who speak French well speak it very well, but most do not. The French and their culture, especially the popular media, are simply not as accessible to the average West German as are the people of the GDR. Moreover, as many West Germans have discovered personally, their language remains a lingua franca in much of eastern Europe, where its use still connotes a certain level of education and culture.[30] The personal stories West Germans tell of holidays in the Netherlands or France, where they were forced to speak English to someone who clearly knew German, are almost never heard from those returning from visits to eastern Europe. For whatever reason—the lingering reputation of German as the language of the Reformation and the universities, the importance of the West German mark to their economies, the attempt to show that their countries are not as isolated in the Soviet bloc as westerners might suppose—the people of eastern Europe seem to many West Germans to want contact with them more than do the French and their other western neighbors.[31]

The situation is further complicated by the personal and family ties that exist between many West and East Germans. Several million families in both countries have a relationship that only a few Franco–West German families have; millions of other West Germans have their family origins in what is now the GDR, Poland, Czechoslovakia, or the Soviet Union. This relationship naturally creates a personal interest in eastern Europe for large numbers of people, young and old, in the Federal Republic. At the same time, much of German history and literature inevitably awakens an interest in the lands east of the Elbe. Moreover, the isolation of this part of Europe from the postwar economic and political development of the European Community countries—Americanization, its critics would say—gives it a certain air of nostalgia for both younger and older West Germans who do not have to live on a daily basis (and without western currency) in the GDR or Poland. Returning visitors often describe their travels as ones in time as well as space, a glimpse of Germany as it once was, at least in their imagination.[32] By contrast, France and the other countries of western Europe seem too familiar, through radio and television, to whet the curiosity of many West Germans.

The impact of this West German fascination with the GDR and the other countries of eastern Europe on Bonn's relationship with Paris is difficult to assess. On the one hand, the French are well aware of, and even sympathetic to, the historical and personal ties that many West Germans feel to eastern Europe. On the other, they have a hard time shaking off the feeling that this attraction could have undesirable political consequences. In October 1988, when Chancellor Kohl visited Moscow, Paris received some indication of whether the Federal Republic's commitment to western European integration and bilateral cooperation with France could withstand the allure of the old German role in Mitteleuropa.[33]

The Image and Legacy of Germany

Despite the somewhat romanticized appeal of the lands east of the Elbe for West Germans, the Kohl-Gorbachev summit, followed a month later by a Mitterrand-Gorbachev summit, boded well for the Franco–West German relationship. Before he left for Moscow, the West German chancellor met informally with the French president to discuss a common approach to the Soviet leader. A regularly scheduled Franco–West German summit was held between the visits of the two western leaders to Moscow and gave them the opportunity to assess the results of Kohl's trip and its implications for the French visit still to come. At the same time, the two allies announced further plans for a joint Franco–West German army brigade, to be established in 1990, as well as plans to open joint embassies in the future, staffed by both West German and French diplomats.[34] Their strategy toward the Soviet Union clearly followed the pattern of the early 1970s, in which the Brandt and Pompidou governments had left no doubt that east-west detente was not a substitute for the construction of the European Community or their bilateral relationship. Continued work on the creation of the EC's single market in 1992 also emphasized Paris's and Bonn's commitment to the Westpolitik.

The two-pronged approach, elaboration of Western European cooperation and east-west detente, was accompanied by West German thrusts on two other fronts: the Atlantic and the historic. In November 1988, Chancellor Kohl visited Washington, the first foreign leader to meet with American president-elect George Bush following his election victory. In Bonn, after the 1987 Soviet-American INF treaty, the opposition SPD had already toned down the highly critical rhetoric it applied from 1982 to 1987 to American foreign policy; its initial reaction to the Republican victory in the 1988 American presidential election was also positive. From the foreign policy perspective, continuity and experience were more important to all mainstream West German parties than ideological affinity.[35] Finally, in late 1988, Bonn turned its attention to NATO nuclear force modernization and the alliance's response to Soviet proposals for further arms and troop reductions in Europe.[36]

The reaffirmation of Bonn's cooperation with Paris and the emphasis on the Atlantic relationship were traditional companions of West German diplomatic initiatives toward Moscow. So was the other dimension of Bonn's foreign policy in late 1988: the articulation of German responsibility for the destruction and division of pre-1945 Europe. The fiftieth anniversary of Kristallnacht, the mob violence against German Jews organized by Berlin on November 9 and 10, 1938, was the opportunity for Bonn to reiterate its consciousness of the unique German stake in both west-west and east-west detente. Despite the inappropriateness of the speech given by the president of West Germany's parliament to commemorate Kristallnacht and his resulting resignation, the anniversary was, in the long run, significant for other reasons. In the context of West German foreign policy, it marked two important new dimensions to Bonn's approach to the German past.

First, the anniversary reaffirmed the nonpartisan West German consensus on German responsibility for the fate of twentieth-century Europe that was first in evidence in the West German president's speech of May 8, 1985.[37] The CDU's internal contradictions, with its origins in the German resistance to Hitler but its dependence on voters from the far right of the political spectrum and emigrés from eastern Europe, had historically made the party more ambiguous than the SPD about Germans' guilt and German responsibility. Weizsäcker's speech had enabled many Christian Democrats to begin to deal with those contradictions.

Chancellor Kohl's 1988 Kristallnacht speeches, at home and in New York on November 14 in honor of Simon Wiesenthal, were a contribution to that process and to ending the political impact in the Federal Republic of the "historians' debate" on the nature of the Third Reich. Abandoning the phrase he had used in earlier years—that the crimes of Nazi Germany had been carried out "in the German name"—the chancellor emphasized in New York, as he had in Moscow in October, that they had been perpetrated "by German hands."[38] His words were less dramatic but no less significant than Willy Brandt's kneeling in Warsaw nearly two decades before; like the nonpartisan Ostpolitik practiced since 1982, they reflected a West German consensus on the origins and goals of Bonn's foreign policy in eastern and western Europe.

Second, the government's approach to the Kristallnacht anniversary clearly signaled its abandonment of a concept that had characterized the first Kohl administration, called, most unfortunately, by the chancellor the "mercy of late birth." The suggestion that Germans born too late to be personally guilty for the crimes of the Third Reich were relieved of the obligation to deal with its historical legacy had caused an uproar at home and abroad in 1984. Followed later that year by Kohl's ceremony of reconciliation with François Mitterrand at Verdun and his failed attempt to do the same with Ronald Reagan at Bitburg in 1985, the "mercy of late birth" idea had left the impression that the chancellor, born in 1930, and West Germans younger than he believed that the past could be put behind them once and for all as the Federal Republic assumed its new role in Europe.[39] In a curious way, the first Kohl administration seemed to be saying that its election marked a new "zero hour," the policies of rapprochement with France in the west, Poland in the east, and West Germany's other neighbors having been accomplished. In October 1988 in Moscow and in November 1988 at the Frankfurt synagogue and in New York, Kohl made clear that he and his government had abandoned any such idea and adopted instead the president's and the foreign minister's frequently articulated concept of a historical legacy shared by all age groups in the Federal Republic.[40]

Speaking to the same issue at a conference of historians in October 1988, the West German president declared that the German nation "cannot make others responsible for what it and its neighbors endured under National Socialism." Germany had been "led by criminals and allowed itself to be led by them," and Weizsäcker asked those who sought historical comparisons to the holocaust, "What, after all would it mean for us if Auschwitz could be compared with the ruthless extermination of other people?" Declaring "the search of young people for self-esteem" a matter "of key importance," the president said:

> They want to and have to know who they are, where they come from and with whom they are to share and shape this world. To them, it is vitally important to know how the moral and political disaster came about in the days of their grandparents. . . . The young certainly do not bear guilt. . . . But liberation will only be possible for them in their own lives if they ask and seek to understand where they come from, if they open up to their history in an attitude of inner freedom.[41]

Clearly, the questions that Kohl and Weizsäcker addressed meant that Bonn's east-west detente policies in the 1990s would differ, as they had in the past, from those of its western allies. The Federal Republic's search for a path to east-west cooperation would continue to be characterized by the need to deal not only with the issues raised by the Cold War but also with those inflicted on Europe by the Third Reich.[42]

Chancellor Kohl's visits to Moscow and Washington, the routine pattern of West German cooperation with France,[43] and the Kristallnacht anniversary made clear that the driving force behind West German foreign policy in the late 1980s remained what it had been in the early 1950s: the legacy of modern German history and the conviction that European civilization came precariously close to self-destruction in the twentieth century. As a symbol for the holocaust brought on Europe by German policies, Auschwitz was already a principal factor in shaping the foreign policy of the Federal Republic in the 1950s. Rebuilding the confidence in German good faith and responsibility that Berlin had destroyed was the first task of that foreign policy in its early years. At the same time, the destruction of World Wars I and II had convinced two generations of Europeans that the continent could not survive a third world war; the birth of the nuclear age reinforced their conviction. In the years after 1945, Hiroshima became the symbol of this conviction, a warning against the use of force to settle Europe's differences.

West Germany is only one of the countries to have reached the conclusion that conflict is counterproductive and cooperation essential to the future well-being of Europe. What gives the symbol of Hiroshima its special meaning in the Federal Republic, however, is the unique German historical context in which it is absorbed, against the background of Auschwitz. West German foreign policy—and the public opinion that supports it—does indeed have its own unique psychology, but it is not principally a psychology of fear, of exposure to attack and invasion on NATO's front line, but a psychology of responsibility. Although West Germans are sensible enough to be uneasy over prospects of their country as a nuclear battlefield, they are even more uneasy over the possibility that the failure of their foreign policy might be responsible one day for turning Europe into a battlefield again.

At Werbellinsee in 1981, Helmut Schmidt and Erich Honecker signed an accord in which both German states committed themselves to the principle that "war should never again originate from German territory."[44] A continuing theme of the West German political debate as a whole is responsibility. The postwar occupation by the western allies did an excellent job of reinforcing the conviction of many Germans that National Socialism and the Third Reich had been possible because individuals had failed to take responsibility for the maintenance of democratic values and human rights.[45] As a result, the concept of individual responsibility for political decisions and skepticism toward political authority are deeply ingrained in the Federal Republic. West German churches, not untouched themselves by responsibility for the crimes of the Third Reich, encourage a critical perspective on foreign policies involving the potential use of force.[46]

West Germans want to be certain that the authority exercised in their name will not plunge Europe into crisis and conflict again. Their seeming obsession with the potential for nuclear war on the continent stems from an awareness that such a war could bring on German responsibility for a genocide greater than that represented by Auschwitz. The destruction of the human race through nuclear war is technologically possible; perhaps it seems more politically possible to West Germans than it does to their allies because they have been forced to confront the historical legacy of one of the most prosperous and literate countries of Europe, their own. The twentieth century's association of their country's name with Auschwitz is a difficult enough burden for Germans to bear; German responsibility for a twenty-first century Hiroshima is almost too painful for them to contemplate.

As a result, the search for new methods and frameworks of cooperation, whether with France and the other members of the European Community in the 1950s and 1960s or with the GDR and the countries of the Warsaw Pact in the 1970s and 1980s, is an essential component of West German foreign policy. The Federal Republic is one of many states—in theory, all the signatories of the U.N. Charter—to have ruled out the use of force in pursuit of its foreign policy goals; unlike them, it has another mission to fulfill: to change the image and legacy of Germany in the history books of Europe. Bonn's concept of the European future says a lot about its interpretation of the German past.

Obsolete Borders, Technological Bridges

Historians of the Wilhelmine period viewed Prussian and German history before 1871 as leading up to and culminating in the establishment of the Second Reich under the Hohenzollerns. The Germans were to have a nation-state, as the French did, and as the "unsuccessful" nations of Europe, Poles and Czechs chief among them, did not. Nevertheless, a people both Catholic and Protestant, urban and rural, united over the years only by their language and its contribution to the westernization and Christianization of eastern Europe, the Germans were not like the French. They were not even like the Czechs or the Poles. On a continent of increasingly autarchical inclinations, the Germans were the indispensable bridge between the nations, until they too capitulated to the particular definition of nationalism sweeping nineteenth-century Europe.

The foreign policy of the Federal Republic is predicated on a fundamentally different concept of nationalism and a radically different interpretation of the German and European past. Far from being seen as a failure or as only the preliminary phase to the state of 1871, the existence of a multipolar state system within German-speaking Europe is increasingly regarded in the Federal Republic as a uniquely German contribution to the peace and stability of Europe.[47] Instead of being the culmination of national development, the nation-state interlude is seen as just that; Bonn's foreign policy postulates a different role for the Germans than the one they sought after 1871. Far from being incompatible with the nationalism of its neighbors, the German role in Europe, interpreted in this light, is not only compatible with their national interests but essential to their advancement.

The critical characteristic of the German multipolar system historically, however, has not characterized east-central Europe in the years since 1945. Within the Austrian Empire, until 1918, "no one had a passport and no one had even heard of a visa."[48] In Germany itself before 1871, borders were commonplace, but they were not the divisive borders of the twentieth century; they did not hinder the flow of ideas or people. The economic centralization required by the Industrial Revolution doomed the miniscule German states of the early nineteenth century, and the autarchical nationalism of the Hapsburg successor states doomed the economic and trade patterns of Austria-Hungary a century later. The result was paradoxically the same: the erection of economic, political, and cultural barriers between the states of Europe.

After 1945, while western Europe began to dismantle its internal frontiers, in the continent's heartland they became even more pronounced. From 1947, when Czechoslovakia under pressure from Moscow rejected participation in the Marshall Plan, through 1961, when the GDR could no longer deal with its economic and political failures without the Berlin Wall, the old frontiers dividing the states of eastern and western Europe became ideological ones. The Iron Curtain was aptly named, but even as it was being erected, it was an historical anachronism. The launching of Sputnik was a better indicator of the future than the watchtowers of the inner-German border; the moment of history had already passed when a totalitarian state could technologically exert control over virtually every activity within its borders and exclude what it deemed politically undesirable.

Goebbels's propaganda machinery and the Soviet and Nazi security organizations of the 1930s and 1940s were unique to their time. They required a level of technology—radio and film were ideal—that enabled them both to manipulate the masses and to invade the privacy of the individual. In the past three decades, however, far from confirming George Orwell's nightmare vision of 1984, technological developments have made attempts to maintain political and economic autarchy self-defeating and suicidal. The economic and environmental failures of the Soviet Union and its eastern European allies, largely self-inflicted, reflect the ideological myopia required by their attempts to resist political pluralism, but the transmission of information by satellite, the revolution in personal computers, and the dangers posed by modern chemicals and nuclear power comprise a technological assault on totalitarian societies. The CSCE Final Act set down principles that had not yet been realized politically in 1975, but it also described a new technological reality, in which the free exchange of persons and information could no longer be prevented.[49] Bonn's Ostpolitik is predicated on the existence of this reality and its inevitable impact on the political leadership of the Warsaw Pact.

The Nature of Europe's Borders

Forty years ago, France and the Federal Republic rejected economic autarchy and West Germans rejected the totalitarian perversion of the German nation-state in their successful attempt to rebuild their bilateral relationship in a free and prosperous western Europe. Both countries, in the acceptance of the Schuman Plan, acknowledged the bankruptcy of their past policies and the disastrous consequences those policies had had for their own nations and for Europe. Until the advent of the Gorbachev years in the Soviet Union, Bonn had no illusions that the leadership of the Warsaw Pact countries was prepared to acknowledge openly its economic and political failures. West Germany was equally convinced, however, that the tangible needs of their citizens would push the countries of eastern Europe in the direction of cooperation with the Federal Republic and that a dynamic of political as well as economic change would begin to take place.[50]

With the arrival of Mikhail Gorbachev in the Kremlin, Bonn's calculation began to appear even more valid than it did in the Brezhnev years. The acknowledgment by the Soviet leadership of the need for domestic economic and political reforms was accompanied by a new Soviet diplomacy, the first sign of which was Moscow's response to the accident at Chernobyl.[51] Since 1986, Soviet pursuit of joint ventures with West German firms, the conclusion of an agreement to link East and West Berlin to the West German electrical supply network, implementation of Bonn's 1976 cultural agreement with Warsaw, the progress made in arms control at Stockholm and Geneva, and the pace of contacts between Bonn and East Berlin have all confirmed the Federal Republic's faith in the process of east-west detente adapted from its Frankreichpolitik.[52] Although not directly related to West Germany, other changes in Moscow's policies, from the rehabilitation of Czechoslovakian leader Alexander Dubček and Soviet physicist Andrei Sakharov to the withdrawal of Soviet forces from Afghanistan, also appeared to mark a turning point in the USSR's recognition of its failure to respond to the economic and political needs of its own citizens and to the foreign policy challenges posed by western Europe and a rapidly changing China.[53] Like its other western European neighbors, Bonn sought to encourage further positive change in the USSR.

In Moscow in October 1988, West Germany and the Soviet Union signed governmental accords dealing with agriculture, cultural exchange, the use of space, environmental and nuclear radiation protection, avoidance of naval incidents on the high seas, and the construction of a high-temperature nuclear reactor. West German industrialists accompanying the chancellor to the summit concluded more than thirty private agreements to do business in the Soviet Union, and a consortium led by the Deutsche Bank extended three billion marks in credit to the USSR. During the chancellor's visit, a satellite television bridge linked Soviet and German veterans of the battle of Stalingrad and soldiers of the Bundeswehr and Red Army today for a discussion that was broadcast live in both countries.[54]

Meanwhile, Bonn's Ostpolitik was entering a new phase at a faster pace with all the countries of eastern Europe, not only because of new leadership in Moscow but also as a result of West German initiatives throughout the region. The Federal Republic became the first western country to establish diplomatic relations with Albania in late 1987, and Bonn and Tirana began developing joint economic ventures to bring Albania the transportation and industrial infrastructure it had shunned for forty years. The Albanian foreign minister paid his first visit to a western country when he arrived in Bonn in September 1988 for the signing of a bilateral cultural agreement.[55]

In October 1988, Hungary and the Federal Republic agreed on an environmental cooperation agreement dealing especially with transborder air pollution, and in November the West German president paid a state visit to Bulgaria, where another bilateral cultural agreement was signed. Working with private industry, Bonn in September had announced the establishment of an east-west foreign trade academy in West Berlin to enhance the city's role as a bridge between the EC's internal market and the COMECON countries after 1992.[56] Pursuant to West Germany's 1976 cultural agreement with Poland, the first exhibit there on the German resistance to Hitler opened in Warsaw in October 1988. It was followed two weeks later by the largest German cultural week ever held in an eastern European country.[57]

In the area of inner-German relations, Bonn agreed to work with East Berlin to develop the GDR's tourist industry—hotels, restaurants, and recreational facilities—for foreign visitors and vacationing East Germans. Another source of western currency for East Berlin, the project was, for Bonn, one more step in the encouragement of contacts between individual East Germans and western Europeans. In August 1988, implementing an agreement reached during Erich Honecker's 1987 visit to West Germany, the two states agreed to a number of specific research projects in, among other areas, nuclear security and high-energy physics. Under the terms of their 1986 cultural agreement, the East German cultural minister attended the November 1988 opening at Charlottenburg Palace of the first GDR historical exhibit, on the Great Elector, to be shown in West Berlin. Two months before, the first member of a GDR government to speak officially in West Berlin did so at the opening of the first major exhibit of East German art in the western half of the city. In the fall of

1988, the book trade associations of Leipzig and Frankfurt organized touring exhibits of each other's books, and their two state libraries planned regular consultations and future common projects.[58]

By 1988, the government of the GDR had been forced to respond to its own citizens' demands for increasing contact with West Germans. In 1987, nearly 20 percent of the population of East Germany visited the Federal Republic—three million individuals.[59] More importantly, over one million visitors were below the pension age, a dramatic increase in the sixty thousand visits allowed to that age group only three years before.[60] In early 1988, Potsdam and Bonn became the nineteenth pair of East and West German sister cities; more than fifty were established or being organized by the end of the year.[61] Largely as a result of the growth of such exchanges, the number of young East Germans visiting the Federal Republic in school, sport, and other youth groups increased from 1,020 in 1985 to 4,000 in 1987.[62] Many of the participants in group exchanges were accommodated in private homes, at the insistence of the West German sponsors, one of whose principal goals was the expansion of contacts between private citizens through home stays.[63]

Progress in the Ostpolitik meant that, for Bonn and Paris, the next few years would also be the beginning of a new period in their relationship. West German press comment on the November 1988 Kohl-Mitterrand summit reflected the Federal Republic's recognition of its valuable relationship with France. One editor wrote:

> We do not know how the economically weakened Soviet Union is to improve things, how it will manage with its nationality problem, whether Gorbachev can stay the reform course he has set out on, and whether he will ever build and decorate that European house he always dreams about. But it is good to know that during this turbulent phase in the Soviet Union the Federal Republic of Germany is not alone at the difficult border of Europe. . . . What the Soviets see are Germans and Frenchmen arm in arm during the creation of peace in Europe.[64]

As contacts between East and West Germans intensify, and as Bonn continues to take an economic lead in the development of *eastern* Europe, France and the Federal Republic will have to confront their aspirations for *western* Europe in a situation that is likely to be radically different from that of the last forty years. In 1992, the European Community expects to become a true internal market, with the implementation of the Single European Act.[65] If the timetable is maintained, the free flow of goods, services, and labor will be the logical next step in the destruction of the economic and political barriers among the states of western Europe that began with the six members of the European Coal and Steel Community forty-two years earlier. The development of the EC has had a significant impact on individual western Europeans, but none more profound than the change it has brought over the past four decades to their national borders. Since the early 1950s, those borders have in fact lost their divisive character, but they have also ceased to be divisive in the imagination of West Germans and their western neighbors.

Between West Germans and their eastern neighbors, borders still divide, psychologically and with deadly force. The actual division of Germany and the symbolic division of Europe were confirmed by the same event: the erection in Berlin of the wall between the western and Soviet sectors in August 1961. With the closing of the Brandenburg Gate, the east-west axis of Unter den Linden lost its purpose, and like the great boulevard, by 1961, Germany too had ceased to be a highway connecting east and west. Another decade passed before the Federal Republic was able to define a foreign policy capable of halting and eventually reversing the factual and psychological division of Europe: a policy that, like its predecessor in the west, renounced a concern for borders and avowed a concern for the nature of those borders.

France found that it could live with a German Ruhr and Saarland, and West Germany with a French Alsace-Lorraine, in the western Europe of the ECSC. Their countries' long-range prosperity and security, as well as the peace of Europe, depended on their willingness to abandon outmoded concepts of territorial control and fortified borders. For its part, in the wake of the Berlin Wall, the Federal Republic discovered that its fixation with borders—Germany's eastern borders of 1937—had become counterproductive. By the 1960s, the borders that mattered in the daily lives of Germans and their eastern European neighbors were on the Elbe and the Spree; modifying their nature required the same willingness to abandon a position once deemed essential to the national interest, this time on the eastern territorial limits of the Reich, which Adenauer had shown in his acceptance of the Ruhr Authority so many years before. Once Bonn had done so, it found that new possibilities for effecting change in eastern Europe opened to West German foreign policy, as a new era of cooperation with France had followed the Federal Republic's first confidence-building measures in the west.

By the 1980s, the goal of Bonn's Ostpolitik was no longer the political reunification of Germany or the demise of the Warsaw Pact per se. It had become, instead, the encouragement of political and economic changes *in* eastern Europe and changes in the character of the borders *between* eastern and western Europe. Breathing life into the CSCE principles of the free flow of ideas and people had replaced the destruction of an ideological enemy and the resurrection of the territory of the Reich as the aim of the Federal Republic's eastern policies. Bonn saw in its western borders, and along its frontier with Austria, the reality it hoped to see in the future on the Elbe and the Oder-Neisse: the expression of the European nations' commitment to both the independence of their countries and the interdependence of their continent.[66] The political borders of such a Europe would reflect, as they do on the Saar and along the once despised frontier between Bavaria and an independent Austria, the fulfillment of both goals to which the people of the new West German democracy committed themselves in the Basic Law of 1949: national self-determination and European cooperation.[67]

Not surprisingly, the president of the Federal Republic found the phrase that best described Bonn's concept of its Ostpolitik: the German question is open as long as the Brandenburg Gate is closed.[68] When the day comes Unter den Linden is once again an east-west axis, Bonn's policies of detente, in the west and the east, will have succeeded. When the borders of central Europe have ceased to divide, the model of Locarno and the Frankreichpolitik will have contributed to the opening of a new era of relations between the states of eastern and western Europe. It will also have enabled West Germans to live more honestly and openly with the legacy of Auschwitz because their country will have helped restore to Europe the future of which it was once nearly deprived by events in Germany's past.

Notes

1. F. Roy Willis, *France, Germany, and the New Europe, 1945–1967* (London: Oxford University Press, 1968), p. 32, wrote that the French occupation "sought to reeducate and democratize the German people, to make them worthy of a place in the moral and cultural community of Europe, notably by cathartic acquaintance with the best of France's own cultural heritage. The mother of arts, arms, and laws was willing to raise a foster child."
2. Fritz Stern, "Germany in a Semi-Gaullist Europe," *Foreign Affairs* 58, no. 4 (Spring 1980): 875–876: "More and more, Germans have come to feel that the memories of past horrors should no longer constrain them from playing an active role in the world. There is an impatience to be rid of the incubus of the past, to tackle the new problems uninhibitedly."
3. See Catherine McArdle Kelleher, "The Federal Republic and NATO: Change and Continuity in the 1980s," in Robert Gerald Livingston, ed., *The Federal Republic of Germany in the 1980s* (New York: German Information Service, 1983), p. 12.
4. In his *Refléxions sur la politique extérieure de la France* (Paris: Fayard, 1986), p. 99, François Mitterrand described France's independent foreign policy role as one it plays "within the Atlantic Alliance."
5. Bernard Oudin, *Aristide Briand* (Paris: Editions Robert Laffont, 1987), pp. 439–472.
6. Stern, "Germany in a Semi-Gaullist Europe," p. 868.

7. Ibid.
8. Ernst Weisenfeld, *Welches Deutschland soll es sein?* (München: C.H. Beck, 1986), pp. 138–140.
9. DeGaulle, wrote Stern ("Germany in a Semi-Gaullist Europe," p. 873), "expected that national interests and historic identity would in time allow for a new relationship with eastern Europe, despite the enmity of two opposing social systems." As Weisenfeld noted (*Welches Deutschland*, p. 116), Pompidou regarded German national sentiment as normal. Mitterrand (*Refléxions*, p. 95) welcomed the fact that the Federal Republic was showing "the will of a nation which declines to be the object" of political decisions made elsewhere.
10. Jon Jacobson, *Locarno Diplomacy* (Princeton: Princeton University Press, 1972), p. 29.
11. Stern, "Germany in a Semi-Gaullist Europe," p. 881: "There is no group in German society that would favor . . . a return to . . . the perpetual game of tilting and jilting between East and West that characterized earlier periods of German foreign policy, especially during the 1920s."
12. Precisely what concerns Hans-Peter Schwarz, *Die gezähmten Deutschen* (Stuttgart: DVA, 1985).
13. On the twenty-fifth anniversary of the Elysée Treaty in January 1988, *L'Express* cast a skeptical eye on the two countries' "community of fate" in "France-Allemagne: le drôle de couple," January 22, 1988, pp. 41–51.
14. Weisenfeld, *Welches Deutschland*, p. 129.
15. Willis, *France, Germany*, pp. 292–299.
16. See, for contrasting views, Maurice Schumann, "France and Germany in the New Europe," *Foreign Affairs* no. 41 (October 1962): 66–77; and Paul-Henri Spaak, "Hold Fast," *Foreign Affairs* 41 (July 1963): 611–622.
17. David Lawday, "France and Germany—The Odd Couple," *Economist* 271, no. 7082 (May 26, 1979): 36: "The argument that close cooperation is indispensable makes so much sense that the relationship must be seen as permanent. The British give the disconcerting impression that they have some kind of workable alternative to Europe up their sleeve. The strength of the bond between France and Germany is that they do not."
18. Stern, "Germany in a Semi-Gaullist Europe," p. 874.
19. Jean Monnet, *Memoirs* (Garden City, NY: Doubleday, 1978), p. 330: "Franco-German reconciliation was the means to the Schuman Plan's goal, which was peace."
20. Weisenfeld, *Welches Deutschland*, p. 178.
21. Schwarz, *Die gezähmten Deutschen*, p. 84: "The possibility of war is and remains the central problem of the modern management of power."
22. Ibid., pp. 84–103, an excellent summary of the classical and modern means used by states to manage power and to order their relations with each other.
23. Weisenfeld, *Welches Deutschland*, p. 109.
24. Willi Emrich, *Französisch-deutsche Freundschaftswoche 1960 in Frankfurt-am-Main* (Frankfurt: W. Krämer, 1961), p. 91: "Both states grew from . . . the Germanic-Roman-Christian Empire of Charlemagne. Both shared the same

name originally, 'Francia,' from the Frankish tribe. Let us remember the western community, which at that time seemed a matter of course."

25. *The Week in Germany* (New York: German Information Center), November 4, 1988. In his speech in Aachen, the West German president praised Kohl and Mitterrand for their coordination of West German and French relations with the Soviet Union. In their speeches, the two leaders both called for the further development of their countries' relations with the countries of eastern Europe. See also *Deutschland-Nachrichten* (New York: German Information Center), November 2, 1988.

26. John J. Maresca, *To Helsinki: The Conference on Security and Cooperation in Europe, 1973–1975* (Durham, NC: Duke University Press, 1987), p. 22, made an interesting point about German as one of the six official CSCE languages:

> German was a special case; it was the only language spoken in both communist and capitalist Europe. This, coupled with the fact that so much of the Conference's work related to German issues, made German useful as an official language. It can even be argued that the German-language text of the Final Act is the most authoritative, since it is the only one on which native-speaking capitalist, communist, and neutral countries agreed. To achieve agreement on the German-language text, a five-nation group (FRG, GDR, Austria, Switzerland, and Liechtenstein) carried on a sporadic parallel negotiation among themselves as sections of the Final Act were agreed.

27. Michael Stürmer, *Bismarck* (München: Piper, 1987), pp. 71–74, quoted a February 1871 speech of Benjamin Disraeli on the Franco-Prussian War: "The balance of power has been entirely destroyed, and the country which suffers most, and feels the effects of this great change most, is England."

28. Conversations in Bonn and Freiburg, 1985 and 1986.

29. *Schwarzwälder Bote* (Freiburg im Breisgau), June 4, 1969.

30. Discussions in Bonn of the role of the German language at the Budapest CSCE Cultural Forum, 1985 and 1986.

31. Discussions in Bonn, West Berlin, Paris, Stockholm, and Vienna, 1985 and 1986.

32. Discussions in Bonn, Saarlouis, and Freiburg, 1986.

33. Franco–West German–Soviet relations were discussed in the following *L'Express* articles: Elie Marcuse, "Des milliards sans concessions," November 4, 1988, pp. 6–8; Yves Cuau, "Emprunts russes," November 4, 1988, p. 7, and "Le hasard et le symbole," January 22, 1988, p. 23; and Alain Besançon, "Ce qui travaille l'Allemagne," October 2, 1987, p. 11.

34. *The Week in Germany*, October 19, 1988, and November 10, 1988; *Deutschland-Nachrichten*, October 26, 1988. Their meeting in Burgundy was the sixtieth between Kohl and Mitterrand.

35. *The Week in Germany*, November 18, 1988.

36. *Deutschland-Nachrichten*, November 23, 1988.

37. Richard von Weizsäcker, "Ansprache in der Gedenkstunde im Plenarsaal des Deutschen Bundestages am 8. Mai 1985," *Nachdenken über unsere Geschichte* (Bonn: Bundespresseamt, 1986).

38. *The Week in Germany*, November 18, 1988. Kohl called the Nazi genocide "without parallel in its cold-blooded, inhuman planning and in its deadly efficiency" and explicitly repudiated atttempts to compare it with other atrocities.
39. "Der Handhalter von Verdun," *Die Spiegel* no. 18 (April 29, 1985): 24–25.
40. Nina Grunenberg, "Die Richtung stimmt," *Die Zeit*, November 4, 1988.
41. Richard von Weizsäcker, "Germans and History: Give It to Us Straight" (excerpts from a speech to the Bamberg historians' conference, October 12, 1988), *International Herald Tribune*, October 29/30, 1988.
42. Theo Sommer concluded otherwise in his *Die Zeit* editorial on the Kohl visit to Moscow, "Unterwegs zu neuen Ufern," November 4, 1988, in which he wrote that Bonn had ended its "special conflict with the east" in "phase 1" of detente, and "phase 2," about to begin, would deal with the issues of the Cold War. Certainly, Bonn set the stage to deal with both sets of issues in the first detente decade, but the West German government seems well aware, contrary to Sommer's conclusion, that the Germans' role in east-west detente in the 1990s, because of Germany's past, will remain more complicated than that of either German state's allies.
43. "The sensation is that there is no sensation," the chancellor said after his November 3–4 meetings with Mitterrand. *The Week in Germany*, November 10, 1988.
44. "Gemeinsames Kommunique über das Treffen von Bundeskanzler Helmut Schmidt mit dem Vorsitzenden des Staatsrates der DDR und Generalsekretär des ZK der SED Erich Honecker vom 13. Dezember 1981," *Dokumentation zur Deutschlandpolitik der Bundesregierung* (Bonn: Bundespresseamt, 1986), pp. 255–260.
45. Carlo Schmid, *Erinnerungen* (Bern: Scherz, 1979), p. 217.
46. Jürgen Schmude, "The Role of the Church in German-German Relations," speech at the Friedrich Ebert Stiftung, Washington, DC, April 27, 1988; Helmut Schmidt, "Ethik und Verantwortung," and Jan-Thorn Prikker, "Nachgedanken zu Tschernobyl," both in *Evangelische Kommentare* no. 9 (September 1986): 533–537 and 540–543. See also the essays "Christentum und Parteipolitik" and "Liebe—Maßstab politischer Ordnung?"in Richard von Weizsäcker, *Die deutsche Geschichte geht weiter* (Berlin: Siedler, 1983), pp. 110–141.
47. Wilfried von Bredow, *Deutschland—ein Provisorium?* (Berlin: Siedler, 1985), argues the case for West German patriotism and the abandonment of reunification as a foreign policy goal.
48. Peter F. Drucker, *Adventures of a Bystander* (New York: Harper & Row, 1978), p. 26.
49. Final Act of the Conference on Security and Cooperation in Europe, Maresca, *To Helsinki*, pp. 261–282.
50. Hans-Dietrich Genscher, "Von der KSZE zur KVAE," in Horst Ehmke, Karlheinz Koppe, and Herbert Wehner, eds., *Zwanzig Jahre Ostpolitik* (Bonn: Verlag Neue Gesellschaft, 1986), p. 125.
51. Discussions in Vienna, 1986.

52. Genscher, "Von der KSZE," pp. 126–127. See also *Der Spiegel*'s interview with Mikhail Gorbachev (October 24, 1988): 20–30.

53. Hans-Adolf Jacobsen, "Deutsch-sowjetische Beziehungen: Kontinuität und Wandel 1945 bis 1987," *Aus Politik und Zeitgeschichte* B 3/88 (January 15, 1988): 42–44.

54. *The Week in Germany*, October 28, 1988, and Grunenberg, "Die Richtung stimmt."

55. *Deutschland-Nachrichten*, September 14, 1988, and *The Week in Germany*, November 20, 1987, and October 30, 1987.

56. *Deutschland-Nachrichten*, November 23, 1988, October 12, 1988, and September 21, 1988; *The Week in Germany*, September 16, 1988.

57. *Deutschland-Nachrichten*, October 19, 1988, and October 12, 1988; *The Week in Germany*, October 21, 1988.

58. *The Week in Germany*, September 16, 1988, and September 11, 1987; *Deutschland-Nachrichten*, November 16, 1988, and September 7, 1988.

59. Carl-Christian Kaiser, "Ein kleines Wunder für die Deutschen," *Die Zeit* (overseas edition), January 8, 1988.

60. Ibid.

61. Ibid., and *The Week in Germany*, November 18, 1988.

62. Ibid.

63. Discussions in Saarlouis and Bonn, 1986.

64. *Aachener Zeitung*, November 5, 1988, quoted in *The Week in Germany*, November 10, 1988.

65. The European Community's magazine features regular articles on implementation of the Single European Act, among them: Lord Cockfield, "E.C.'s Internal Market Is Just the Beginning," *Europe* no. 277 (June 1988): 28–30.

66. Nearly all of the chancellor's and foreign minister's speeches strike this note; two among them are: Helmut Kohl, "Rede zur Eröffnung der VI. Interparlamentarischen KSZE-Konferenz," Bonn, May 26, 1986 (*Bulletin* no. 59 [May 28, 1986]: 498–501); and Hans-Dietrich Genscher, "Deutschamerikanischer Beitrag zu Frieden und Verständigung," Heidelberg, February 8, 1986 (*Bulletin* no. 15 [February 13, 1986]: 109–113).

67. Preamble, *Grundgesetz für die Bundesrepublik Deutschland* (Bonn: Bundeszentrale für politische Bildung, 1984), p. 21.

68. Richard von Weizsäcker has used the phrase many times, among them in discussion with the 1985–86 American fellows of the Robert Bosch Foundation at Villa Hammerschmidt, Bonn, September 18, 1985.

bibliography

One of the advantages to anyone writing about West German foreign policy is the amount of documentation issued on a daily basis by the press and information offices of the West German government and parliament. Much of the primary documentary material used in the writing of this book came from material reprinted in the *Bulletin* of the Federal Press and Information Service (Bundespresseamt), which publishes the full text of important speeches by, among others, the federal president, the chancellor, and the foreign minister. Texts normally appear in the *Bulletin* two to three days after delivery, as do important letters, communiqués, and documents. Those issues quoted, cited, or used extensively for background are listed below.

The Bundespresseamt also publishes several series of books and pamphlets (*Berichte und Dokumentationen, Bürger-Informationen, Politik-Informationen*) that contain treaties and other documents relevant to West German foreign policy, each government's program, important speeches organized topically, summaries of official policies, and discussions of topical items in the West German political debate. Those cited or quoted in the text are listed below.

The Bundeszentrale für Politische Bildung publishes documents, such as the Grundgesetz, and commentaries on West German foreign policy that proved invaluable as background information. As a supplement to its excellent weekly newspaper *Das Parlament*, the Bundeszentrale issues *Aus Politik und Zeitgeschichte*, which contains articles, frequently on issues of foreign policy or diplomatic history, by West German and foreign authors. Those articles quoted or cited in the text or used extensively for background are listed in full below.

I had a personal opportunity to participate in the research and discussions sponsored by the Bundeszentrale in November 1986 and May

1987, when I was invited to join two seminars on the German question at the Bundeszentrale's Ostkolleg in Cologne. Those seminars enabled me to discuss the ideas contained in this book with, among others, Renata Fritsch-Bournazel, Hans-Ulrich Wehler, Wolfgang Seiffert, and Peter Danylow. My thanks to W. Maibaum, Barbara Kamutzki, and Heinrich Bartel for the invitation to take part in the Ostkolleg's programs.

The documents of three conferences were used in the preparation of this book. They included those of the opening session of the Conference on Security and Cooperation in Europe's (CSCE) review meeting in Vienna, which I attended in November 1986. The U.S. Ambassador to the CSCE meeting, Warren Zimmerman, gave an excellent summary of U.S. CSCE policy in a speech at the German Society for Foreign Affairs (DGAP) in Bonn on October 28, 1986, which I was privileged to attend. My thanks to the Society's director, Karl Kaiser, and to its library staff for their help in locating material on Franco–West German political and security cooperation.

In addition to attending the opening session of the CSCE meeting, I had the opportunity in Vienna to discuss the two September 1986 sessions of the International Atomic Energy Agency (IAEA) devoted to the implications of the accident at Chernobyl for national policy and international cooperation. Hans-Friedrich Meyer and James Dalgleisch of the IAEA staff and Rüdiger Freiherr von Preuschen zu Liebenstein of the Federal Republic's mission to the IAEA gave generously of their time. I am especially grateful to Freiherr von Preuschen for his insights into the post-Chernobyl political process and to Herr Meyer for access to the IAEA documents cited in the text, including the statements by national delegations at the two September meetings and the texts of the Federal Republic's initial proposals for the special session.

Hellmut Hoffman of the West German delegation to the Mutual and Balanced Force Reduction (MBFR) talks graciously took time to discuss with me western consultations in Vienna and to provide advice on appointments and assistance in locating documentation, despite my inconvenient arrival in the city at the same time as his foreign minister.

The third group of meeting documentation used was that issued by the CSCE Conference on Confidence-building Measures and Disarmament in Europe (CDE) in Stockholm, which concluded in September 1986. My thanks to Folke Löfgren of the Swedish Ministry of Foreign Affairs/CDE Secretariat for his time and for the material he provided. My thanks also for discussions with Walther Stützle, Director of the Stockholm International Peace Research Institute (SIPRI), and to Jan-Olof Pettersson of Swedish National Radio, who took time to discuss the Stockholm Conference with me, despite his imminent departure for the U.S.-USSR summit in Reykjavík. Special thanks to the staff of the

United States Information Service (USIS) library at the American Embassy in Stockholm, who provided background information on CDE and statements by the American delegation, and to Herr Metscher of the West German CSCE/CDE delegation, who made time to discuss the CSCE process with me in the midst of his own preparations for the move to Vienna later that month. Herr Altenburg at the Auswärtiges Amt in Bonn helped steer me in the right direction.

The fourth group of documents and interviews that completed the primary unpublished material used for this book was provided by the Franco-German Youth Office (DFJW/OFAJ) and the cities of Saarlouis and Bremen on the implementation of Franco—West German sister cities and cultural exchange programs established in the 1950s and 1960s and the development of such programs with the GDR and Poland. Thanks to Hartmut Gimmler of the German-American Institute in Saarbrücken, I spent an exceptionally pleasant and valuable day with the mayor of Saarlouis, Manfred Henrich, and his colleague on the city council Hans-Joachim Fontaine in December 1986. I am grateful for their insights and perspectives on the nature of the sister cities relationship, across the Rhine and across the inner-German border, and for the documentation they provided.

Former Mayor of Bremen Hans Koschnick was kind enough to spend several hours with me at the Bremen state representation in Bonn in December 1986 and discuss the establishment of Bremen's sister city relationship with Gdansk during his administration in the 1970s. His insights into the importance to individual West Germans of *Vergangenheitsbewältigung* and the Locarno from below were invaluable, as was the documentation provided to me, at his request, by Gertrud Exner of the city of Bremen.

Gert Hammer, Deputy Director of the Franco-German Youth Office in Bad Honnef, generously gave a half-day in September 1985 to a discussion of Franco–West German sister cities and youth exchanges. His office provided substantial documentation on the work of the DFJW. In Stuttgart in December 1986, Michael Hagenmeyer of the Baden-Württemberg state ministry of economics also took a half-day to discuss with me the role of the West German states in east-west trade and cooperation and the political issues associated with the development of east-west cultural and economic relations.

In the framework of my Robert Bosch fellowship in 1985 and 1986, I had the opportunity to participate in seminars at the Bundesakademie für öffentliche Verwaltung in Bonn, which included discussions with Michael Stürmer, Dieter Lattmann, and Paul Noack. The most valuable of these discussions were undoubtedly an informal meeting with Chancellor Helmut Kohl and an insightful two hours with President Richard von Weizsäcker on the terrace of his residence, Villa Hammerschmidt. The Bundesakademie program was arranged by Reinhold Geimer, whose insights into his country's history and its relationship with France provided some of the most memorable moments of the Bosch fellowship year.

The Ecole Nationale d'Administration (ENA) made possible ten productive days in France for the Robert Bosch fellows in December 1985, including discussions with Alfred Grosser and with Bonn's ambassador to Paris, and a two-day visit to Chartres to discuss local government and planning with city and regional officials. I am also indebted to M. Nora, Mme. Terroir, and Mme. de Chabot of ENA for arranging an interview for me with Jacques Chaban-Delmas, then president of the French National Assembly and former prime minister, who graciously spent an hour discussing Franco–West German relations from his perspective as a national and local (as mayor of Bordeaux since 1947) political leader.

I could not list the hundreds of West German public officials and private individuals with whom I discussed the issues raised in this book between August 1985 and May 1987. In addition to numerous colleagues at the Bundestag and the Auswärtiges Amt, over lunch, coffee, and the copying machine, they included the officers at the Bundeswehr Zentrum für Innere Führung and the parliamentary party leaders of the Saarland state legislature, but also teachers, students, labor leaders, artists, and many others whose names were never known to me. Their questions, comments, and presentations at the seminars I attended under the auspices of USIS Bonn all helped clarify my perspective on the events and concepts discussed in this book.

Needless to say, the conclusions I have reached on the broadening and deepening of the Frankreichpolitik, the emergence of an understanding of Locarno as a process of detente-entente-cooperation in West German foreign policy, and especially the relevance of a Locarno from below to the establishment of a new German self-image and European cooperation are mine alone. None of the individuals mentioned above or in the preface bears any responsibility for those interpretations; their contribution was to my knowledge of their countries and continent and to the warm personal memories I have of my years in Europe.

Books

ABENHEIM, DONALD. *Reforging the Iron Cross: The Search for Tradition in the West German Armed Forces*. Princeton: Princeton University Press. 1988.

ADENAUER, KONRAD. *Erinnerungen*. Stuttgart: Deutsche Verlags-Anstalt. 1964–68.

ALLARDT, HELMUT. *Moskauer Tagebuch*. Frankfurt am Main: Ullstein. 1980.

ARON, RAYMOND. *Mémoires*.: Paris: Julliard. 1983

BARTOSZEWSKI, WLADYSLAW. *Aus der Geschichte lernen?* München: DTV. 1986.

BECKER, JOSEF, and HILLGRUBER, ANDREAS. *Die Deutsche Frage im 19. und 20. Jahrhundert.* München: Ernst Vögel. 1983.

BENDER, PETER. *Das Ende des ideologischen Zeitalters.* Berlin: Severin and Siedler. 1981.

———. *Die Ostpolitik Willy Brandts.* Hamburg: Rowohlt. 1972.

BÖLLING, KLAUS. *Die Fernen Nachbarn: Erfahrungen in der DDR.* Hamburg: Stern. 1984

BRACHER, KARL DIETRICH. *Die deutsche Diktatur.* Köln: Kiepenheuer & Witsch. 1969.

BRANDT, WILLY. *Auf der Zinne der Partei.* Bonn: J. H. W. Dietz, 1984.

———. *Begegnungen und Einsichten.* Hamburg: Hoffman und Campe Verlag. 1976.

———. *Geschichte als Auftrag: Willy Brandts Reden zur Geschichte der Arbeiterbewegung.* ed. Iring Fetscher. Bonn: J. H. W. Dietz. 1981.

———. *". . . wir sind nicht zu Helden geboren."* Zurich: Diogenes. 1986.

VON BREDOW, WILFRIED. *Deutschland—ein Provisorium?.* Berlin: Siedler. 1985.

BUCHSTAB, GÜNTER; KAFF, BRIGITTE; and KLEINMANN, HANS-OTTO, eds. *Verfolgung und Widerstand, 1933–1945: Christliche Demokraten gegen Hitler.* Düsseldorf: Droste. 1986.

BULLOCK, ALAN. *Ernest Bevin, Foreign Secretary 1945–1951.* New York: W. W. Norton. 1983.

BYRNES, JAMES F. *Speaking Frankly.* New York: Harper. 1947.

CALLEO, DAVID. *Europe's Future: The Grand Alternatives.* New York: Norton. 1967.

———. *The German Problem Reconsidered: Germany and the World Order, 1870 to the Present.* Cambridge: Cambridge University Press. 1978.

CAMPBELL, EDWINA S. *Consultation and Consensus in NATO: Implementing the Canadian Article.* Lanham, MD: University Press of America. 1985.

CAMUS, ALBERT. *Resistance, Rebellion, and Death.* New York: Vintage Books. 1974.

CASDORFF, CLAUS HINRICH. *Weihnachten 1945: Ein Buch der Erinnerungen.* München: DTV. 1984.

COOK, DON. *Ten Men and History.* New York: Doubleday. 1981.

CRAIG, GORDON, and GILBERT, FELIX. *The Diplomats: 1919–1939.* Princeton: Princeton University Press. 1953.

DAGERMAN, STIG. *Deutscher Herbst '46.* Köln: Hohenheim Verlag. 1981.

DAHRENDORF, RALF. *Society and Democracy in Germany.* New York: Doubleday. 1967.

DAWISHA, KAREN. *Eastern Europe: Gorbachev and Reform, The Great Challenge.* Cambridge: Cambridge University Press. 1988.

DEAN, JONATHAN. *Watershed in Europe.* Boston: Union of Concerned Scientists. 1986.

DELCOUR, ROLAND. *Konrad Adenauer.* Paris: Seghers. 1966.

DÖNHOFF, MARION GRÄFIN. *Namen die keiner mehr nennt.* München: DTV. 1986.

———. *Von Gestern nach Übermorgen.* München: DTV. 1986.

DOUGHERTY, JAMES E., and PFALTZGRAFF, ROBERT L., JR., eds. *Shattering Europe's Defense Consensus.* McLean, VA: Pergamon-Brassey's. 1985.

DRUCKER, PETER F. *Adventures of a Bystander.* New York: Harper & Row. 1979.

VON ECKARDT, FELIX. *Ein unordentliches Leben.* Frankfurt am Main: Ullstein. 1971.

EDINGER, LEWIS J. *Kurt Schumacher.* Stanford: Stanford University Press. 1965.

EHMKE, HORST; KOPPE, KARLHEINZ; and WEHNER, HERBERT, eds. *Zwanzig Jahre Ostpolitik: Bilanz und Perspektiven*. Bonn: Verlag Neue Gesellschaft. 1986.

FEILER, OSWALD. *Moskau und die Deutsche Frage*. Krefeld: Sinus. 1984.

FERELL, ROBERT H. *Peace in Their Time: The Origins of the Kellogg-Briand Pact*. New Haven: Yale University Press. 1952.

FRITSCH-BOURNAZEL, RENATA. *Das Land in der Mitte*. München: iudicium verlag. 1986.

DE GAULLE, CHARLES. *The Complete War Memoirs*. New York: Simon and Schuster. 1968.

———. *Memoirs of Hope: Renewal and Endeavor*. New York: Simon and Schuster. 1976.

GAUS, GÜNTER. *Die Welt der Westdeutschen*. Köln: Kiepenheuer & Witsch. 1986.

———. *Wo Deutschland liegt*. München: DTV. 1986.

GLOTZ, PETER. *Manifest für eine Neue Europäische Linke*. Berlin: Siedler. 1985.

GOLDSTEIN, WALTER., ed. *Reagan's Leadership and the Atlantic Alliance*. McLean, VA: Pergamon-Brassey's. 1986.

GRAML, HERMANN. *Europa zwischen den Kriegen*. München: DTV. 1969.

GRESS, DAVID. *Peace and Survival*. Stanford: Hoover Institution Press. 1985.

GREWE, WILHELM G. *Die deutsche Frage in der Ost-West Spannung*. Herford: Busse/Seewald. 1986.

GROSSER, ALFRED. *Affaires Extérieures: La Politique de la France, 1944/1984*. Paris: Flammarion. 1984.

———. *The Western Alliance: European-American Relations since 1945*. New York: Vintage Books, 1982.

HAFFNER, SEBASTIAN. *Anmerkungen zu Hitler*. München: Kindler Verlag. 1978.

———. *Im Schatten der Geschichte*. Stuttgart: Deutsche Verlags-Anstalt. 1985.

———. *Preussen ohne Legende*. Hamburg: Stern. 1979.

———. *Der Selbstmord des Deutschen Reiches*. Bern: Scherz. 1970.

———. *Zur Zeitgeschichte*. München: Kindler. 1982.

HERZFELD, HANS. *Die Weimarer Republik*. Frankfurt am Main: Ullstein. 1969.

HEUSS, ALFRED. *Versagen und Verhängnis*. Berlin: Siedler. 1984.

HILLGRUBER, ANDREAS. *Deutsche Geschichte, 1945–1982: Die "deutsche Frage" in der Weltpolitik*. Stuttgart: W. Kohlhammer. 1983.

———. *Endlich genug über Nazionalsozialismus und Zweiten Weltkrieg?* Düsseldorf: Droste. 1982.

———. *Die Last der Nation*. Düsseldorf: Droste. 1984.

———. *Zweierlei Untergang: Die Zerschlagung des Deutschen Reiches und das Ende des europäischen Judentums*. Berlin: Siedler. 1986.

HOLBORN, HAJO. *Hajo Holborn: Inter Nationes Prize 1969*. Bonn: Inter Nationes. 1969.

IRELAND, TIMOTHY P. *Creating the Entangling Alliance*. Westport, CN: Greenwood Press. 1981.

JACOBSON, JON. *Locarno Diplomacy: Germany and the West, 1925–1929*. Princeton: Princeton University Press. 1972.

JENS, WALTER. *Ort der Handlung ist Deutschland*. München: Knaur. 1981.

JUNKER, DETLEF, ed. *Deutschland und die USA, 1890–1985*. Heidelberg: German-American Institute. 1985.

KAHN, HERMAN, and REDEPENNING, MICHAEL. *Die Zukunft Deutschlands*. Stuttgart: Horst Poller Verlag. 1982.

KAISER, KARL, and LELLOUCHE, PIERRE, eds. *Deutsch-französische Sicherheitspolitik: Auf dem Wege zur Gemeinsamkeit?* Bonn: Europa Union Verlag. 1986.

KATZENSTEIN, PETER J. *Disjoined Partners: Austria and Germany Since 1815*. Berkeley: University of California Press. 1976.

KELLEHER, CATHERINE M., and MATTOX, GALE A., eds. *Evolving European Defense Policies*. Lexington, MA: D. C. Heath. 1987.

KENNAN, GEORGE F. *Memoirs, 1950–1963*. New York: Pantheon. 1983.

KREISKY, BRUNO. *Zwischen den Zeiten: Erinnerungen aus fünf Jahrzehnten*. Berlin: Siedler. 1986.

VON KROKOW, CHRISTIAN GRAF. *Die Stunde der Frauen*. Stuttgart: Deutsche Verlags-Anstalt. 1987.

LACOUTURE, JEAN. *De Gaulle, 2. Le politique, 1944–1959*. Paris: Seuil. 1985.

―――. *Pierre Mendès France*. Paris: Seuil. 1981.

LEICHT, ROBERT, ed. *Im Lauf des Jahres: Deutsche Texte und Dokumente 1981*. München: DTV. 1982.

―――. *Im Lauf des Jahres: Deutsche Texte und Dokumente 1982*. München: DTV. 1983.

LEINEMANN, JÜRGEN. *Die Angst der Deutschen*. Reinbek bei Hamburg: Rowohlt/Spiegel. 1982.

LIVINGSTON, ROBERT GERALD, ed. *The Federal Republic of Germany in the 1980s*. New York: German Information Center. 1983.

LÖWENTHAL, RICHARD. *Social Change and Cultural Crisis*. New York: Columbia University Press. 1984.

――― and SCHWARZ, HANS-PETER, eds. *Die zweite Republik*. Stuttgart: Seewald Verlag. 1974.

MARESCA, JOHN J. *To Helsinki: The Conference on Security and Cooperation in Europe, 1973–1975*. Durham, NC: Duke University Press. 1987.

MARTIN, ERNST. *Zwischenbilanz: Deutschlandpolitik der 80er Jahre*. Stuttgart: Verlag Bonn Aktuell. 1986.

MASER, WERNER. *Deutschland, Traum oder Trauma, Kein Requiem*. München: Drömer Knaur. 1984.

MASTNY, VOJTECH, ed. *Helsinki, Human Rights, and European Security*. Durham, NC: Duke University Press. 1986.

―――. *Russia's Road to the Cold War*. New York: Columbia University Press. 1979.

McGEEHAN, ROBERT. *The German Rearmament Question*. Urbana: University of Illinois Press. 1971.

McKENZIE, JOHN R. P. *Weimar Germany, 1918–1933*. Totowa, NJ: Rowman & Littlefield. 1971.

MEE, CHARLES L., JR. *Meeting at Potsdam*. New York: M. Evans and Co. 1975.

MERKL, PETER, ed. *West German Foreign Policy: Dilemmas and Directions*. Chicago: Council on Foreign Relations. 1982.

MILOSZ, CZESLAW. *Native Realm*. New York: Doubleday. 1968.

MIREK, HOLGER. *Deutsch-Französische Gemeindepartnerschaften*. Kehl am Rhein: N.P. Engel Verlag. 1984.

MITTERRAND, FRANÇOIS. *Refléxions sur la politique extérieure de la France*. Paris: Fayard. 1986.

MONNET, JEAN. *Memoirs*. Garden City, NY: Doubleday. 1978.

NEUMANN, WILLIAM L. *After Victory: Churchill, Roosevelt, Stalin and the Making of the Peace*. New York: Harper and Row. 1967.

NIPPERDEY, THOMAS. *Nachdenken über die deutsche Geschichte*. München: C. H. Beck. 1986.

OUDIN, BERNARD. *Aristide Briand*. Paris: Robert Laffont, 1987.

PICHT, ROBERT. *Das Bündnis im Bündnis: Deutsch-Französische Beziehungen im internationalen Spannungsfeld*. Berlin: Severin und Siedler. 1982.

PIERRE, ANDREW J., ed. *A Widening Atlantic?*. New York: Council on Foreign Relations. 1986.

RAFF, DIETHER. *Deutsche Geschichte vom Alten Reich zur Zweiten Republik*. München: Max Hüber Verlag. 1985.

ROUSSEL, STEPHANE. *Les collines de Berlin: Un regard sur l'Allemagne*. Paris: Mazarine. 1985.

ROVAN, JOSEPH. *L'Allemagne n'est pas ce que vous croyez*. Paris: Seuil. 1978.

SAUZAY, BRIGITTE. *Le Vertige Allemand*. Paris: Olivier Orban. 1985.

SCHLÖGEL, KARL. *Die Mitte liegt ostwärts: Die Deutschen, der verlorene Osten und Mitteleuropa*. Berlin: Siedler. 1986.

SCHMID, CARLO. *Erinnerungen*. Bern: Scherz Verlag. 1979.

SCHMIDT, HELMUT. *A Grand Strategy for the West*. New Haven: Yale University Press. 1985.

———. *Die nüchterne Leidenschaft zur praktischen Vernunft*. Berlin: Pharus Verlag. 1987.

SCHULZE, HAGEN. *Weimar Deutschland 1917–1933*, volume 4 of the six volume *Die Deutschen und ihre Nation*. Berlin: Severin und Siedler. 1982.

SCHWARZ, HANS-PETER. *Adenauer, Der Aufstieg: 1876–1952*. Stuttgart: Deutsche Verlags-Anstalt. 1986.

———. *Die gezähmten Deutschen: Von der Machtbesessenheit zur Machtvergessenheit*. Stuttgart: Deutsche Verlags-Anstalt. 1985.

SIEBURG, FRIEDRICH. *Abmarsch in die Barbarei*. Frankfurt am Main: Ullstein. 1986.

SIEDLER, WOLF JOBST. *Auf der Pfaueninsel: Spaziergänge in Preussens Arkadien*. Berlin: Siedler. 1986.

SPEIDEL, HANS. *Aus unserer Zeit*. Berlin: Propylaen. 1977.

DE STAEL, MADAME. *De l'Allemagne*. Oxford: Clarendon Press. 1906.

STEININGER, ROLF. *Eine vertane Chance: Die Stalin-Note vom 10. März 1952 und die Wiedervereinigung*. Bonn: J. H. W. Dietz. 1985.

STRESEMANN, WOLFGANG. *Mein Vater Gustav Stresemann*. Berlin: Ullstein. 1985.

STÜRMER, MICHAEL. *Bismarck*. München: Piper. 1987.

———. *Dissonanzen des Fortschritts*. München: Piper. 1986.

———. *Die Reichsgründung: Deutscher Nationalstaat und europäisches Gleichgewicht im Zeitalter Bismarcks*. München: DTV. 1984.

———. *Das ruhelose Reich: Deutschland 1866–1918*, vol. 3 of the six volume series *Die Deutschen und ihre Nation*. Berlin: Severin und Siedler. 1983.

———, ed. *Die Weimarer Republik: Belagerte Civitas*. Königstein: Verlagsgruppe Athenaeum, Hain, Scriptor, Hanstein. 1980.

TURNER, HENRY AHSBY. *Stresemann and the Politics of the Weimar Republic.* Princeton: Princeton University Press. 1963.

VENOHR, WOLFGANG, ed. *Ohne Deutschland geht es nicht.* Krefeld: Sinus. 1985.

VOGELSANG, THILO. *Das geteilte Deutschland.* München: DTV. 1973.

WEBER, ALFRED. *Haben wir Deutschen nach 1945 versagt?.* München: Piper. 1979.

WEIDENFELD, WERNER, ed. *Die Identität der Deutschen.* Bonn: Bundeszentrale für politische Bildung. 1983.

————. *Konrad Adenauer und Europa.* Bonn: Europa Union Verlag. 1976.

WEISENFELD, ERNST. *Welches Deutschland soll es sein? Frankreich und die deutsche Einheit seit 1945.* München: C. H. Beck. 1986.

VON WEIZSÄCKER, RICHARD. *Die deutsche Geschichte geht weiter.* Berlin: Siedler. 1983.

WILKINSON, JAMES D. *The Intellectual Resistance in Europe.* Cambridge, MA: Harvard University Press. 1981.

WILLIS F. ROY. *France, Germany, and the New Europe, 1945–1967.* London: Oxford University Press. 1968.

WILLMS, BERNARD. *Die Deutsche Nation.* Köln: Hohenheim Verlag. 1982.

WILMS, DOROTHEE. *The German Question and Inner-German Relations.* Washington, D.C.: Konrad Adenauer Stiftung. 1987.

DE ZAYAS, ALFRED M. *Nemesis at Potsdam.* London: Routledge and Kegan Paul. 1977.

Journals and Magazines

BRZEZINSKI, ZBIGNIEW. "The Future of Yalta." *Foreign Affairs* 63, no. 2 (Winter 1984/5): 279–302.

CALLEO, DAVID P. "NATO's Middle Course." *Foreign Policy* no. 69. (Winter 1987/8): 135–147.

CAMPBELL, EDWINA S. "The Ideals and Origins of the Franco-German Sister Cities Movement, 1945–70." *Journal of the History of European Ideas* 8, no. 1 (1987): 77–95.

CHABAN-DELMAS, JACQUES. "Perspektiven für die politische Zukunft Europas." *Europa-Archiv* no. 5 (March 1985): 121–132.

GLEES, ANTHONY. "Churchill's Last Gambit." *Encounter* 64, no. 4 (April 1985): 27–31.

GRESS, DAVID. "Whatever Happened to Willy Brandt?" *Commentary* (July 1983): 55–58.

HOFFMANN, STANLEY. "Choices." *Foreign Policy.* no. 12 (Fall 1973): 3–42.

KAGAN, DONALD. "World War I, World War II, World War III." *Commentary* (March 1987): 21–40.

KENNEDY, PAUL. "What Gorbachev Is Up Against." *Atlantic* (June 1987): 29–43.

KIEP, WALTHER LEISLER. "The New Deutschlandpolitik." *Foreign Affairs* 63, no. 2 (Winter 1984/5): 316–329.

LAWDAY, DAVID. "France and Germany—The Odd Couple." *Economist* 271, no. 7082 (May 26, 1979): 27–36.

LIVINGSTON, ROBERT G. "A Wounded Nation." *The National Interest* (Winter 1987/8) 90–94.

LÖWENTHAL, RICHARD. "The German Question Transformed." *Foreign Affairs* 63, no. 2 (Winter 1984/5): 303-315.

MAY, ERNEST R. "The Nature of Foreign Policy: The Calculated vs. the Axiomatic." *Daedalus* no. 91 (Fall 1962): 653–667.

MOSETTIG, MICHAEL D. "Reflections on Jean Monnet" (Interview with François Duchène). *Europe* no. 281 (November 1988): 30–48.

RUIZ PALMER, DIEGO A. "Between the Rhine and the Elbe: France and the Conventional Defense of Central Europe." *Comparative Strategy* 6, no. 4 (1987): 471–512.

SCHMIDT, HELMUT. "Ethik und Verantwortung." *Evangelische Kommentare* no. 9 (September 1986): 533–537.

SOUTOU, JEAN-MARIE. "Paris-Bonn: le fil de l'Histoire." *Le Point* no. 612 (June 11, 1984).

STENT, ANGELA. "Soviet Relations with Europe are Changing," *Europe* (January-February 1988): 32–33, 51.

STERN, FRITZ. "Germany in a Semi-Gaullist Europe." *Foreign Affairs* 58, no. 4 (Spring 1980): 867–886.

WALL, PATRICK. "The Fallout from Chernobyl." *Sea Power*. pp. 24–6.

BULLETIN.

Presse- und Informationsamt der Bundesregierung (commonly, Bundespresseamt), Bonn:

SPEECHES BY HANS-DIETRICH GENSCHER

"Besuch des Aussenministers von Jugoslawien." Bonn, January 20, 1986. no. 8 (January 24, 1986): 49–50.

"Deutsch-amerikanischer Beitrag zu Frieden und Verständigung." Heidelberg, February 8, 1986. no. 15 (February 13, 1986): 109–113.

"Europas Verantwortung als gleichgewichtiger Partner der USA." Stuttgart, September 6, 1986. no. 99 (September 10, 1986): 833–835.

"Initiativen und Impulse für Rüstungskontrolle und Abrüstung." Geneva, June 10, 1986. no. 68. (June 12, 1986): 573–576.

"Kooperative Sicherheitsstrukturen für Europa." Bonn, July 11, 1986. no. 86 (July 16, 1986): 725–728.

"Perspektiven einer europäischen Friedensordnung." Vienna, August 27, 1986. no. 96 (August 29, 1986): 807–813.

"Rede des Aussenministers vor den Vereinten Nationen." New York, September 25, 1986. no. 113. (September 30, 1986): 953–958.

SPEECHES BY HELMUT KOHL

"Auftrag und Verpflichtungen des Erbes Robert Schumans." Strasbourg, July 8, 1986. no. 87 (July 18, 1986): 733–735.

"Ecksteine deutscher Politik." Mainz, September 17, 1986. no. 106 (September 23, 1986): 897–900.

"Leitlinien und Grundüberzeugungen deutscher Aussenpolitik." Bonn, June 25, 1986. no. 78 (July 1, 1986): 657–663.
"Rede des Bundeskanzlers vor dem Deutschen Bundestag." Bonn, September 5, 1985. no. 95 (September, 6, 1985): 829–836.
"Zur Eröffnung der VI. Interparlamentarischen KSZE-Konferenz." Bonn, May 26, 1986. no. 59 (May 28, 1986): 498–501.

SPEECHES BY RICHARD VON WEIZSÄCKER

"Ansprache vor beiden Häusern des Parlaments." London, July 2, 1986. no. 84 (July 10, 1986): 706–709.
"Bankett des Lord Mayor of London," London, July 2, 1986. no. 84 (July 10, 1986): 709–711.
"Die Bedeutung der Friedensfunktion der Vereinten Nationen." Bonn, July 11, 1986. no. 86. (July 16, 1986): 721–722.
"Die Bedeutung des Gesprächs zwischen Politik und Literatur." Hamburg, June 22, 1986. no. 75 (June 25, 1986): 633–634.
"Staatsbankett im Buckingham Palace." London, July 1, 1986. no. 84 (July 10, 1986): 705–706.

MISCELLANEOUS

"Ansprache von Bundespräsident a. D. Walter Scheel zum Gedenken an den 17. Juni 1953," Bonn, June 17, 1986. no. 73 (June 19, 1986): 613–619.
"Arbeitsprogramm der Bundesregierung zur Verbesserung der Reaktorsicherheit." no. 97 (September 5, 1986): 821.
"Bericht über die Auswirkungen des Reaktorunfalls in Tschernobyl." no. 78 (July 1, 1986): 663–664.
"Deutsch-französische Konsultationen in Paris." no. 24 (March 7, 1986): 180–181.
"Dokument der Stockholmer Konferenz (KVAE)." no. 110 (September 26, 1987): 929–936.
"15 Jahre Viermächte-Abkommen." no. 97 (September 5, 1986): 820.
"Grundlagen und Prinzipien der freiheitlichen Demokratie." Speech by Interior Minister Friedrich Zimmermann, Berlin, September 7, 1986. no. 99 (September 10, 1986): 836–839.
"Die kulturelle Dimension des deutsch-französischen Verhältnisses." no. 8 (January 24, 1986): 51.
"Rede des Bundestagspräsidenten Philipp Jenninger zur Eröffnung der VI. Interparlamentarischen Konferenz über Europäische Zusammenarbeit und Sicherheit." Bonn, May 26, 1986. no. 59 (May 28, 1986): 497–498.
"Stiftung 'Haus der Geschichte der Bundesrepublik Deutschland.' " no. 87 (July 18, 1986): 735–736.
"Verpflichtung zur nationalen Solidarität." no. 73 (June 19, 1986): 619.
"Wiener Expertentreffen über den Reaktorunfall in Tschernobyl." no. 97 (September 5, 1986): 821–822.

"Zielstrebiger Ausbau der innerdeutschen Beziehungen." no. 73 (June 19, 1986): 619.

AUS POLITIK UND ZEITGESCHICHTE

(Beilage zur Wochenzeitung *Das Parlament*). Bundeszentrale für politische Bildung, Bonn.

BLÄNSDORF, AGNES. "Zur Konfrontation mit der NS-Vergangenheit in der Bundesrepublik, der DDR und Österreich." B 16–17/87 (April 18, 1987): 3–18.

GRESS, DAVID R. "Die deutsch-amerikanischen Beziehungen von 1945 bis 1987." B 3/88 (January 15,1988): 16–27.

HACKE, CHRISTIAN. "Traditionen und Stationen der Aussenpolitik der Bundesrepublik Deutschland." B 3/88 (January 15, 1988): 3–15.

HANRIEDER, WOLFRAM F. "Die deutsch-amerikanischen Beziehungen in den Nachkriegsjahrzehnten." B 26/86 (June 28, 1986): 16–28.

HRBEK, RUDOLF. "30 Jahre Römische Verträge." B 18/87 (May 2, 1987): 18–33.

JACOBSEN, HANS-ADOLF. "Deutsch-sowjetische Beziehungen: Kontinuität und Wandel 1945 bis 1987." B 3/88 (January 15, 1988): 28–44.

KORTE, KARL-RUDOLF. "Deutschlandbilder—Akzentverlagerungen der deutschen Frage seit den siebziger Jahren." B 3/88 (January 15, 1988): 45–53.

MOMMSEN, HANS. "Die Geschichte des deutschen Widerstands im Lichte der neueren Forschung." B 50/86 (December 13, 1986): 3–18.

MÜLLER, KLAUS-JÜRGEN. "Die nationalkonservative Opposition 1933–1939." B 50/86 (December 13, 1986): 19–30.

VAN ROON, GER. "Der Kreisauer Kreis und das Ausland." B 50/86 (December 13, 1986): 31–46.

SCHRÖDER, HANS-JÜRGEN. "Marshallplan, amerikanische Deutschlandpolitik und europäische Integration 1947–1950." B 18/87 (May 2, 1987): 3–17.

SCHWAN, GESINE. "Das deutsche Amerikabild seit der Weimarer Republic." B 26/86 (June 28, 1986): 3–15.

WOLFFSOHN, MICHAEL. "Die Wiedergutmachung und der Westen—Tatsachen und Legende." B 16–17/87 (April 18, 1987): 19–29.

DER SPIEGEL

COUDENHOVE-KALERGI, BARBARA. "Wie deutsch sind die Österreicher?" no. 39 (September 26, 1988) 176–177.

KOCKA, JÜRGEN. "Der Bruch war tiefer als 1918/19." no. 36 (September 5, 1988): 45–54.

"Kompetent am Huf." no. 38 (September 19, 1988): 99–105.

"Eine Kooperation auf neuem Niveau." no. 26 (July 6, 1987): 19–31.

"Länger schlaffen." no. 16 (April 18, 1988): 45.

LEINEMANN, JÜRGEN. "Eine der grossen Leitfiguren der Welt." no. 4 (January 23, 1989): 31–32.

"Mit Knobelbechern durch die Geschichte." no. 46 (November 14, 1988): 22–28.

"Noch eins drauf." no 40. (October 3, 1988): 58–60.

" 'Politiker sollten ihre Worte wägen' " (Interview with Mikhail Gorbachev). no. 43 (October 24, 1988): 20–31.

"Slawisches im Blut." no. 40 (October 3, 1988): 21–22.

"Trostreiche Tüttelchen." no. 4 (January 23, 1989): 47.

L'EXPRESS

BESANÇON, ALAIN. "Catastroika: le programme extérieur." no. 1901 (December 18, 1987): 15.

———, "Ce qui travaille l'Allemagne." no. 1890 (October 2, 1987): 11.

CASANOVA, JEAN-CLAUDE. "Les leçons de Yalta." no. 1948 (November 11, 1988): 62.

CUAU, YVES. "Emprunts russes." no. 1947 (November 4, 1988): 7.

———. "Et l'autre Europe?" no. 1901 (December 18, 1987): 9.

———. "Les années du destin." no. 1890 (October 2, 1987): 9.

———. "Le hasard et le symbole." no. 1906 (January 22, 1988): 23.

FERRY, LUC. "Comprendre la RFA." no. 1963 (February 24, 1989): 21.

FONTAINE, FRANÇOIS. "Jean Monnet: l'Europe, cette idée simple." no. 1951 (December 2, 1988).

"France-Allemagne: le drôle de couple." no. 1906. (January 22, 1988): 41–51.

MARCUSE, ELIE. "Des milliards sans concessions." no. 1947. (November 4, 1988): 6–8.

MINC, ALAIN. "Où va l'Allemagne?" no. 1963 (February 24, 1989): 20.

NEW YORK REVIEW OF BOOKS

ASH, TIMOTHY GARTON. "Does Central Europe Exist?" (October 9, 1986): 45–52.

———. "From World War to Cold War" (June 11, 1987): 44–50.

———. "Which Way Will Germany Go?" (January 31, 1985): 33–40.

CRAIG, GORDON A. "The War of the German Historians." (January 15, 1987): 16–19.

HOFFMANN, STANLEY. "Coming Down from the Summit." (January 21, 1988): 21–25.

KENNAN, GEORGE. "The Gorbachev Prospect." (January 21, 1988): 3–7.

STERN, FRITZ. "Remembering the Uprising." (December 3, 1987): 14–19.

Newspapers

FRIEDMANN, BERNHARD. " 'Wiedervereinigung Deutschlands als Sicherheitsgarantie für Ost und West.' " *Die Welt.* November 13, 1986.

GATERMANN, RAINER. "Gefordert ist europäisches Denken und Handeln, sonst spielen wir keine gebührende Rolle mehr." *Die Welt.* Feburary 26, 1986.

GILLIES, PETER. "Überall ist Krähwinkel." *Die Welt.* May 13, 1986.

KREMP, HERBERT. "Die Wiedervereiningung als Mittel zu mehr Sicherheit?" *Die Welt.* November 14, 1986.

VON LAUE, THEODORE H. "It's in Our Power to Ease East-West Tensions" (letter). *New York Times.* October 26, 1986.

MAASS, PETER. "Comecon Courting Western Europe." *New York Times.* September 22, 1986.

MACGREGOR, DOUG. "The New Soviet-German Pact." *Christian Science Monitor.* February 18, 1987.

MARKHAM, JAMES M. "East and West Germany Strive to Build Ties." *New York Times.* March 18, 1987.

————. "French Fall in Step Under a German." *New York Times.* September 24, 1987.

————. "Missile Diplomacy: Europe Prepares." *New York Times.* April 2, 1987.

NITSCHKE, EBERHARD. "Ein Zeichen der Hoffnung am Ort des Entsetzens." *Die Welt.* December 9, 1986.

OVERESCH, MANFRED. "Deutsche Frage und politische Kultur—Dilemmata der Deutschen und ihre Geschichte." *Das Parlament.* nos. 16–17. April 18–25, 1987.

POND, ELIZABETH. "For West Berlin Mayor, Nipping across the Wall Is a Big Decision." *Christian Science Monitor.* March 9, 1987.

————. "Pursuing the Ideal of a Central Europe." *Christian Science Monitor.* March 6, 1987.

"Les rélations inter-européennes et le dialogue est-ouest." *Le Monde.* December 9, 1985.

REUMANN, KURT. "Warum sind die Deutschen anders?" *Frankfurter Allgemeine.* September 4, 1985.

SCHULZE-REIMPELL, WERNER. "Die Schleier zu zerreissen." *Frankfurter Allgemeine.* December 10, 1986.

STÜRMER, MICHAEL. "Gibt es Mitteleuropa?" *Frankfurter Allgemeine.* December 10, 1986.

"Versöhnen ohne zu vergessen." *Das Parlament.* no. 16–17. April 18–25, 1987.

LE MONDE DIPLOMATIQUE

"L'Allemagne prospère et inquiète." March 1983.

CHAUVIER, JEAN-MARIE. "Le mouvement communiste en declin." December 1986.

————. "Un 'vent de fraîcheur' souffle sur Moscou." February 1986.

DE LA GORCE, PAUL-MARIE. "La diplomatie ouest-allemande à l'avant-garde de la détente." February 1989.

"Dissuasion française et défense européene." September 1985.

DRACH, MARCEL, "Une nouvelle donne dans les relations entre les deux Europes." February 1989.

JULIEN, CLAUDE. "Sécurité," September 1985.

LAVIGNE, MARIE. "Une vision globalement pessimiste." February 1986.

MANALE, MARGARET. "L'Allemagne de l'Est en quête de devises pour entreprendre sa révolution technologique." September 1985.

WAUTHIER, CLAUDE. "Les sommets franco-africains, symboles de continuité." November 1986.

INTERNATIONAL HERALD TRIBUNE

"Bonn and Paris Weigh Opening a Joint Embassy." October 14, 1988.
DARNTON, ROBERT. "Glasnost: Echoes of a Republic of Letters." October 11, 1988.
JOFFE, JOSEF. "Germans and Russians: Far from Rapallo." October 28, 1988.
LEWIS, FLORA. "How Do They Get Out of Communism?" October 14, 1988.
LIVINGSTON, ROBERT GERALD. "Kohl Goes to Moscow: What Will the Chancellor Be After?" October 21, 1988.
PFAFF, WILLIAM. "The New Europe May Doom the Soviet System." October 29/30, 1988.
PODHORETZ, NORMAN. "Munich 1938: The Lesson About Military Strength Stands." October 21, 1988.
STÜRMER, MICHAEL. "Germany: A Nation of Two States in Slow Motion." November 17, 1988.
VON WEIZSÄCKER, RICHARD. "Germans and History: Give It to Us Straight" (excerpt from a speech to the Bamberg historians' congress, October 12, 1988). October 29/30, 1988.
YODER, EDWIN M., JR. "Munich: Two Misconceptions Endure." October 21, 1988.

GENERAL ANZEIGER, BONN:

ANTWERPEN, MARIANNE. "Hauptstadtnotizen." May 16–17, 1987.
"Aussenminister Frankreichs erneuert Berlin-Garantien." December 9, 1986.
BELL, WOLF J. "Bonn und Paris müssen vorangehen." October 30, 1986.
BENECKE, DIETER W. "Glänzende Steinchen im Mosaik Deutschlandbild." December 12, 1986.
CHALUPA, GUSTAV. "Schatten des Gipfels auch in Budapest." October 14, 1986.
EICH, HERMANN. "Cattenom: Vergebliche Warnungen" (editorial). September 27/8, 1986.
"Honecker-Rede zum Berliner Jubiläum." September 27/8, 1986.
JACOBSEN, HANS-ADOLF. "Der Dialog war offener und konstruktiver." May 16–17, 1987.
"Jugendbegegnungsstätte als Schritt zur Versöhnung mit Polen." December 8, 1986.
KEMNA, FRIEDHELM. "Ehrgeiziges Angebot" (editorial). December 12, 1986.
"Kohl an gutem Verhältnis zur UdSSR interessiert." December 9, 1986.
KORFF, CHRISTIANE. "Friedrich der Grosse gibt Rätsel auf." October 16, 1986.
"Kulturangebot an die DDR: Knifflige Themen ausgespart." October 16, 1986.
"NATO schlägt dem Osten Verhandlungen vor." December 12, 1986.
"Die positive vertrauensbildende Bedeutung des Stockholmer Dokuments" (editorial). September 26, 1986.
SEMJONOW, WLADIMIR. "Wir werden eine zweite Sowjetunion aufbauen." February 25, 1986.
SMETS, FRANZ. "Parteitag der begrenzten Möglichkeiten." February 25, 1986.
"Städtepartnerschaft Trier-Weimar für Frühjahr geplant." December 8, 1986.

WASHINGTON POST:

BOHLEN, CELESTINE. "Chernobyl Parley Asks Safety Steps." August 30, 1986.
————. "Chernobyl Was First Test of Gorbachev's Policy of Openness." April 26, 1987.
BRZEZINSKI, ZBIGNIEW. "Reagan's INF Treaty Moves Us toward a New Europe." September 27, 1987.
CANNON, LOU, and OBERDORFER, DON. "Reagan Praises Helsinki Pact's Achievements." May 28, 1988.
CODY, EDWARD. "France, West Germany Expand Defense Cooperation." January 23, 1988.
————. "French Urge Honecker to Tear down Berlin Wall." January 9, 1988.
————. "Paris, Bonn Broaden Military Cooperation." January 13, 1988.
DEYOUNG, KAREN. "Britain and France to Strengthen Military Ties." January 30, 1988.
DIEHL, JACKSON. "Bonn Official Sees Progress in Polish Ties." January 14, 1988.
————. "Eastern Europeans Turn to West in Effort to End Technology Gap." February 28, 1988.
————. "Honecker's Trip Unsettles Poland." September 13, 1987.
————. "Kremlin Decides It Can Learn from Its Allies." October 13, 1987.
————. "Poland Eases Restrictions on Travel to West." April 3, 1988.
DOBBS, MICHAEL. "Gorbachev Turns Anew to Western Europe." July 8, 1986.
GADDIS, JOHN LEWIS. "Mikhail Gorbachev's Manifesto." November 29, 1987.
GETLEIN, FRANK. "Keep Germany Divided." June 14, 1987.
KALB, MADELEINE G. "Ban 'La Bombe'!" December 27, 1987.
LEE, GARY. "Bonn Chief Challenges East-West Split." July 7, 1987.
————. "A New Mix of Independence and Anxiety." October 12, 1987.
————. "Soviets Ease Travel and Emigration." September 6, 1987.
LEWIS, DAVID. "East, West Peace Blocs Hold Budapest Meeting." November 22, 1987.
McCARTNEY, ROBERT J. "Bonn Embraces Detente." January 17, 1988.
————. "Bonn, Paris Widen Martial Cooperation." September 25, 1987.
————. "Bonn Receives East German Leader." September 8, 1987.
————. "Bonn Says It Paid East Germany to Free Record 2,500 in 1985." December 10, 1986.
————. "Cold Shoulder to Glasnost." March 22, 1987.
————. "Fleeing East Germans No Longer Being Shot." December 9, 1987.
————. "Meeting of German Leaders Seen Acceptance of Partition." September 6, 1987.
————. "Modest Results Mark Honecker's Visit to Bonn." September 9, 1987.
————. "Two Germanys Frame Long-Term Agenda." September 14, 1987.
————. "West Berliners' Interest in Better Ties with Eastern Sector Worries Allies." March 11, 1987.
SERVAN-SCHREIBER, JEAN-JACQUES. "Complex Crises, Simple Solutions." August 30, 1987.
SHCHARANSKY, NATAN. "Why Is the West So Dazzled by Gorbachev?" September 13, 1987.

SIMES, DIMITRI K. "Tearing down the Berlin Wall." March 1, 1987.
TUOHY, WILLIAM. "Paris, Bonn to Coordinate Economic Policy." November 14, 1987.

DIE ZEIT, HAMBURG
(OVERSEAS EDITION, UNLESS OTHERWISE NOTED)

ARTICLES/EDITORIALS BY MARION GRÄFIN DÖNHOFF

"Ein Dach für ganz Europa." April 8, 1988.
"Durchs offene Tor." July 10, 1987.
"Mauer und Einheit: Zeit zum Umdenken." May 1, 1987.
"Mit Zögern ist es nicht getan." May 15, 1987.
"Nach dem Feindbild die Wunschbilder?" March 27, 1987.
"Nicht für die Ewigkeit bestimmt." August 22, 1986.
"Nicht nur Waffen verderben die Welt." January 15, 1988.
"Ob endlich die Zukunft beginnt?" September 18, 1987.
"Vom Unfug der Feindbilder." December 4, 1987.
"Von der Geschichte längst überholt." January 27, 1989.
"Die Weltpolitik vor der Wende?" February 5, 1988.
"Der Wind des Wandels aus dem Osten." May 5, 1987 (domestic edition).
"Zwei Männer, zwei Reden, zwei Welten." February 13, 1987.

ARTICLES/EDITORIALS BY HELMUT SCHMIDT

"Einer unserer Brüder." July 31, 1987.
"Europa ist nicht dekadent." July 11, 1986.
"Europa muss sich selbst behaupten." November 28, 1986.
"Das gemeinsame Dach bleibt das Ziel." November 7, 1986.
"Der General und seine Erben." May 8, 1987.
"Die Nachbarn im Alltag." May 15, 1987.
"Null-Lösung im deutschen Interesse." May 15, 1987.
"Wirtschaft als Schicksal." May 15, 1987 (domestic edition).

ARTICLES/EDITORIALS BY THEO SOMMER:

"Auf dem langen Marsch—wohin?" April 10, 1987.
"Aus dem Traum in die Tragödie." March 18, 1988.
"Bis die Krabben pfeifen lernen." September 13, 1985 (domestic edition).
"Deutschland: gedoppelt, nicht getrennt?" September 11, 1987.
"Deutschland: nichts Halbes und nichts Ganzes." August 22, 1986.
"Die Einheit gegen Freiheit tauschen." July 3, 1987.
"Fäusteschütteln, Händedrücken." October 28, 1988.
"Ein gutes Ende—kein neuer Anfang?" February 12, 1988.
"Hausieren mit einem alten Hut." June 5, 1987.
"Jenseits von Potsdam." June 24, 1988.

"Nach der Wende die Spitzkehre?" December 12, 1986.
"Eine Rolle sucht ihren Darsteller." June 19, 1987.
"Schwach aus Stärke." January 23, 1987.
"Unterwegs zu neuen Ufern." November 4, 1988.
"Wenn die Welt in den Angeln knarrt." January 9, 1987.

OTHER AUTHORS:

BECK, ULRICH. "Die Gefahr verändert alles." October 3, 1986.
BECKER, HELLMUT. "Physik und Frieden." July 3, 1987.
BECKER. KURT. "Das Ende der Alten Sicherheit." November 14, 1986 (domestic edition).
――――. "Europas Gewicht." July 25, 1986.
――――. "Kohl muss die Scherben kitten." August 1, 1986.
BECKURTS, KARL HEINZ. "Nach Tschernobyl weiter?" July 25, 1986.
BENDER, PETER. "Sind wir unschuldig an dem Monstrum?" August 15, 1986.
――――. "Versöhnung mit dem alten Gegner." March 13, 1987
BERTRAM, CHRISTOPH. "Akrobat auf dem Schwebebalken." February 17, 1989.
――――. "Bedenkträger aus Europa." October 31, 1986 (domestic edition).
――――. "Ein Deutschlandkenner im Kreml." November 4, 1988.
―――― "Mit dem Pfunde nicht gewuchert." January 16, 1987.
――――. "Ein Oscar für die beste Nebenrolle." October 3, 1986.
――――. "Rendezvous mit der Geschichte." January 29, 1988.
――――. "Unbehagen am Katzentisch." April 10, 1987.
――――. "Zu schnell verdammt?" May 16, 1986 (domestic edition).
――――. "Zwei Diener ihrer Herren." December 4, 1987.
―――― and DE WECK, ROGER. " 'Es ist wichtig, Zweideutigkeiten auszuräumen.-' " May 1, 1987.
BREMKES, WILLI. "Grosser Andrang beim Jugendaustauschprogramm." May 15, 1987 (domestic edition).
BROSZAT, MARTIN, and FRIEDLÄNDER, SAUL. "Historisierung des Nationalsozialismus?" April 29, 1988.
BRZEZINSKI, ZBIGNIEW. "Europa ist nicht mehr der Brennpunkt." June 26, 1987.
BUCERIUS, GERD. "Als die Bomben-Angst noch nachwirkte." October 10, 1986.
――――. "Aus der Vergangenheit nichts gelernt?" September 18, 1987.
――――. "Farewell America?" May 29, 1987.
BUHL, DIETER. "Mit dem Mut zur Utopie." June 26, 1987.
BURT, RICHARD. "Ein Loblied auf die Differenzen." December 5, 1986 (domestic edition).
BUTENSCHÖN, MARIANNA. "Der Geist ist aus der Flasche." May 1, 1987.
DÜRRENMATT, FRIEDRICH. "Georg Büchner und der Satz vom Grunde." October 17, 1986 (domestic edition).
ECO, UMBERTO. "Pascal und die Kernenergie." August 22, 1986.
FREESE, GUNHILD. "Tragbar für Moskau." March 6, 1987.
GENSCHER, HANS-DIETRICH. "Ein Plan für das ganze Europa." October 28, 1988.

GERSTE, MARGRIT. "Die Angst vor den Beton-Türmen." May 16, 1986 (domestic edition).

GREINER, ULRICH. "Ach Europa!" January 29, 1988.

———. "Wir leiden an dem Hassverhältnis zwischen Geist und Macht." January 15, 1988.

GRUNENBERG, NINA. "Der König von Strassburg." January 23, 1987

———. "Die Richtung stimmt." November 4, 1988.

HABERMAS, JÜRGEN. "Eine Art Schadensabwicklung." July 23, 1986.

———. "Vom öffentlichen Gebrauch der Historie." November 14, 1986.

HANKE, THOMAS, and HOFFMANN, WOLFGANG. "Der teure Rest des Risikos." May 16, 1986 (domestic edition).

"Hat die Hoffnung noch eine Zukunft?" January 2, 1987.

HIRSCH, HELGA. "Suche nach dem Kompromiss." January 22, 1988.

HIRSCHFELD, OSWALD. "Schweden hat lange gezögert." September 13, 1985 (domestic edition).

HOFFMANN, WOLFGANG. "Ausstieg, aber wann?" May 16, 1986 (domestic edition).

———. "Ein langer Abschied." August 15, 1986.

HOFMANN, GUNTER. "Das lästige Leitbild." December 12, 1986.

———. "Ein Leben lauter Abschiede." June 12, 1987.

———. "Der Präses und der Populist." May 24, 1985 (domestic edition).

———. "Ein Präsident fürs Prinzipielle." January 8, 1988.

———. "Unruhe—hüben wir drüben." February 26, 1988.

———. "Unter dem Kanzler schwankt der Boden." May 16, 1986 (domestic edition).

———. "Unterwegs in eine böse Zukunft." November 7, 1986 (domestic edition).

———. "Von Perspektiven keine Rede." March 6, 1987.

———. " 'Das Zuschauen bekommt mir ganz gut.' " February 5, 1988.

HUBER, MARIA and SCHMIDT-HÄUER, CHRISTIAN. "Ist Russland noch zu reformieren?" April 17, 1987.

JÄCKEL, EBERHARD. "Die elende Praxis der Untersteller." September 19, 1986.

JANSSEN, KARL-HEINZ. "Als ein Volk ohne Schatten?" November 28, 1986.

———. "Im Schatten der Vergangenheit." March 27, 1987.

JENS, WALTER. "Vaterländischer Missklang." September 26, 1986.

KAISER, CARL-CHRISTIAN. "Ein kleines Wunder für die Deutschen." January 8, 1988.

———. "Eine Ouvertüre, noch keine Partitur." April 24, 1987.

———. "Späte Entdeckung." January 15, 1988.

———. "Viele Wahrheiten, kein Augenzwinkern." September 18, 1987.

———. " 'Wir sind Nachbarn.' " October 24, 1986 (domestic edition).

KENNAN, GEORGE. "Eine Wasserscheide zwischen Angst und Hoffnung." July 10, 1987.

KEWENIG, WILHELM. "Quo vadis Berlin?" February 27, 1987.

KNOLL, JOACHIM H. "Die Vergesslichkeit sollte uns Angst machen." May 1, 1987.

KÖHLER, HENNING. "Adenauer wollte doch den Rheinstaat." December 5, 1986 (domestic edition).

KRZEMINSKI, ADAM. "So oder so gehören wir zueinander!" April 3, 1987.

————. "Was uns unterscheidet, worin wir ähnlich sind." August 1, 1986.

KÜHNERT, HANNO. "In politischen Fällen etwas schüchtern." September 19, 1986.

VON KÜNHEIM, HAUG. "Friedrich und sein Erbe." September 19, 1986.

LÄMMERT, EBERHARD. "Wem gehört die Geschichte?" January 29, 1988.

LEGGEWIE, CLAUS. "Antifaschisten sind wir sowieso." February 26, 1988.

LEICHT, ROBERT. "Eines Deutschen Sonderweg." April 3, 1987.

————. "Gute Deutsche und gute Europäer?" September 18, 1987.

————. "Jetzt wissen wir was auf dem Spiele steht." May 16, 1986 (domestic edition).

————. "Ein Korb zu Ostern." April 24, 1987.

————. "Der Mühlstein der Vergangenheit." February 26, 1988.

————. "Niemals normal." April 17, 1987.

————. "Nur das Hinsehen macht uns frei." January 2, 1987.

————. "Über alle Mauern der Stadt hinweg." March 20, 1987.

LEONHARDT, RUDOLF WALTER. "Das doppelte Deutschland im Ausland." September 26, 1986.

————. "Der Kampf um die deutsche Sprache." October 3, 1986.

LIVINGSTON, ROBERT GERALD. "Drängen auf einen deutschen Patriotismus." June 19, 1987.

LÖWENTHAL, RICHARD. "Vom Wert eines 'hoffnungslosen' Kampfes." January 2, 1987.

MANN, GOLO. " 'Ein Volk, Ein Reich, Ein Führer.' " March 11, 1988.

MAYER-VORFELDER, GERHARD. "Wie viele Strophen hat die deutsche National-hymne?" July 25, 1986.

MENGE, MARLIES. "Beiderlei Deutsche—zweierlei Deutsche." August 15, 1986.

————. "Deutschland—wo liegt es?" February 20, 1987.

————. "Was soll uns das schon bringen?" November 4, 1988.

————. " 'Wir haben zu grosse Erwartungen.' " February 26, 1988.

"Mitterrand: Pläne gegen den Krieg." October 30, 1987.

"Nach Reykjavik: Wie soll es weitergehen?" November 7, 1986.

NAWROCKI, JOACHIM. "Ein alter Brief als Vorwand." April 24, 1987.

————. "Gewalt zum Geburtstag." June 26, 1987.

————. "Zauberformeln für Berlin." December 12, 1986 (domestic edition.).

NIPPERDEY, THOMAS. "Unter der Herrschaft des Verdachts." October 17, 1986 (domestic edition).

NOLTE, ERNST. "Die Sache auf den Kopf gestellt." October 31, 1986 (domestic edition).

POGGE VON STRANDMANN, HARTMUT. "Warum die Deutschen den Krieg wollten." March 11, 1988.

POND, ELIZABETH. "Sind wir verraten und verkauft?" July 3, 1987.

RIBHEGGE, WILHELM. "Stellenweise Glatteis." February 13, 1987.

SALEWSKI, MICHAEL. "Der Draht nach St. Petersburg." June 26, 1987.

SCHMIDT-HÄUER, CHRISTIAN. "Der Kampf um die toten Seelen." March 6, 1987.

————. "Eher harsch als huldvoll." November 4, 1988.

————. "Ein neues Blatt aufgeschlagen." August 1, 1986.

————. "Werben um West und Ost." August 8, 1986.

Schmude, Jürgen. "Die Einheit in der Teilung." December 4, 1987.
Schulze, Hagen. "Fragen, die wir stellen müssen." October 3, 1986.
Schwan, Gesine. "Mitten im ganzen Europa." January 27, 1989.
Sichtermann, Barbara. "Die Mauern beben." July 3, 1987.
Spörl, Gerhard. "Ordnung muss herrschen im Land." August 1, 1986.
Stehle, Hansjakob. "Dass Hitler auch die Polen ausrotten wollte." November 7, 1986 (domestic edition).
Tatu, Michel. "Gute Reise, Kanzler!" October 28, 1988.
Tugendhat, Ernst. "Überlegungen zum Dritten Weltkrieg." December 4, 1987.
de Weck, Roger. "Alle drei Jahre Kultur." November 7, 1986.
———. "Als wäre nichts geschehen." September 26, 1986.
———. "Angst vor einem 'europäischen München.' " March 20, 1987.
———. "Chirac machte seinem Ärger Luft." August 1, 1986.
———. "Freundschaft halten im Spagat." November 27, 1987.
———. "Eine Freundschaft ohne Wärme." January 29, 1988.
———. "Honneurs für Honecker." January 15, 1988.
———. "Misstöne und Verstimmungen." October 31, 1986.
Wehler, Hans Ulrich. "Bevor der Funke der Revolution aus Frankreich übersprang." August 29, 1986.
Weidenfeld, Werner. "Deutschland, Deutschland—und kein Ende." July 24, 1987.
———. "Zähneknirschen im Detail." September 4, 1987.
Wördehoff, Bernhard. "Träumereien in der Kapuzinergruft." August 15, 1986.
Zundel, Rolf. "Rückfall in die Dampfplauderei." November 14, 1986.

Reports

Berlin: A Double Celebration (*International Herald Tribune* special news report). December 16, 1986.
Boldt, Frank; Geiss, Immanuel; Januszajtis, Andrzej; and Potocki, Stanislaw, eds. *Deutsch-polnische Jahrbücher* (reports of the German-Polish Society). Bremen: Deutsch-polnische Gesellschaft Bremen-Bremerhaven. 1980–85.
Das Deutsch-französische Jugendwerk 1985. Bad Honnef: General Secretariat. 1985.
"Die 47. deutsch-französischen Konsultationen in Paris." *Frankreich-Info.* Number 12/86. March 7, 1986.
Groscolas, Daniel. "Initiativen zur Europäischen Öffnung." *Internationale Partnerschaft.* Bonn: Europa Union Verlag. Number 1. April 1985.
Köhler, Anne, and Eppinger, Rudolf. *Einstellungen von Jugendlichen zur DDR und zur Deutschlandpolitik.* (Schriften und Materialien zur Deutschlandpolitik und Europapolitik 3/1984). München: Studienstätte für Politik und Zeitgeschehen. 1984.
Mittendorfer, Rudolf. "Zum 35. Jahrestag der Erklärung Robert Schumans am 9. Mai 1985." *Internationale Partnerschaft.* Bonn: Europa Union Verlag. Number 2. June-July 1985.

The 1984–1988 French Defence Programme. Paris: Ministry of Defense. 1983.
NORTH ATLANTIC ASSEMBLY. *NATO in the 1990s.* Brussels. 1988.
The Right to Smile: A Survey of West Germany (Special *Economist* supplement). December 6, 1986.
SCHMALSTIEG, HERBERT. "Kommunale Zusammenarbeit zwischen Hannover und Poznan." *Internationale Partnerschaft.* Bonn: Europa Union Verlag. Number 1. April 1985.
La visite en France de M. Gorbatchev (*Le monde* special section). October 3, 1985.
Was ist der Deutschen Vaterland? (Special first issue of *Wir in Ost und West*). Wiesbaden: Arbeitsgemeinschaft Jugend und Bildung. Number 1. September 1985.
WÖSLER, DIETMAR M. "Motto und Taten." *Internationale Partnerschaft.* Bonn: Europa Union Verlag. Number 2. June–July 1985.
Zwanzig Jahre Deutsch-französisches Jugendwerk—Europäische Jugendpolitik (Special issue of *Jugendpolitik*). Number 2. June 1983.

BERICHTE UND DOKUMENTATIONEN, BUNDESPRESSEAMT, BONN.

Dokumentation zur Deutschlandpolitik der Bundesregierung: Verträge und Vereinbarungen mit der DDR. 1986.
Dokumentation zur Ostpolitik der Bundesregierung: Verträge und Vereinbarungen. 1986.
Erinnerung, Trauer und Versöhnung: Ansprachen und Erklärungen zum vierzigsten Jahrestag des Kriegsendes. June 1985.
Nachdenken über unsere Geschichte: Reden zum vierzigsten Jahrestag des 8. Mai 1945. June 1986.
Zur Lage der Nation im geteilten Deutschland: Bericht der Bundesregierung vom. 14. März 1986. May 1986.

Unpublished Material

BOLUKBASIOGLU, SUHA. *The Legitimacy Problem of the German Democratic Republic.* M.A. Thesis. University of Virginia. 1984.
HAMMER, GERT. *Das Deutsch-französische Jugendwerk.* 1985.
SCHMUDE, JÜRGEN. "The Role of the Church in German-German Relations." Speech at the Friedrich Ebert Stiftung, Washington, DC, April 27, 1988.

index

about the author

Edwina Campbell, currently a senior analyst at Eagle Research Group, Inc., Arlington, Virginia, received her Ph.D., M.A.L.D., and M.A. from the Fletcher School of Law and Diplomacy and her B.A. from the American University. She was a summer fellow at Worcester College, Oxford, and a Fulbright Fellow at the University of Freiburg. A member of the American Council on Germany/Atlantik-Brücke's first group of German-American young leaders, Dr. Campbell was a Robert Bosch Fellow in the West German parliament and foreign office. She has also received grants from the German Marshall Fund and the Stiftung für die Deutsche Wissenschaft.

Before joining Eagle Research Group, Dr. Campbell was a U.S. foreign service officer and an assistant professor of government and foreign affairs at the University of Virginia. Her other publications include *Consultation and Consensus in NATO* (1985) and chapters in *Germany Through American Eyes* (1989) and *Security Perspectives of the West German Left: The SPD and the Greens in Opposition* (1988), as well as articles and book reviews in *National Review*, *Foreign Service Journal*, *Defense News*, *Fletcher Forum*, *Journal of the History of European Ideas*, and *News for Teachers of Political Science*.